T0331094

Renewable Energy Enterprises in Emerging Markets

This book highlights the challenges faced by renewable energy enterprises (REEs) in emerging markets by reflecting on the enterprises' own stories and experiences.

Research into REEs has focused largely on successful businesses and business models and developed markets. With significant opportunities for renewable energy enterprise in emerging markets, this book presents a unique business-level perspective. It highlights the key barriers and outlines the strategic and operational solutions for success articulated by the entrepreneurs themselves. The research draws on interviews with entrepreneurs in twenty-eight emerging markets, including Barbados, Cambodia, Chile, Ghana, Indonesia, India, Kenya, South Africa and Uganda. The book concludes by summarising the key solutions for success and illustrating how successful REEs put them into practice.

This book will be of great interest to students and scholars of renewable energy, sustainable business and the sustainability agenda in emerging markets.

Cle-Anne Gabriel, PhD, is a researcher at The University of Queensland (UQ) Business School in Australia. She is UQ Business School's Director for the United Nations Principles for Responsible Management Education (UN PRME) and a Director of the North American Case Research Association (NACRA). She has worked on sustainable development projects and assignments funded by Australian Aid (AusAID), the European Union (EU), the Japanese Ministry for Environment and New Zealand's Ministry of Business, Innovation and Employment (MBIE).

Routledge Research in Sustainability and Business

For more information about this series, please visit: www.routledge.com/
Routledge-Research-in-Sustainability-and-Business/book-series/RRSB

Renewable Energy Enterprises in Emerging Markets
Strategic and Operational Challenges

Cle-Anne Gabriel

Routledge
Taylor & Francis Group

LONDON AND NEW YORK

First published 2020
by Routledge
2 Park Square, Milton Park, Abingdon, Oxon OX14 4RN

and by Routledge
52 Vanderbilt Avenue, New York, NY 10017

Routledge is an imprint of the Taylor & Francis Group, an informa business

First issued in paperback 2021

British Library Cataloguing-in-Publication Data
A catalogue record for this book is available from the British Library

Library of Congress Cataloging-in-Publication Data
A catalog record for this book has been requested

ISBN: 978-1-138-34829-5 (hbk)
ISBN: 978-1-03-208326-1 (pbk)
ISBN: 978-0-429-43674-1 (ebk)

Typeset in Sabon
by Apex CoVantage, LLC

Contents

Figures

Tables

Preface

Storytelling is important. Those who master it use it to bring and keep people and communities together, introduce and legitimise shared values and encourage cooperation towards reinforcing these values (Yong, 2017). Described by Charlemae Rollins (1957: 165) as the "breathing of life into literature", storytelling is also an effective means of acquainting newcomers with a topic or issue and helping them see values and value they would not or could not otherwise envision in the world around them (Rollins, 1957). My aim is twofold: to acquaint those unfamiliar with the challenges of renewable energy enterprise in emerging markets and to familiarise you, the reader, with their values and value as they engage in the work of sustainable human thriving.

Renewable energy enterprises in emerging markets are notoriously difficult to access for research purposes. They are mostly very small ventures, whose founders are so dedicated to addressing the ecological and social issues of the worlds around them, and so consumed by the demands of the daily running of their enterprises, that they generally offer little time to be the subject of academic research. For this reason, the challenges of running such enterprises had remained largely speculated about and theorised in academic and development circles, with little voice given to the enterprises themselves in some of the world's least developed markets. Therefore, when these elusive entrepreneurs agreed to tell me their stories, it was of paramount importance that I listened and studied keenly, and in this book, I share those stories in good faith.

However, the story cannot easily be divorced from the lens and preferred techniques of the storyteller. My own personal and professional experiences have influenced my approach to telling these stories. Personally, I was born and raised in an emerging market. On the islands of Trinidad and Tobago, I became acquainted with several sustainability challenges at an early age. In my formative years, I took a keen interest in and was determined to address the often-bewildering challenges of sustainable human thriving we faced then and continue to face today. As I grew older, I became concerned about Trinidad and Tobago's ecological sustainability primarily, and my work and academic pursuits soon aligned with these interests. However, I soon learned that ecological and socioeconomic challenges are inexorably and intricately connected. As I traveled internationally, I became perplexed by the global nature of these complex and interrelated grand challenges and, in particular, their exacerbated effects on emerging markets like Trinidad and Tobago. I believe the world needs holistic solutions that tackle several of these challenges simultaneously. Eventually, renewable energy emerged as an area of interest and a solution to these challenges in emerging markets.

Professionally, I undertook this research during my time as a doctoral student, then as a tertiary educator and scholar at two mainstream business schools in New Zealand and Australia. Thus, influenced by the knowledge acquired and my experiences at these institutions, I chose the business model as the lens through which I made sense of renewable energy enterprises in emerging markets. I found the concept of a business model – that is, the logic of how enterprises create and retrieve value from their endeavours – a useful frame to organise what I learned about these enterprises and the people leading them. I believed then, as I do today, that renewable energy enterprise is a crucial conduit of sustainable human thriving in emerging markets. Therefore, it is important that stakeholders of the transition concern themselves with ensuring the value-creating success of such enterprises. It is also important to understand the challenges that hinder their success. Even some of the biggest critics of capitalist markets and enterprise agree that perhaps certain types of enterprises must flourish and proliferate to realise a sustainable future for all. In my opinion, renewable energy enterprises are such enterprises. Thus, the business model is an important lens to frame the stories of how these enterprises have organised themselves, and the resources at their disposal, for success.

This book highlights the key strategic and operational challenges faced by renewable energy enterprises in emerging markets and outlines the solutions for success articulated by the entrepreneurs themselves. To my knowledge, it is the first book to offer a firm-level perspective on this issue by it addressing the challenge of running a renewable energy enterprise in emerging markets directly. The book is timely because there is a success bias in existing research on renewable energy enterprise in emerging markets. Researchers tend to focus on successful businesses and business models. There is good reason for this. After all, almost two-thirds of all of the world's new power generation capacity added in 2018 came from renewables, led by emerging markets (IRENA, 2019), and there is still much to learn. Yet, more than 25 percent of the enterprises in my study have failed. Technological maturity is no longer a challenge and there is no shortage of demand and innate need for renewable energy in these markets. Some of the challenges encountered are simply symptomatic of the difficulty of starting and running a successful enterprise. However, alarmingly, many of the enterprises I studied perceived they had ineffective recipes for success: ineffective or irrelevant performance metrics, overdependence on aid and development funding and ineffective distribution channels, for instance. Therefore, I challenged myself: how could I help with the tools at my disposal as a researcher? More poignantly, how could the entrepreneurs who start and run such enterprises help themselves? For me this book was the answer to both questions.

In this book, I tell the stories entrusted to me and share my own insights into the experiences of the renewable energy enterprises I studied for eight years. I aim to influence research and practice of renewable energy enterprise in emerging markets by

1   Establishing renewable energy entrepreneurship in emerging markets as a legitimate and distinctive area of research
2   Explicating the challenges encountered by renewable energy enterprises in emerging markets and
3   Providing guidance from and for best-practice renewable energy enterprise in emerging markets

However, I could not complete this project without the support, assistance, input and guidance of several people. Most importantly, I am grateful for and to my son, Edan – although you were still too young to know it, you provided invaluable support and encouragement when I needed it most.

I am grateful to the entrepreneurs who participated in my research over the years and agreed to share their time and stories with me – in particular, Clive Jones of Power Providers, Tanzania and Ananda Setiyo Ivannanto of A-Wing, Indonesia. I am also grateful to Kathryn Davies and Joshua Hartmann, who provided professional graphics support when I needed it and to my research assistants, Utkarsh Kiri, Danfeng Zhu and Samira Nazar for their dependable support, hard work and initiative. I must also thank those who provided mentorship and support during the conduct of some of the research that informs this book, including Dr Jodyanne Kirkwood, Professor Elizabeth L Rose, Associate Professor Sara Walton and Associate Professor Adam Doering.

Finally, in the difficult process of completing this book, a few friends, family and colleagues provided direct support, feedback and/or inspiration for which I am extremely grateful. They are Afiya Holder, Aldon Jasper, Dr Carol Janson Bond, Dr Danielle De Merieux and Janine Narbutas. Thank you for your time, encouragement and support.

References

IRENA (International Renewable Energy Agency), 2019. *Renewable Capacity Statistics 2019*. Abu Dhabi: IRENA.

Rollins, C., 1957. Storytelling: Its value and importance. *Elementary English*, 34(3), pp. 164–166.

Yong, E., 2017. The desirability of storytellers. *The Atlantic*, 05 December. Retrieved from www.theatlantic.com/science/archive/2017/12/the-origins-of-storytelling/547502/ (accessed 02 June 2019).

Part I

Introduction

Chinua Achebe (1930–2013) on "the danger of not having your own stories":

There is that great proverb – that until the lions have their own historians, the history of the hunt will always glorify the hunter. That did not come to me until much later. Once I realized that, I had to be a writer. I had to be that historian. It's not one man's job. It's not one person's job. But it is something we have to do, so that the story of the hunt will also reflect the agony, the travail – the bravery, even, of the lions.

I wrote this book to tell the stories of the people – the courageous 'lions' as Achebe (1994) described them in the preceding quote – who start and run renewable energy ventures under challenging circumstances in emerging markets every day. These people engage unrewarded in the hard work of sustainable human thriving, yet their voices were rarely heard above those from developed markets – that is, developed market donors, enterprises, researchers, advisors and their agents. Prior to my research, renewable energy entrepreneurs in the world's least developed emerging markets (that is, beyond India and China) were often talked about but rarely ever talked *to*. I endeavoured to break that trend. This book, along with several prior publications on the subject,[1] is the result of that endeavour. I hope it gives you, the reader, some insight into the lives and livelihoods of renewable energy entrepreneurs and their enterprises in emerging markets. Indeed, I have woven their stories into the pages of this book.

Sustainability and the renewable energy enterprise

The world is counting down to 2030. At the time of writing, we, as a global community, have 11 years left to meet our 17 Sustainable Development Goals (SDGs).[2] A large part of the difficult battle to achieve these goals must be fought and won in the world's so-called least developed countries, or emerging markets.[3] Addressing the World Energy Council's 'trilemma' of sustainable energy – security, equity and environmental sustainability (World Energy Council, 2018) – is closely and deeply entwined with the achievement of not only SDG 7 Affordable and Clean Energy,[4] but many other SDGs as well. Indeed, many view energy as a 'golden thread' that connects many facets of human thriving (*eudemonia*), social equity and environmental sustainability (World Bank and IEA, 2017). Therefore, facilitating the transition towards sustainable energy in emerging markets is a top priority globally.

The Industrial Revolution relied on exploiting the planet's many finite resources, including fossil fuels such as petroleum, natural gas and coal, to scale-up production. Even in the present age, growing trends in human consumption rely heavily on petrochemical-derived products such as plastics. However, the use of these fossil resources has caused severe and irreversible environmental damage to Earth's ecosystems. With rising demands for energy, these adverse environmental effects will continue, unless our civilisation embraces more sustainable alternatives. Renewable energy is chief amongst these alternatives. Renewable energy is energy harvested from sources that are replenished naturally and indefinitely on a human timescale in a manner that ensures these sources will never be depleted. Increasing the share of renewable energy produced and consumed is pivotal to the success of the sustainable energy transition everywhere in the world. Not only is renewable energy a cleaner and more ecologically sustainable option than incumbent fossil energies, but it is also especially important in emerging markets. Certainly, renewable sources and technologies (renewables) are noted for their overwhelmingly positive socioeconomic effects in emerging markets. For instance, in remote regions of the world without twentieth century electricity distribution infrastructure (that is, without an electricity 'grid'), renewable energy installations help create a sense of communal self-sufficiency and independence. Remote communities with their own renewable supply of energy live, quite literally, off the grid. Families who would otherwise live without (or with poor quality) light during the night-time hours gain a few extra hours in the day to develop and build enterprise, socialise with neighbours, or for children to complete homework at night. Even in communities connected to electricity distribution infrastructure, households may generate their own electricity using renewable energy technologies and sell any excess back to the grid. Indeed, renewables foster enterprise as well as enhanced prosperity and well-being.

However, a successful transition to renewable energy in emerging markets relies on the vision, dedication and initiative of individual and community-based renewable energy enterprises. The renewable energy transition must happen in partnership with these enterprises, or it will not happen at all. The transition is characterised by the enhanced legitimacy of renewable energy technologies and resources in emerging markets, prompted by the simultaneous de-legitimisation of fossil energies. The activities of each individual enterprise contribute to the aggregate transitioning of emerging markets. Yet, while the aggregate effects of such enterprises have been studied at length on macro-economic, socio-systemic and even communal scales, we still know very little about the inner value generating mechanisms and infrastructures within renewable energy enterprises themselves, even more so in emerging markets. How do the owners and managers of these enterprises orchestrate success in emerging markets notorious for their challenging commercial and infrastructural environments? What leads to failure, and how can this failure be avoided?

Within the *academe* of business and management, one assumes such enterprises have a plan – a strategy, a roadmap to overcome the constraints faced and materialise their vision. This roadmap is often referred to as a business model. It is the logic or reasoning for the activities undertaken and engaged in by enterprises to realise their vision. In emerging markets undergoing the transition to more sustainable forms of energy, there is no vision worth studying and sharing more than that of renewable energy enterprises. Renewable energy enterprises assume a considerable share of the responsibility for ushering in the transition by toiling, deliberately or inadvertently, to realise their own vision for renewable energy in emerging markets.

I spent much of the last eight years, from 2012 to 2019, studying renewable energy enterprises in emerging markets. This book is anchored in the research and insights from the last eight years, in which I interviewed and studied 43 renewable energy entrepreneurs and their enterprises in 28 emerging markets: Barbados, Belize, Cambodia, Cameroon, Chile, Costa Rica, Ecuador, Ethiopia, Fiji, Ghana, Guatemala, India, Indonesia, Kenya, Laos, Nigeria, Panama, Philippines, Papua New Guinea, Senegal, Somalia, South Africa, Tanzania, Thailand, Tonga, Trinidad and Tobago, Uganda and Zambia. A comparison of selected indicators of human development at the time of completion of the interviews highlights some of the development challenges enterprises grapple with in these emerging markets. In the compilation of indices presented in Appendix 1, I highlight grand challenges related to issues such as education, security, life expectancy and poverty. Indeed, these challenges constitute the context in which REEs operate in the world's emerging markets. In addition, to respect their desire for anonymity, the participants were assigned codes and pseudonyms as shown in Table 0.1. Attentive readers will notice that I use these pseudonyms throughout this book to highlight the key insights they contribute individually. Thus, towards the aim of contributing to the renewable energy transition, herein I present and discuss the findings from two studies of these renewable energy enterprises in emerging markets.

Study I (2012–2016)

When I started this research in January 2012, I had two aims. First, I wanted to understand the challenges faced by renewable energy enterprises in emerging markets: What were the main challenges faced? Which enterprises were most affected? Which countries, regions and conditions did renewable energy enterprises find the most challenging? Second, I was deeply curious about the strategies used by the entrepreneurs themselves to overcome these

Table 0.1 Identifiers used for the territories represented in the study

Territories Represented in Study	Country Identifiers	Names[1]
Barbados	BBS	Arthur
Belize	BZ	Günther
Cambodia, Kingdom of	CAM	Chea
Cameroon, Republic of	CMN	Delphine, Jean
Chile, Republic of	CHL	Vicente, Martín
Costa Rica, Republic of	CR	Tim
Ecuador, Republic of	EC	Ángel
Ethiopia, Federal Democratic Republic of	ETH	Aaron, Daniel
Fiji, Republic of	FJ	Vijay, Sam
Ghana, Republic of	GH	Kofi, Abeiku
Guatemala, Republic of	GUA	Luis
Indonesia, Republic of	INA	Arif, Iwan
India, Republic of	IND	Dhruv, Sai, Ajay
Kenya, Republic of	KE	Thomas, Clive, Adamu
Lao People's Democratic Republic	LA	Chris
Nigeria, Federal Republic of	NIG	Jonathan, Chiagozie
Panama, Republic of	PAN	Matías
Philippines, Republic of the	PH	Ernesto
Papua New Guinea, Independent State of	PNG	David
South Africa, Republic of	SA	Henry
Senegal, Republic of	SEN	Alain
Somalia	SOM	Liam
Tanzania, United Republic of	TZ	Elton, Mark
Thailand, Kingdom of	TLD	Raphael, Chaow
Tonga, Kingdom of	TON	Tane
Trinidad & Tobago, Republic of	TT	Kenneth
Uganda, Republic of	UG	Hans, Joshua
Zambia, Republic of	ZA	Francis

1 Disguised for anonymity.

challenges: How did the enterprises adjust the products and services they offered, or types of customers they served, based on the challenges they faced? How did the enterprises adjust supply chain relationships to cope? Although I provide a more detailed definition and delimitation of renewable energy enterprise in Chapter 1, it suffices at this stage to declare, simply, that I consider the renewable energy entrepreneur an individual who has started and runs a renewable energy enterprise.

This study focuses strictly on the downstream, end-user side of the industry – that is, the end-user interface, which is the commercial, technological, social and organisational space in which interaction between the final users and the generators or suppliers of renewable energy (technologies) occurs. Activities occurring at the end-user interface may include, for example, technology retail or service, energy supply or service, consultancy, maintenance and repair (refer to Chapter 2 for a typology of renewable energy enterprises operating at the end-user interface). The decision to focus on the renewable energy end-user interface and, within this delimitation, to maintain a broad definition of entrepreneurship, reflects my primary focus on renewable energy uptake in emerging markets, instead of its emergence (Elzen, Geels and Green, 2004). Thus, I set out, purposely, to recruit individuals owning and operating businesses and ventures at the renewable energy end-user interface in emerging markets. I identified potential research participants in several ways, including by systematic web-based searches and by enlisting the assistance of several renewable energy-related organisations with operations and contacts in emerging markets. These included, for example, Deutsche Gesellschaft für Internationale Zusammenarbeit (GIZ) GmbH, the Organisation of American States (OAS) Department of Sustainable Development, the Renewable Energy and Energy Efficiency Partnership (REEEP)'s South Asia, Southeast Asia and the Pacific and Southern Africa offices, Renewable Energy and Environmental Experts – African Network (REEE-AN), Energy and Environment Partnership (EEP) with Indonesia, Secretariat of the Pacific Community (SPC) and Die Deutsch-Ecuadorianische Industrie- und Handelskammer (AHK Ecuador). Upon completing each interview, I asked each participant to recommend other renewable energy enterprises who might be willing to participate (snowballing technique). By the end of 2014, of the 122 enterprises I contacted and invited to participate in the study, 43 agreed.

Once an entrepreneur agreed to be interviewed, I gathered contextual information about his/her enterprise. I scoured their websites and perused publicly available documentation related to either the enterprise or the entrepreneur. Equipped with this information, I was then prepared to meet and discuss each entrepreneur's unique situation. The discussions were structured around a survey and semi-structured interview. However, qualitative research methods can be fiddly. So much depends on the interpretation of the research participant, and one never knows what insights and new angles will be uncovered. Therefore, in addition to background research, refining the research instruments before approaching participants was also of paramount importance. To be certain of the entrepreneurs' interpretation of my questions, and identify any potentially problematic questions, I engaged two New Zealand renewable energy enterprises in a test study. The test study informed a number of subsequent changes to my approach but most importantly, it helped me arrive at the crucial opening question for the interviews: "Tell me, what would you say is the biggest challenge or challenges you face while running this business?". I observed during the test study that this question was pivotal to reassure participants that I was indeed interested in their opinions and experiences and to encourage them to begin by discussing the challenges that were most important to their enterprises.

I first presented participants with the survey, which gave the entrepreneurs the opportunity to identify the biggest challenge(s) they faced while running their renewable energy enterprises. My strategy was this: I presented the challenges previously identified in the scholarly and grey literatures to the entrepreneurs, then asked them to rank these pre-determined challenges based on their own experiences in the industry. By doing this, I could compare the challenges identified in literature (mostly, I must say, by researchers based in developed countries) to those experienced in practice in emerging markets. Next, I asked the entrepreneurs to identify any other challenges of significance to their enterprises.

In the same survey, I also invited the entrepreneurs to rate the importance of ten commonly considered financial indicators to the performance of their enterprises: sales level, sales growth rate, cash flow, return on shareholder equity, gross profit margin, net profit margin from operations, profit to sales ratio, return on investment, ability to fund business growth from profits and overall firm performance. I also asked them to indicate how satisfied they were with their enterprise's performance on the same ten indicators. I considered 'satisfaction' an important aspect of my analysis of the importance of these financial indicators to renewable energy enterprises in emerging markets. Indeed, it was important to consider the entrepreneurs' 'importance' and 'satisfaction' ratings in light of each other for two reasons. First, it provided a subjective indication of their enterprises' overall financial health from the perspective of their owner-managers. Second, it indicated the fitness for purpose of these financial indicators to the aims of the enterprises. Thus, I could arrive at much richer insight into the expectations and experiences of the renewable energy enterprises regarding their performance.[5]

I used the technique of semi-structured interview as a way to follow-up and clarify participants' responses to the survey questions and as an opportunity for discussion. Semi-structured interviews meant I prescribed only some questions in advance, generally around a few key, but broad, themes. I found this approach advantageous; although predetermined questions limited the discussions broadly within the theme of the research, participants had ample room to raise and explore any issue on the subject. Whenever I needed to explore an issue more deeply, I asked probing follow-up questions. The enterprise owner-managers appeared at ease providing personal opinions and experiences because, I reasoned, they retained some control over the pace and thematic directionality of conversation. Therefore, the interview was a useful complement to the survey instrument, permitting a much deeper exploration of how renewable energy enterprises cope with the challenges faced in emerging markets over their lifetimes. I conducted these interviews face-to-face and via Skype or telephone. A number of factors determined how I chose to conduct the interviews, including convenience and ease of access to the entrepreneurs who ran the enterprises.

I also collected a considerable amount of secondary data about each enterprise, and about the journey of their entrepreneurs and owner-managers, as appropriate. These data included, for example, any documents of significance to the history, reputation or web and market presence of the venture as well as any information that could provide further insight into their entrepreneurial experiences and opinions, such as articles or opinion papers. I also collected development data for each of the countries and regions represented by the enterprises in the study including, notably, human development indicators[6] and World Bank contextual information on the ease of doing business in each country and region (World Bank and IFC, 2014).

There are several advantages to using a mix of approaches (that is, a mix of survey, interview and secondary data) to conduct the research. Chief among these, in my opinion, is the opportunity for triangulation. Indeed, I could cross-check interview responses with the ranked survey data and the secondary data acquired. For instance, where an entrepreneur ranked "access to finance" as a major challenge, I referred to the details provided in their interview responses to understand why it was a challenge and how the enterprise was designed to overcome this challenge. The appearance of issues related to this challenge in the secondary data collected would further corroborate its severity and importance to the enterprise.

Study II (2017–2018)

In Study I, I investigated the strategies used by the enterprises to overcome the challenges they faced and also uncovered their perceived ability to inspire and lead the changes required within their respective contexts to eradicate these challenges. However, there was no way to tell if the enterprises had indeed succeeded in doing so or whether they had managed to contribute in some way to the faster uptake of renewable energy technologies in emerging markets, thus contributing to the sustainable energy transition. Therefore, I sought to approach the same enterprises again, to enquire how their efforts to increase renewable energy uptake had progressed since 2013/2014.

Thus, four years later I designed a much simpler study, Study II, with the aim to follow-up with the same enterprises. I aimed to understand if they faced the same challenges they did four years prior and how they were progressing in their respective markets. To each entrepreneur who agreed to participate I posed only four questions:

1 (How) has your business progressed since 2013?
2 Do you think the challenges you face today are the same challenges you faced in 2013?
3 Please rank the following challenges in order of importance to your business, starting with the MOST challenging:

    a   Access to finance
    b   Price of the technology
    c   Local demand
    d   Renewable energy skill shortages
    e   Physical infrastructure

    f   Power of existing players on energy market
    g   Other (please specify) _____

4   Why do you think institutional conditions and challenges have improved (or worsened)?

Upon inviting the entrepreneurs to participate in the research, I noticed that many were no longer in business. Overall, over one-quarter of the enterprises involved in Study I failed by the time I began Study II. Thus, I set out to explore the differences between the 32 surviving enterprises (12 of which agreed to participate in Study II) and those that did not survive (based on data collected from the non-survivors in Study I). It is this comparison that allowed me to draw the preliminary conclusions that are the subject of this book, to problematize and recommend factors that enhance renewable energy enterprises' chances of survival in emerging markets. I used a discourse analysis to compare the successful and failed REEs in the study.

Renewable energy enterprises in emerging markets aim to contribute to the sustainable energy transition in countries in which they operate. The strategies used by REEs to realise this transition include resource mobilisation, new institutional arrangements and discursive strategies (Gabriel et al., 2016; Gabriel et al., 2019). While studying the renewable energy enterprises, I noticed that discursive strategies are an important means of influencing change used by REEs in emerging markets. Discursive strategies are the discourses – words, language and speaking turns within interactions – used in interactions with others that enable renewable energy enterprises to influence and potentially contribute to the sustainable energy transition in emerging markets. However, relatively little is known about the discursive strategies used by these enterprises. This is concerning because understanding the discursive strategies used by renewable energy enterprises, particularly those who survive and continue to influence the sustainable energy transition in emerging markets, will provide much needed insight to strengthen the impact of other nascent enterprises around the world.

At the centre of discursive strategies are discursive objects. These objects may be documents, monologues or technologies, for example, which are the means by which people communicate with target audiences. When I conducted Study II, I considered the interviews with surviving entrepreneurs an important discursive object. However, as many did not agree to be interviewed in the second study, I searched for an alternative discursive object that would allow me to understand and compare the discourses and business approaches of successful and failed enterprises. Thus, I used the enterprises' business websites as the discursive objects by which I could understand the discursive strategies they used in emerging markets. By analysing the words, images and overall content and organisation of their websites, I gained a deeper understanding of how renewable energy enterprises intended to contribute to the sustainable energy transition in emerging markets. That is, what, exactly they aimed to achieve or change in such markets, and with whom they intended to engage in dialogue in order to achieve their desired goals. I uncovered insightful differences between the discursive strategies used by the renewable energy enterprises that survived and those that did not survive in emerging markets. Therefore, in the final chapter of Part II, Chapter 6, I offer an evidence-based summary of the features, discourses and overall business model approaches used by successful renewable energy enterprises in emerging markets.

How this book is organised

I have organised the book as follows: Part I provides an overview of the field of renewable energy enterprise in emerging markets. In it the reader will find two chapters. Chapter 1 focuses on introductory and definitional issues. It defines the renewable energy enterprise and other core concepts, such as renewable energy sources and technologies, and justifies the focus on these enterprises in the emerging market context in particular. Chapter 2 outlines a typology of renewable energy enterprises. Indeed, it builds upon previously published work that merely identifies the four types without contextualising or characterising them fully.

The next major section of this book, Part II, provides details of the strategic and operational challenges faced by REEs in emerging markets in the course of trying to sell renewable energy products in emerging markets. Specifically, Chapter 3 outlines the logistical challenges of navigating the supply chain for RETs (i.e. operational challenges related to value creation and delivery). Chapter 4 enters into a discussion about the competitive landscape for REEs in emerging markets (i.e. strategic challenges related to value proposition and revenue generation). Chapter 5 describes how REEs' engagement with international aid influences their business models (i.e. strategic and operational challenges related to all aspects of their business models). Finally, Chapter 6 offers a description of successful renewable energy enterprises as well as alternative metrics to measure their success in emerging markets.

Finally, I conclude with Part III, which includes two case studies of real entrepreneurs and their enterprises and their success in emerging markets. Specifically, the case enterprises are Power Providers (Tanzania) and A-Wing (Indonesia). Both enterprises have demonstrated different but effective approaches to contributing to the aim of sustainable human thriving in emerging markets. These case studies should be read together with the case on Shane Thatcher and his enterprise, Illumination Solar, which provides yet another perspective (see Gabriel, Stanley and Thatcher (2018)). It is a pleasure to share the stories of these enterprises.

Notes

1 *Cf.* Gabriel (2016), Gabriel and Kirkwood (2016), Gabriel et al. (2016) and Gabriel et al. (2019).

2 The global 2030 agenda for sustainable development includes 17 Sustainable Development Goals (SDGs):

1 – No Poverty
2 – Zero Hunger
3 – Good Health and Well-being
4 – Quality Education
5 – Gender Equality
6 – Clean Water and Sanitation
7 – Affordable and Clean Energy
8 – Decent Work and Economic Growth
9 – Industry, Innovation and Infrastructure
10 – Reduced Inequalities
11 – Sustainable Cities and Communities
12 – Responsible Consumption and Production
13 – Climate Action
14 – Life Below Water
15 – Life on Land
16 – Peace, Justice and Strong Institutions
17 – Partnerships for the Goals

3 There is a caveat about the developed versus developing/emerging market dichotomy that I must raise here. I acknowledge that these designations, especially as descriptors of national well-being, are problematic for many reasons, not the least of which is the considerable grey area between 'developed' and 'emerging' that such dichotomous designations trivialise. Therefore, for research purposes only, I define and identify 'emerging markets' based on the countries listed in Table E (list of 'emerging and developing economies') in the International Monetary Fund (IMF)'s 2012 World Economic Outlook (WEO) Report (IMF, 2012) on pages 182–183. At the time of writing, this list may be considered outdated. However, at the time of participant selection and interviews, this list was the most relevant.

4 Sustainable Development Goal (SDG) 7: to ensure access to affordable, reliable, sustainable and modern energy for all. More information about SDG 7 can be retrieved from the United Nations Sustainable Development website: https://sustainabledevelopment.un.org/sdg7 (accessed 02 June, 2019).

5 The approach I used was a variation of the Importance-Performance Analysis (IPA) diagnostic decision tool first developed by Martilla and James (1977) in the field of marketing and used by many others since (see Tonge and Moore (2007) and Verreynne (2006) for example). Ultimately, I decided on the version developed by Gupta and Govindarajan (1984) and Covin and Slevin (1989). The work of Azzopardi and Nash (2013) can be consulted for a meta-analytic overview of the benefits of this method.

6 The Human Development Index (HDI) is used by the United Nations Development Programme (UNDP) to measure and communicate countries' progress on development.

References

Achebe, C., 1994. The art of fiction 139: Interview with Jerome Brooks. *The Paris Review*, 36(133), Winter, pp. 142–166.

Azzopardi, E. and Nash, R., 2013. A critical evaluation of importance: Performance analysis. *Tourism Management*, 35, pp. 222–233.

Covin, J.G. and Slevin, D.P., 1989. Strategic management of small firms in hostile and benign environments. *Strategic Management Journal*, 10(1), pp. 75–87.

Elzen, B., Geels, F.W. and Green, K. (Eds.), 2004. *System Innovation and the Transition to Sustainability: Theory, Evidence and Policy*. Northampton, USA: Edward Elgar Publishing.

Gabriel, C.A., 2016. What is challenging renewable energy entrepreneurs in developing countries? *Renewable and Sustainable Energy Reviews*, 64, pp. 362–371.

Gabriel, C.A. and Kirkwood, J., 2016. Business models for model businesses: Lessons from renewable energy entrepreneurs in developing countries. *Energy Policy*, 95, pp. 336–349.

Gabriel, C.A., Kirkwood, J., Walton, S. and Rose, E.L., 2016. How do developing country constraints affect renewable energy entrepreneurs? *Energy for Sustainable Development*, 35, pp. 52–66.

Gabriel, C., Stanley, M. and Thatcher, S., 2018. *Illumination Solar: Delivering Energy Poverty Solutions*. Case Study, Ivey Publishing.

Gabriel, C.A., Nazar, S., Zhu, D. and Kirkwood, J., 2019. Performance beyond economic growth: Alternatives from growth-averse enterprises in the Global South. *Alternatives: Global, Local, Political*, 44(2–4), 119–137.

Gupta, A.K. and Govindarajan, V., 1984. Business unit strategy, managerial characteristics, and business unit effectiveness at strategy implementation. *Academy of Management Journal*, 27(1), pp. 25–41.

IMF (International Monetary Fund), 2012. *World Economic Outlook April 2012*. World Economic and Financial Surveys. Washington, DC, USA: International Monetary Fund.

Martilla, J.A. and James, J.C., 1977. Importance-performance analysis. *Journal of Marketing*, 41(1), pp. 77–79.

Tonge, J. and Moore, S.A., 2007. Importance-satisfaction analysis for marine-park hinterlands: A Western Australian case study. *Tourism Management*, 28(3), pp. 768–776.

Verreynne, M.L., 2006. Strategy-making process and firm performance in small firms. *Journal of Management & Organization*, 12(3), pp. 209–222.

World Bank and IEA (International Energy Agency), 2017. *Sustainable Energy for All Global Tracking Framework*. Progress toward Sustainable Energy. Washington, DC, USA: International Bank for Reconstruction and Development.

World Bank and IFC (International Finance Corporation), 2014. Doing business: Ease of doing business index. *Doing Business*. Retrieved from www.doingbusiness.org/rankings (accessed 30 June 2014).

World Energy Council, 2018. *World Energy Trilemma Index 2018*. London, UK: World Energy Council.

1 Renewable energy enterprises in emerging markets

Overview of renewable energy sources, technologies and enterprise

Renewable energy technology (RET) refers to the equipment used to harness and transform energy from existing and ongoing natural processes such as sunshine, flowing water, wind and geothermal processes. This equipment may be installed and used either as part of the larger electricity transmission and distribution infrastructure (that is, grid integrated or 'grid-tied') or independently as standalone technology installations (that is, 'off-grid' installation). The five most common types of renewable energy are solar, wind, hydro, biomass and geothermal energy. Of the 43 enterprises included in the studies, 39 focused primarily on varieties of solar energy technology while also having someexpertise in other forms of renewable energy. Indeed, only four entrepreneurs specified technological expertise and services that did not include solar power: two offered various forms of biomass; one focused on supplying micro-hydropower to rural communities and one focused on the distribution of wind turbines. The aim of this chapter is to outline the basics of these five types of renewable energy sources and their associated technologies as they relate to the initiation and conduct of enterprise in emerging markets.

The renewable energy enterprise

First, I will identify and address some definitional issues around the renewable energy enterprise (REE), especially as it operates within the world's emerging markets. In development and business practice, as well as academia, these enterprises have received increasing attention. However, noticeably, the topic remains somewhat neglected in the context of emerging markets. In addition, few scholarly contributions on the subject are based on the first-hand voices and experiences of REEs themselves. It is important, therefore, to draw some definitional boundaries around what precisely I mean by renewable energy enterprise to begin to render clarity to a research subfield hitherto marred by conceptual and operational opacity.

I am partial to the following definition of renewable energy entrepreneurship: *the starting up and running of a growth-aspiring renewable energy enterprise*. In turn, I define renewable energy enterprise as the following: *a set of activities coordinated with the aim to develop, design, produce and/or distribute renewable energy and/or renewable energy systems or technologies*. Attentive readers will notice I distinguish between the terms "entrepreneurship" and "enterprise". The enterprise is a set of activities, a project or undertaking, sometimes structured as a profit-seeking business (though not necessarily so), which is coordinated to carry out some commercial activity. The entrepreneur is the person who initiates and manages the enterprise; entrepreneurship is, therefore, the set of processes and experiences undertaken by the entrepreneur to initiate and manage the enterprise. In sum, the enterprise is the venture, or set of activities, started by the entrepreneur. Whereas the locus of entrepreneurship is the person, the locus of the enterprise is the venture itself. Throughout this volume, in instances where the positionality of both person and venture is the same, I refer simply to the enterprise, which is the unit of analysis for the research that informed this volume.

Renewable Energy Sources (RES) and Technologies (RETs)

Solar energy is perhaps the most recognisable form of renewable energy. Most people can easily recognise active solar technologies, which are designed to capture the sun's rays directly. These technologies include solar photovoltaic (PV) cells and concentrated solar systems that use mirrors to direct and concentrate sunlight in a specific spot. The sunlight captured by these technologies is used to generate the electricity that powers lives and communities. It can be used for heating, lighting, and powering devices and machines. Solar energy can also be captured passively, without the use of technology. For instance, positioning windows to receive sunlight during the day is an effective way to heat a building, thereby reducing the need to actively generate heat. However, in emerging markets, most small renewable energy enterprises (REEs) offer products and services that capture solar energy actively. Active solar energy (hereafter referred to simply as "solar energy") offers a significant business opportunity. Solar energy delivers much needed electricity to communities in emerging markets that are either neglected by conventional electricity grid infrastructure or experience unreliable or an intermittent supply of grid-tied electricity. In such contexts, solar energy is the most popular off-grid solution, which gives its users the independence of generating their own electricity for use in homes or community buildings. In addition, PV cells are durable with a lifetime of approximately 20 years, and solar lights are usually easy to use and integrate into the lifestyles of individuals and communities. Offering solar energy products and services requires knowledge of the technology itself as well as the amount and changes in sunlight available at different times and locations.

Humans have used wind energy for thousands of years. There is evidence that ancient Egyptians harnessed the power of the wind to propel their boats along the Nile River around 5000 BC (US EIA, 2018). Wind turbines are the technology used to convert the force of the wind, as it turns the blades of the turbine into a force that can be used to run a generator to produce electricity. Wind turbines are distinct from windmills. Windmills produce more physical work to pump water or grind grain on farms, for example. Wind turbines are used to produce electrical force. It is increasingly familiar to see clusters of wind turbines installed over a large area of land (wind farms) or in the ocean (offshore wind farms). The electricity generated by these wind farms is distributed to buildings and communities for consumption. In areas with steady winds, wind power provides a cheap and reliable source of electricity. However, as wind is not always steady in all locations, on its own it is not a panacea for all electricity needs. In emerging markets, I found that enterprises offering wind energy technologies and services are usually larger and better established within the global renewable energy market than those offering solar energy, for example. Certainly, there were fewer enterprises focused mainly on wind energy technologies and services in the studies described in this volume.

Hydropower is one of the world's oldest and most inexpensive sources of renewable energy. Hydroelectricity is generated by using dams to control the flow of water from a large river. Hydroelectric power plants force controlled amounts of water through tunnels in a dam, and the water then turns turbines that generate electricity. Hydropower is especially appropriate in emerging markets; rivers are available all over the world, and the dams themselves are relatively easy to build and manage, leading to a reliable source of electricity that can be scaled to the needs of communities. In my research, I found only two enterprises specialising in hydropower, with their work focused on educating communities to become self-reliant by building their own micro-hydro dams to generate just enough electricity to meet their needs. Specialised hydropower technologies and services are not usually offered by small scale enterprises because hydropower generation and the considerable dam building effort required is largely undertaken as a state-owned and -operated enterprise. In other words, large scale hydroelectricity generation is usually run by utilities instead of individuals and communities.

Biomass energy (also referred to as 'bioenergy') is generated by converting the energy that has been stored in biomass (plants and microorganisms) through photosynthesis. Burning different forms of biomass, such as wood or woodchips, manure, crops such as corn or sugarcane and garbage, creates heat and generates electricity. However, often, biomass is also converted into forms of biofuel that can be mixed with regular fuels such as gasoline to power vehicles. Biomass is an important source of energy in emerging markets where traditional biomass such as vegetation and manure are used widely for household purposes (IEA, 2017). One of the challenges associated with the use of biomass for household purposes, however, is the air quality and related health concerns that ensue by burning fuel indoors without adequate ventilation. This presents an important opportunity for enterprise in emerging markets. In the research that informs this volume, the enterprises offering biomass solutions and advice focus on clean cook stoves (a healthier alternative to using traditional biomass for indoor cooking) or electricity generation from biogas (gases produced by the process of breaking down biomass in the absence of oxygen – that is, anaerobic digestion).

Geothermal energy is harnessed from the natural underground geothermal heat of the Earth. The Earth's geothermal heat is evident in the lava and hot water (geysers) that rise to the surface. Where steam rises to the surface naturally, it is captured and piped to power plants to power turbines that generate electricity. Water can also be injected deep underground, where it heats up and creates steam for power plants. Geothermal heat pumps are a system of pipes that cycle water between underground heat sources and a building or other heat-consuming infrastructure. Cool water is warmed underground and returns to the surface with enough heat to meet the building's heating needs. In the research that informed this volume, I found no examples of enterprises focused on geothermal energy in emerging markets. This is not necessarily because they do not exist. Instead, I speculate that the situation is similar to that of hydroelectricity; that is, large scale geothermal generation is usually run by utilities or established by large commercial or government entities instead of individuals and communities in emerging markets.

Perhaps the best known and most widely reported advantages of renewable energy are its superior ecological benefits to the natural environment, comparative to fossil energies. For instance, RETs that harness energy from wind or solar sources produce negligible amounts of polluting substances. In emerging markets in particular, air quality is a crucial concern, especially in regions where households are dependent on traditional forms of biomass such as wood and charcoal for cooking and igniting the fires that heat their homes. Indeed, the use of these fossil energies in emerging market households significantly deteriorates indoor air quality in homes and is responsible for a considerable portion of respiratory health issues reported in these nations. Therefore, although renewables such as biomass do emit some pollutants, through the use of improved cookstoves made with advanced technology, emissions can be cut by up to 95 percent.[1]

However, arguably a lesser known advantage of RES and RETs is they also produce considerable socioeconomic benefits and contribute to social and technological transformation. Indeed, their socioeconomic value is one of the most potent insights derived from the development and use of renewable energies in socioeconomically disadvantaged communities all over the world, but specifically in emerging markets. For instance, on both macro- (e.g. country or regional scale) and micro-(e.g. on the scale of individual households or communities) levels, integrating RES and RETs into electricity grid infrastructure leverages locally exploitable native energy sources, and this process also diversifies and ensures the independence and security of energy supply for those dependent on them. Off-grid distributed renewable energy installations are also advantageous because they offer independence and resilience to extreme events, and they can be deployed quickly in emergency cases. Indeed, they offer flexibility of supply. In addition, the International Renewable Energy Agency (IRENA) estimates that in 2016 the global renewable energy industry contributed to the employment of a record 9.8 million people (IRENA, 2017). Indeed, investment in renewables has increased to $2.9 trillion since 2004, improving its attractiveness for enterprise, especially in emerging markets (Frankfurt School, 2018). More poignantly, however, RES and RETs are lauded globally for their contribution to addressing a myriad of challenges associated with energy poverty in emerging markets. Energy poverty is the lack of access to modern energy services. It affects more than 1 billion people globally, mostly in emerging markets (IEA, 2017).To capture these benefits, therefore, efforts to support and proliferate renewable energy enterprise have grown steadily, especially in emerging markets. These enterprises offer valuable solutions to the socio-economic and ecological challenges faced in such markets.

Renewable energy enterprises in emerging markets are different

I have often been asked this question: are renewable energy enterprises in emerging markets really *that* different? In fact, an anonymous reviewer once advised me, "It needs to be tested that there is a significant difference between [developed market] and [emerging market] REEs". Empirically, it was an astute observation. To date, I have found no studies that empirically test the significance of postulated differences between REEs in developed and emerging markets. That is, I found no studies that acquired a representative sample of REEs from both contexts, and undertake empirical testing of differences in experience, aims, business structure, and context, for example. Indeed, to undertake such a study of REEs would no doubt provide significant advantages, and would clarify our understanding of the features that make these enterprises truly unique, especially in emerging market contexts. However, I consider that although such research would have the advantage of statistical significance, it would do little to illuminate and signal the significance, too, of the voices and nuanced experiences of individual REEs. In addition, one does not require a direct feature-by-feature comparison to observe that REEs face significantly more difficult contextual challenges and strategize and operate differently in emerging markets. Allow me to put it this way: the narratives about renewable energy enterprise have largely been influenced by developed market hegemony to date. Indeed, as scholars we have curated a considerable corpus of knowledge on developed market RES, RETs and enterprise; to such an extent, even, that this corpus has admittedly framed my own enquiry in emerging markets. I am of the opinion, therefore, that understanding the features of REE as conceived and described in developed markets provides ample premise to identify strategic and operational differences in those in emerging markets. In the 8 years of qualitative study on this topic, I observed three areas of distinction common to REEs in emerging markets: generally, they are institutional, infrastructural and socioeconomic differences, which challenge REEs in emerging markets. Within these three categories, one may find answers to the question of not only how, but *why*, REEs in emerging markets are different.

Institutional differences in emerging markets

Renewable energy enterprises are ubiquitous today, as they continue to define an ever-growing industry. They are especially important in emerging markets, particularly in regions and locales characterised by dysfunctional institutions, including incumbent market players and governments (Estrin, Mickiewicz and Stephan, 2016). REEs provide innovative solutions to the social, political and environmental challenges faced, often filling deep institutional voids in such markets. For instance, some of the literature on social enterprise suggests that emerging markets in sub-Saharan Africa are complex social and cultural contexts that influence enterprises' self-perceptions, venture organisations and activities on the ground (Rivera-Santos et al., 2015; Ault and Spicer, 2014; Bruton, Ahlstrom and Obloj, 2008). In emerging markets, enterprises are challenged by a number of issues related to both public and private institutions locally. For instance, the overall ease of doing business in emerging markets (or lack thereof) is a major challenge for REEs. Emerging markets have fared consistently poorly in the International Finance Corporation's (IFC) rankings of the ease of doing business in countries all over the world (World Bank and IFC, 2014). The IFC's rankings consider factors such as the ease of starting a business, getting credit, paying taxes, trading across borders and enforcing contracts. Other constraining conditions in emerging markets include corruption and poor legal structures (Adomako and Danso, 2014; Gupta et al., 2014), weak property rights (Herrera-Echeverri, Haar and Estévez-Bretón, 2014) and lack of access to information or education on how to start a new business (Baumol, Schilling and Wolff, 2009; Carlos Díaz Casero et al., 2013). Historically, there has been a bias in renewable energy investment in favour of Europe, China and the United States (UNEP, 2012b). These significant challenges persist for entrepreneurs doing business in such contexts due to various forms of institutional neglect, chief among which, I argue, is political support.

Political support (or lack thereof) strongly influences the conduct of REE in emerging markets. A lack of political facilitation and support can be detrimental to enterprise in emerging markets. For instance, REEs' ability to meet the logistical demands of the enterprise could be hindered by political and trade barriers and restrictive foreign policies. However, conversely, heavy handed governance and stringent regulation may also stymy entrepreneurial endeavour in emerging markets. This is especially the case in those least developed markets where nascent renewable energy enterprises are still gaining foothold in the local renewable energy industry. Indeed, policy making and governance are hegemonic processes, the outcomes of which often reflect incumbent and dominant interests. In the case of renewable energy enterprise, those dominant interests are generally those of the institutions that benefit from the proliferation of fossil energies in emerging markets. To illustrate the effects of this hegemonic process on the ability of REEs to influence the renewable energy transition in emerging markets, allow me to reflect upon the paradox of embedded agency. The paradox is a concept that has occupied the imaginations of institutional entrepreneurship theorists in recent times. In 2007, the paradox of embedded agency was described by three of institutional entrepreneurship's most prominent scholars as such:

> *The theoretical puzzle is as follows: if actors are embedded in an institutional field, how are they able to envision new practices and then subsequently get others to adopt them? Dominant actors in a given field may have the power to force change but often lack the motivation; while peripheral players may have the incentive to create and champion new practices, but often lack the power to change institutions.*
>
> (Garud, Hardy and Maguire, 2007: 961)

Indeed, debate endures abundantly about whether it is actors at the centre of their industries (e.g. dominant incumbent actors such as fossil fuel institutions) (Greenwood and Suddaby, 2006; Maguire, Hardy and Lawrence, 2004) or those on the periphery (Boxenbaum and Battilana, 2005; Garud, Jain and Kumaraswamy, 2002) (e.g. new REEs), who are most likely to express agency and act as change makers within the industry. This *aporia* has created a false polarity: those who constitute the institutional status quo (dominant actors) versus those wishing to change the status quo (peripheral actors). The resulting "us versus them" narrative has led to the (self-) characterisation of enterprises such as REEs as a peripheral and aggrieved "us", standing in opposition to the dominant institutional "them". However, while there are indeed institutional tensions between dominant and peripheral actors, I posit that it is the frustration of experiencing the combined effect of dominant, incumbent self-preservation and protracted peripheral insistence that eventually motivate REEs to persist and successfully influence institutional change. Moreover, I surmise that, unfortunately, the same combined effect may be the cause of failure for many REEs in emerging markets.

The challenge of accessing credit or investment to start or maintain a renewable energy enterprise in emerging markets is a fair example. On one hand, unavailability and inaccessibility of affordable credit has dissuaded many nascent REEs from developing their enterprises, often leading to failure. On the other hand, unavailability and inaccessibility of affordable credit has prompted REEs in emerging markets to find innovative ways to ensure the survival of their businesses. In my studies, I have noted that many REEs try strategies such as crowdfunding, microfinance and micro-franchising to innovatively overcome such challenges. However, not all have used them successfully. For instance, although three REEs attempted to use crowdfunding as a way of financing one or more of their businesses' projects, only one was able to use it successfully. "Luis" used a crowdfunding platform successfully to "fund a change in our business model" for his REE to facilitate access and suitability of his distribution mechanisms for extremely remote regions in Guatemala. Luis' crowdfunding campaign gained worldwide attention, and due to its success, he generated enough seed capital to adapt his business model to the context of end-users in Guatemala.

In short, constraints in their institutional environment have the potential to restrict the agency (that is, the ability to act freely) of REEs. However, the agency of the entrepreneurs who run these enterprises may be viewed as *embedded* agency, a paradox, which emphasises that institutional challenges play a dual role. These challenges simultaneously constrain and encourage REEs to influence the renewable energy transition; see Powell and DiMaggio (2012), Garud, Hardy and Maguire (2007), Battilana (2006) and Battilana and D'Aunno (2009). Thus, as REEs endeavour to overcome institutional challenges, they simultaneously create new institutions themselves, leveraging the knowledge acquired through the experience of embeddedness despite the power and influence of incumbent fossil fuel institutions (Garud, Hardy and Maguire, 2007; Hockerts and Wüstenhagen, 2010; Lovio, Mickwitz and Heiskanen, 2011).

I surmise that these arguments gather support when confronted with international observation that although REEs in emerging markets are consistently challenged by difficult institutional constraints, emerging markets have been found to have among the world's highest rates of socially-and environmentally-motivated enterprise (Global Entrepreneurship Monitor Consortium, 2017). Indeed, despite the institutional challenges faced, REEs persist. It is also extremely important to understand REEs in the world's least developed regions, as the challenges faced are likely more difficult (Gabriel, 2016). Yet, a considerable portion of the corpus on enterprise in emerging markets has been built on a foundation of research from larger, quickly developing countries such as India (e.g. Datta and Gailey, 2012, China (highlighted by Kolk, Rivera-Santos and Rufín, 2014 and Kolk and Rivera-Santos, 2018) and South Africa (e.g. Littlewood and Holt, 2018). If we are to distinguish the features that characterise emerging market versus developed market renewable energy enterprise in a manner that effectively and usefully informs practice in emerging markets; it is important to draw upon a wider variety of economic and institutional contexts and draw lessons from research in these under-represented, least developed regions.

Infrastructural differences in emerging markets

There are some infrastructural challenges in emerging markets that make it more difficult to achieve universal energy access than in many of the world's more developed markets. Most importantly, emerging markets suffer from the absence of twenty-first century infrastructure, particularly those required to establish and develop electricity distribution grids. Therefore, to assist with the renewable energy transition in emerging markets and facilitate the uptake of renewable technologies, decentralised off-grid supply is widely regarded as most appropriate, especially among remote communities.

Renewable energy sources are plentiful and advantageous in emerging markets. For instance, biomass can be stored and used when needed and is a familiar resource to many communities in emerging markets, especially those still reliant on traditional forms of biomass. Likewise, solar is advantageous because of its abundance as a resource, its appropriateness for decentralised generation and supply and relative ease of installation. Indeed, micro-grids of solar PV, pico-solar lighting products and cleaner, more efficient cook stoves are appropriate technologies in emerging markets. However, to harness this energy, many individuals and communities in emerging markets rely on reverse innovation, which ensures that the technologies available in such markets are tailored to the contexts in which they will be used. Reverse innovation is viewed as an opportunity to overcome these infrastructural challenges. It refers to the design and commercialisation of products, services and technologies in emerging markets first before spreading to more developed markets. It involves a process of tailoring such innovations to suit the needs of users in emerging markets.

Energy deprived communities in emerging markets live with either no basic energy services, or when available these services are unreliable. Such communities often rely on polluting and unhealthy fuels such as kerosene for lighting and biomass for cooking and other household needs (Koch and Hammond, 2013; Albi and Lieberman, 2013). Despite the many infrastructural improvements achieved in recent years, energy poverty persists in some of the world's most remote and socioeconomically deprived communities, especially in parts of sub-Saharan Africa and Asia (IEA, 2017). Renewable energy enterprise is seen as an important solution to some of these challenges not only because they increase availability and distribution of RETs, but also because they contribute significantly to technological and business model innovation in emerging markets (Gabriel, 2016).

Socioeconomic differences in emerging markets

Many of the institutional constraints faced by entrepreneurs in developing and emerging countries are due to issues related to poverty. Therefore, allow me at this point to introduce and outline a concept that highlights business conduct under such conditions: that is, the concept of the 'Base of the Pyramid' or 'Bottom of the Pyramid' (BOP). The term was first introduced by C. K. Prahalad in the late 1990s as a way to refer to those segments of the global population that live under USD2.00 per day – that is, the world's poorest socioeconomic category. Scholarly work on the BOP initially focused on multinational enterprises (MNEs) and the strategies that can be used to not only tap into this segment of the global market, but also help alleviate poverty. Prahalad and other proponents of BOP principles claim that doing business at the BOP required moving past business as usual to the development of unique products, services and strategies that were suited to the unique characteristics of BOP populations (Prahalad, 2006; Prahalad and Hammond, 2002). These ideas included microcredit schemes and the reconceptualization of the poor as strategic partners rather than as simply poor customers. However, recently, the study of business at the BoP has shifted in focus from the actions of MNEs to a focus on local and regional enterprise and entrepreneurship. In 2014, Kolk, Rivera-Santos and Rufín (2014) produced the first comprehensive review of scholarly articles focusing on the BOP concept, which confirmed this shift in focus. Kolk, Rivera-Santos and Rufín (2014) demonstrated that over the last decade the focus of scholarly research has been fairly broad, embracing and investigating a variety of means of conceptualising how enterprises engage with the poor as customers in emerging markets.

One of the issues faced at the BOP in emerging markets is that of energy poverty (the lack of access to modern energy services). Indeed, energy poverty is experienced by one billion people all over the world who do not have access to energy for the purposes of lighting, heating, powering household devices and as a fuel for cooking and other household uses. Indeed, this urgent issue is one of the most compelling arguments for off-grid solutions in emerging markets. Energy poverty within BOP communities also raises issues of the affordability of RETs (Gabriel, 2022). RET prices can be prohibitive among BOP communities. Therefore, to solve the issues related to affordability for end-users in these communities, REEs often rely on co-designing their business models and adapting their technologies together with BOP communities. In addition, these issues are also addressed by improving the availability and accessibility of various forms of financial assistance for socioeconomically disadvantaged end-users.

In addition, REEs must consider the appropriateness of the technologies offered for end-users at the BOP locally. REEs attentive to issues of local appropriateness must consider the functionality, durability and life cycle of the products offered (Gabriel, 2022). Inclusive business models such as micro-franchising are an important means of addressing the challenges of affordability and appropriateness in emerging markets by involving end-users in the distribution and maintenance of renewable energy products and equipment. Inclusive business models (see Chapter 2 for a detailed explanation) also have the additional advantage of leveraging and developing the technical skills of end-users in emerging markets.

Therefore, as communities in emerging markets grapple with not only issues of ecological importance and urgency, but also crucial social challenges, the use of RES and RETs in such markets also raises certain ethical concerns that do not normally arise in more developed markets. For instance, the use of biomass as a source of renewable energy remains relatively controversial in emerging markets for two reasons. First, the drive to plant and harvest crops for use as biofuels requires large swathes of land, which could be used for food instead. In countries marred by poverty and nutritional concerns, the use of arable land for fuel has ignited a passionate "food versus fuel" debate that remains largely unsettled to date (*cf.* Tomei and Helliwell, 2016; Zhang et al., 2010 and Graham-Rowe, 2011). Second, many consider biomass energy akin to a non-renewable resource because it relies on plant matter as feedstock, which must be harvested, processed and burned to create electricity. If this plant matter is not replanted at a rate compatible with the rate of extraction, then indeed biomass may be considered non-renewable. A similar ethical dilemma has been raised about the use of geothermal energy in emerging markets. If geothermal energy is used in parts of the world where the only available source is underground dry heat, then freshwater must be used to generate the steam needed to convert this energy to electricity. There are two issues here. First, in such arid parts of the world (such as in parts of sub-Saharan Africa and Latin America), freshwater may not be available in large enough quantities to ensure a steady supply of geothermal energy. Second, reminiscent of the "food versus fuel" dilemma, the use of this freshwater in regions where large portions of the population lack potable water is ethically questionable.

Common features of renewable energy enterprise in emerging markets

The institutional, infrastructural and socioeconomic differences of renewable energy enterprises in emerging markets mean there are some features that these enterprises have in common. The next chapter elaborates on the specific features of REE business models in emerging markets. However, here I outlined three of the common features that those working with REEs are likely to encounter in the structure and operations of REEs. One may not encounter all these features in the same enterprise, and these three in no way constitute an exhaustive list. Instead, those working with REEs may observe different combinations of these features among such enterprises in emerging markets.

Distributed installations

Distributed (decentralised), off-grid energy installations are common throughout the developing world. In emerging markets, the infrastructural challenges related to unreliable or non-existent energy distribution infrastructure and socioeconomic challenges such as energy poverty, affordability and technological appropriateness often point to off-grid, decentralised installation as an effective and quick solution.

Solar technologies

I have found, overwhelmingly, that REEs in emerging markets mostly offer solar energy products and equipment. However, this comes as no surprise because there is immense solar energy resource potential in emerging markets. Therefore, most REEs aim to leverage this abundant resource to create value for end-users in emerging markets. Moreover, the abundance of solar resource enhances its ease of exploitation as well as its efficiency and effectiveness as a solution to many of the socioeconomic challenges encountered in emerging markets.

Aid and NGO involvement

A common feature of REEs in emerging markets is their dependence on and/or collaboration with international aid and development organisations (IDOs) or non-governmental organisations (NGOs). In Chapter 5 of this volume, I describe the aid-centric business model used by many REEs in emerging markets. As a solution, I recommend shifting aid to the periphery and propose an alternative aid-peripheral business model.

Small-scale enterprises

Most REEs operating in emerging markets are small in size in terms of the number of people they employ. In the studies on which this volume is based, the average number of employees in the 43 enterprises engaged was 17. However, the enterprise run by Dhruv was an exception, employing over 224 employees at the time of interview. Dhruv's enterprise was much larger than the average because it used a very successful micro-franchising approach. The small size of most REEs usually has the advantage of allowing them to focus more meaningfully on locally relevant issues, ensuring that their products and services are tailored to the needs of end-users in emerging markets.

Whenever I am asked to identify quintessential examples of renewable energy enterprise in emerging markets, three come immediately to mind: *Grameen Shakti*, *d.light* and *Solar Dynamics*. I use these examples because they represent an array of REE features, including those described previously, and they are well-known; therefore, information about them is easily accessible across the industry. Here is a summary of their approaches and achievements, including indication of whether and how they integrated the aforementioned features into their business models.

Before Muhammad Yunus started the award-wining enterprise, *Grameen* in Bangladesh, the conventionally held wisdom was that doing business with the poor was not a tenable option for enterprise (Wimmer, 2012; Yunus, 1998). Nonetheless, Yunus' Grameen became a successful microfinance enterprise, offering small loans to people living at the BOP in emerging markets to improve their lives and livelihoods. Yunus' "doing business with the poor" ethos led to the creation of Grameen subsidiary, *Grameen Shakti*, which focuses on offering ecologically benign, cleaner solutions. For instance, Grameen Shakti offers small-scale solar home systems (SHSs) and clean cook stoves. One of the most important insights from the experiences of Grameen Shakti is that the poor can and do repay their loans faithfully if loan systems are coupled with other features. These other features included, for example, group accountability (groups of women, for example, could borrow together and assist or encourage each other to repay their loans). In addition, Grameen Shakti offered comprehensive services tailored to the specific needs of its end-users in Bangladesh's BOP communities. Grameen's business model has since been replicated in countries all around the world, not only in emerging markets.

d.light[2] offers portable pico solar lighting products in the decentralised renewables industry in emerging markets. Pico solar products are those that rely on very small, compact and light weight solar photovoltaic panels to generate very small amounts of power needed for tasks such as lighting. Pico solar products are generally portable and can be used not just for lighting, but also for charging devices and radios. d.light is a REE that is well known globally for delivering affordable solar products and equipments to BOP communities affected by energy poverty in emerging markets. Given this context, d.light's products are tailored for distributed generation in remote areas, and the Lighting Global initiative[3] has increased the popularity of d.light's products. In addition to its products, d.light and other similar REEs around the world are transforming the way such enterprises interact with socioeconomically challenged end-users in emerging markets. d.light's first product was delivered to emerging markets in 2008. The company claims to have distributed "over 20 million solar light and power products in 65 countries, improving the lives of over 93 million people".[4] However, d.light operates on a much larger international scale than most other REEs in emerging markets. Indeed, although it is significantly larger than the enterprises included in this study, d.light exemplifies the aspirations of the small-scale REEs whose stories are included in this volume.

Solar Dynamics,[5] operating in Barbados in the Eastern Caribbean, is a typical profit-oriented distributor of renewable energy products and equipment. In operation for 45 years since 1974, Solar Dynamics has grown into one of the best known REEs in the Caribbean region. They supply solar hot water systems for residential and commercial use in Barbados and across other Caribbean countries as well. Solar Dynamics has received financial support from many regional NGOs and international IDOs over its lifetime. For instance, the REE received a loan from an NGO, Christian Action for Development in the Caribbean, a division of the Caribbean Conference of Churches. In addition, James Husbands (Managing Director of Solar Dynamics) has explained that along with other financial entities, the World Bank also supported a revolving fund to demonstrate the effectiveness of solar hot water systems in Jamaica. Husbands explained that "the concept of solar water heating as an appropriate technology was the brainchild of Canon Andrew Hatch, who built one of The Brace Research designs of the "Low Cost" solar water heaters in the early 1970's".[6] Solar Dynamics has since sold and installed over 30,000 solar hot water systems on homes and resorts in Barbados, St Lucia and Grenada, university campuses in Grenada and Jamaica and for the Barbados Defence Force, for example. Indeed, the REE has made a significant contribution to the renewable energy transition, especially for heating purposes in the Caribbean.

Common myths about renewable energy enterprise in emerging markets

Renewable energy enterprises are the same as utilities

Typically, utilities function to supply energy (electricity and/or heat) via centralised grid infrastructure. While REEs may supply energy on a scale similar to utilities (refer to "Integrators (Type IV)"), in Chapter 2), utilities rarely become involved in distributed generation. Large utility-scale renewable energy enterprises are common in more developed markets, where they design and develop communal scale wind farms, as well as large scale solar installations, for instance.

Renewable energy enterprises are solely development oriented enterprises

I was astounded by the shear variety of motivations for starting and running REEs in emerging markets. Some, do in fact, start their enterprises with the motivation to contribute to human development in their locales. However, the reasons also include ecological "green" motivations, independence, profitability and necessity. Regardless of their motivations, REEs in emerging markets use their experience and growing influence in these markets to usher in transformative change in the sustainable energy systems in emerging markets.

Renewable energy enterprises are microfinance enterprises

I believe this misconception comes from the global popularity of Indian renewable energy enterprises such as *Grameen Shakti*. Indeed, it is only larger REEs who are able to offer microfinance services to their customers as well. Because most are extremely small, microfinance is not commonly offered by REEs in emerging markets. I have observed, however, that many REEs will partner with local microfinance institutions to provide customers in need with access to financing. However, this is in no way applies to all REEs. In addition, in cases where they do engage microfinance institutions, the relationship with such institutions is usually at an arm's length only. That is, they simply refer customers to the microfinance institution, then supply the products if the customer is approved to receive finance.

Most renewable energy enterprises operate in India and China

It is difficult to test this statement empirically. Indeed, the vast majority of renewable energy enterprises in emerging markets are so small and purposely operating "under the radar" that those who might seek to quantify the number of REEs existing in emerging markets would find it a challenging task. It is therefore problematic to determine unequivocally whether most are operating in large markets such as India and China. However, I posit that there is greater "psychic distance" (O'Grady and Lan, 1996; Brewer, 2007) between entities in the developed world and the least developed parts of sub-Saharan Africa, Asia and the Pacific, and Latin America and the Caribbean than between the developed world and India and China. Therefore, I surmise that this misconception stems from a combination of the relative popularity of REEs in India and China (such as *Grameen Shakti*), the relative ease of accessing these markets from the developed world and the shorter psychic distance between the developed world and India and China.

Renewable energy enterprise in emerging markets can never be financially self-sustaining

The attentive reader will note, as they progress through the pages of this book, that there are many examples of renewable energy enterprises that are self-sustaining. In fact, I provide some examples of such in the case studies highlighted in Part III of this book. With the quickly reducing cost of RETs, wider variety of options for generation and steadily improving institutional conditions, renewable energy enterprise is becoming increasingly attractive and lucrative. Indeed, I would say, unequivocally, renewable energy sources, technologies and the enterprises that leverage them are here to stay.

Notes

1 Project Drawdown, available from: www.drawdown.org/solutions/food/clean-cook stoves (accessed 02 June 2019).
2 d.light's business website: www.dlight.com/products/ (accessed 02 June, 2019)
3 Lighting Global is an initiative of the World Bank, which aims to quickly improve access to distributed off-grid energy for those living in energy poverty in the emerging markets of the world. Part of the initiative is a unique quality standard for off-grid solar products. Only companies, such as d.light, who have their products certified by Lighting Global's standards can receive the support of the initiative. Companies and products registered with Lighting Global benefit from significant market advantages in emerging markets.
4 d.light 'About Us': www.dlight.com/about/ (accessed 02 June, 2019).
5 Solar Dynamics' business website: www.solardynamicslimited.com/ (accessed 02 June 2019).

6 Biography of James Husbands GCM available here: http://siteresources.world-bank.org/INTLAC/Resources/257803-1340980367976/Bio-JamesHusbands.pdf (accessed 02 June, 2019).

References

Adomako, S. and Danso, A., 2014. Regulatory environment, environmental dynamism, political ties, and performance: Study of entrepreneurial firms in a developing economy. *Journal of Small Business and Enterprise Development*, 21(2), pp. 212–230.

Albi, E. and Lieberman, A.E., 2013. Bringing clean energy to the base of the pyramid: The interplay of business models, technology, and local context. *Journal of Management for Global Sustainability*, 1(2), pp. 141–156.

Ault, J.K. and Spicer, A., 2014. The institutional context of poverty: State fragility as a predictor of cross-national variation in commercial microfinance lending. *Strategic Management Journal*, 35(12), pp. 1818–1838.

Battilana, J., 2006. Agency and institutions: The enabling role of individuals' social position. *Organization*, 13(5), pp. 653–676.

Battilana, J. and D'aunno, T., 2009. Institutional work and the paradox of embedded agency. In T. Lawrence, R. Suddaby and B. Leca (Eds.), *Institutional Work: Actors and Agency in Institutional Studies of Organizations* (Vol. 31, p. 58). Cambridge, UK: Cambridge University Press.

Baumol, W.J., Schilling, M.A. and Wolff, E.N., 2009. The superstar inventors and entrepreneurs: How were they educated? *Journal of Economics & Management Strategy*, 18(3), pp. 711–728.

Boxenbaum, E. and Battilana, J., 2005. Importation as innovation: Transposing managerial practices across fields. *Strategic Organization*, 3(4), pp. 355–383.

Brewer, P.A., 2007. Operationalizing psychic distance: A revised approach. *Journal of International Marketing*, 15(1), pp. 44–66.

Bruton, G.D., Ahlstrom, D. and Obloj, K., 2008. Entrepreneurship in emerging economies: Where are we today and where should the research go in the future. *Entrepreneurship Theory and Practice*, 32(1), pp. 1–14.

Carlos Díaz Casero, J., Almodóvar González, M., de la Cruz Sánchez Escobedo, M., Coduras Martinez, A. and Hernández Mogollón, R., 2013. Institutional variables, entrepreneurial activity and economic development. *Management Decision*, 51(2), pp. 281–305.

Datta, P.B. and Gailey, R., 2012. Empowering women through social entrepreneurship: Case study of a women's cooperative in India. *Entrepreneurship Theory and Practice*, 36(3), pp. 569–587.

Estrin, S., Mickiewicz, T. and Stephan, U., 2016. Human capital in social and commercial entrepreneurship. *Journal of Business Venturing*, 31(4), pp. 449–467.

Frankfurt School (FS-UNEP Collaborating Centre), 2018. Global trends in renewable energy investment 2018. Frankfurt School of Finance & Management gGmbH, Frankfurt, Germany.

Gabriel, C.A., 2016. What is challenging renewable energy entrepreneurs in developing countries? *Renewable and Sustainable Energy Reviews*, 64, pp. 362–371.

Gabriel, C.A., 2022. Reverse innovation. In W. Leal Filho (Ed.), *Encyclopedia of the UN Sustainable Development Goals (SDGs)*. SDG 7 Affordable and Clean Energy. Springer: Switzerland.

Garud, R., Hardy, C. and Maguire, S., 2007. Institutional entrepreneurship as embedded agency: An introduction to the special issue. *Organization Studies*, 28(7), pp. 957–969.

Garud, R., Jain, S. and Kumaraswamy, A., 2002. Institutional entrepreneurship in the sponsorship of common technological standards: The case of Sun Microsystems and Java. *Academy of Management Journal*, 45(1), pp. 196–214.

Global Entrepreneurship Monitor Consortium, 2017. *Global Entrepreneurship Monitor 2016/2017 Global Report*. Retrieved from www.gemconsortium.org/report/49812 (accessed 02 June 2019).

Graham-Rowe, D., 2011. Beyond food versus fuel. *Nature*, 474(7352), p. S6.

Greenwood, R. and Suddaby, R., 2006. Institutional entrepreneurship in mature fields: The big five accounting firms. *Academy of Management Journal*, 49(1), pp. 27–48.

Gupta, V.K., Guo, C., Canever, M., Yim, H.R., Sraw, G.K. and Liu, M., 2014. Institutional environment for entrepreneurship in rapidly emerging major economies: The case of Brazil, China, India, and Korea. *International Entrepreneurship and Management Journal*, 10(2), pp. 367–384.

Herrera-Echeverri, H., Haar, J. and Estévez-Bretón, J.B., 2014. Foreign direct investment, institutional quality, economic freedom and entrepreneurship in emerging markets. *Journal of Business Research*, 67(9), pp. 1921–1932.

Hockerts, K. and Wüstenhagen, R., 2010. *Greening Goliaths versus Emerging Davids: Theorizing about the Role of Incumbents and New Entrants in Sustainable Entrepreneurship*, 25(5), pp. 481–492.

IEA (International Energy Agency), 2017. *Energy Access Outlook 2017: From Poverty to Prosperity*. OECD/IEA.

IRENA (International Renewable Energy Agency), 2017. *Renewable Energy and Jobs: Annual Review 2017*. Abu Dhabi: IRENA.

Koch, J.L. and Hammond, A., 2013. Innovation dynamics, best practices, and trends in the off-grid clean energy market. *Journal of Management for Global Sustainability*, 1(2), pp. 121–139.

Kolk, A. and Rivera-Santos, M., 2018. The state of research on Africa in business and management: Insights from a systematic review of key international journals. *Business & Society*, 57(3), pp. 415–436.

Kolk, A., Rivera-Santos, M. and Rufín, C., 2014. Reviewing a decade of research on the "base/bottom of the pyramid" (BOP) concept. *Business & Society*, 53(3), pp. 338–377.

Littlewood, D. and Holt, D., 2018. Social entrepreneurship in South Africa: Exploring the influence of environment. *Business & Society*, 57(3), pp. 525–561.

Lovio, R., Mickwitz, P. and Heiskanen, E., 2011. Path dependence, path creation and creative destruction in the evolution of energy systems. In R. Wuestenhagen and R. Wuebker (Eds.), *Handbook of Research on Energy Entrepreneurship*. Cheltenham, UK: Edward Elgar Publishing.

Maguire, S., Hardy, C. and Lawrence, T.B., 2004. Institutional entrepreneurship in emerging fields: HIV/AIDS treatment advocacy in Canada. *Academy of Management Journal*, 47(5), pp. 657–679.

O'Grady, S. and Lane, H.W., 1996. The psychic distance paradox. *Journal of International Business Studies*, 27(2), pp. 309–333.

Powell, W.W. and DiMaggio, P.J. (Eds.), 2012. *The New Institutionalism in Organizational Analysis*. Chicago, USA: University of Chicago Press.

Prahalad, C.K., 2006. *The Fortune at the Bottom of the Pyramid*. New Jersey, USA: Wharton School Publishing.

Prahalad, C.K. and Hammond, A., 2002. What works: Serving the poor, profitably. A private sector strategy for global digital opportunity. World Resources Institute. Retrieved from http://web.mit.edu/sp.784/www/DOCUMENTS/serving_profitably%20-%20paper%20Jorge%20sent.pdf (accessed 02 June 2019).

Rivera-Santos, M., Holt, D., Littlewood, D. and Kolk, A., 2015. Social entrepreneurship in sub-Saharan Africa. *Academy of Management Perspectives*, 29(1), pp. 72–91.

Tomei, J. and Helliwell, R., 2016. Food versus fuel? Going beyond biofuels. *Land Use Policy*, 56, pp. 320–326.

UNEP (United Nations Environment Programme), 2012b. Global trends in renewable energy investment 2012. U.C. Centre (Ed.). Frankfurt School, UNEP Collaborating Centre for Climate and Sustainable Energy Finance, Bloomberg New Energy Finance, German Federal Ministry for the Environment, Nature Conservation and Nuclear Safety, Germany.

US EIA (U.S. Energy Information Administration), 2018. Wind explained: History of wind power. Retrieved from www.eia.gov/energyexplained/index.php?page=wind_history (accessed 19 March 2019).

Wimmer, N., 2012. *Green Energy for a Billion Poor*. MCRE Verlag UG.

World Bank and IFC (International Finance Corporation), 2014. Doing business: Ease of doing business index. *Doing Business*. Retrieved from www.doingbusiness.org/rankings (accessed 30 June 2014).

Yunus, M., 1998. *Banker to the Poor: The Story of the Grameen Bank*. India: Penguin Books.

Zhang, Z., Lohr, L., Escalante, C. and Wetzstein, M., 2010. Food versus fuel: What do prices tell us? *Energy Policy*, 38(1), pp. 445–451.

2 A typology of renewable energy enterprises

Four types of renewable energy enterprise: a business model typology

The case has been made for typologies in social science research. Typologies organise otherwise disparate fragments of information according to specified dimensions. The aim is to identify similarities and differences towards the objective of creating a set of characteristics by which different types can be distinguished. A typology of renewable energy enterprises is especially important and timely because although there is a growing corpus of knowledge around renewable energy enterprise in emerging markets, much of this knowledge exists and is passed on only tacitly. Where repositories, discourses and cadres of explicit knowledge do exist, said knowledge exists for antidotal rather than explanatory purposes. Indeed, the knowledge curated in the renewable energy industry in emerging markets to date focuses on remedying the socioeconomic challenges faced in these markets. Yet, this knowledge has been curated without insight from the enterprises themselves. It is timely, therefore, to reflect on the lessons learned from and about renewable energy enterprises so far and take stock of who, exactly, renewable energy enterprises are and what they do in emerging markets.

I encountered four types of renewable energy enterprise (REE) in emerging markets: (I) Consultants, (II) Innovators, (III) Distributors and (IV) Integrators (Gabriel and Kirkwood, 2016). There are two distinct supply chains pertaining to renewable energy enterprises in emerging markets: the renewable energy sources (RES) and renewable energy technology (RET) supply chains. On one hand, the RES supply chain is responsible for the harvesting of energy from renewable sources such as the sun and wind and transforming it into electricity and heat for end-users. On the other hand, the RET supply chain supplies the equipment used to generate and distribute energy for end-users. Renewable energy enterprises operate across one or both of these supply chains. Figure 2.1 illustrates the four types of renewable energy enterprise along the RES and RET supply chains.

Renewable energy consultants are enterprises that leverage the knowledge and experiences of their founders and employees to provide advice to

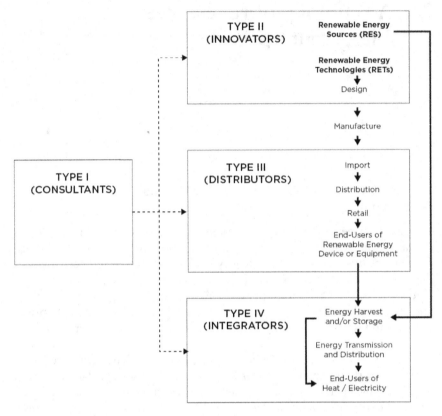

Figure 2.1 A typology of renewable energy enterprises in emerging markets

system designers, managers, providers and end-users of renewable energy technologies and sources. These Type I enterprises are not limited to a single aspect of renewable energy supply chains (refer to Figure 2.1). Instead, they offer advice on all aspects, including renewable energy system design, sources of renewable energy, its end uses, storage and maintenance. Indeed, the renewable energy consultant is a relative generalist, applying a wide range of renewable energy specific knowledge and know-how to provide solutions and make recommendations to those investing in or embarking upon renewable energy projects around the world. In sum, consultants are REEs who offer advice and design services as the value proposition for their businesses.

Renewable energy (RES and RET) innovators (Type II) invent and develop their own new renewable energy technology or source of renewable energy. Thus, 'innovators' refers to those enterprises with value propositions based on the development and sale of new RETs and RESs invented or discovered by the entrepreneur.

Renewable energy distributors perform a specific role within renewable energy supply chains. These Type III enterprises operate along all aspects of the end-user facing distribution activities of the RET supply chain (Figure 2.1). Essentially, distributors bring renewable energy products, devices and equipment to the end-users who will use them to generate energy. Distributors are involved in all or some of a country or region's renewable energy import, wholesale distribution and retail activities. For instance, they might sell solar panels, solar lights, biomass cook stoves, batteries and other equipment in emerging markets. Many of the enterprises supported and certified by the Lighting Global initiative operate under distributor business models, making solar lighting equipment more widely available in these markets. Therefore, distributors are those whose value proposition and customer relationships focus on the direct sale and exchange of RETs for capital.

Finally, renewable energy integrators (Type IV) operate along the RES supply chain, often engaging in off-grid renewable energy supply in emerging markets. Integrators are slightly similar to utilities only in the sense that they are primarily involved in the supply of energy *services*, not equipment. For instance, when emerging market governments and NGOs wish to provide electricity to off-grid communities, they seek the services of integrators, who then do the work of system design, deciding the most appropriate RES and mix for the community's needs, based on available resources, acquiring the appropriate technology (either from a distributor, or sourcing and importing themselves), then building and setting up the system to deliver energy to end-users. Therefore, integrators run scaled-up distribution enterprises delivering renewable energy services and focusing on the design, installation and management of micro-and mini-grids in emerging markets.

In this volume, I characterise the four types based on their position along the RES and RET supply chains and the features of their business models. A business model captures and reflects *how* an enterprise *implements* the business strategy or plans conceived by its owners and/or managers (Casadesus-Masanell and Ricart, 2010). The business model describes the logic of how value is created and retained by the enterprise (Hall and Wagner, 2012). In practice, Osterwalder, Pigneur and Clark (2010) observed four key pillars of a business model: Infrastructure Management, Value Proposition, Customers and Financial Aspects. Theoretically, these four pillars emanate from the three main constructs observed within business models: the *configuration of value creation* (Infrastructure Management), the *value proposition* (including Customers) and the *model of revenue generation* (Financial Aspects) (Wustenhagen and Boehnke, 2008).

The configuration of value creation refers to the physical and human infrastructure needed to produce a product or service and deliver it to customers (that is, the supply chain). It refers to all resources and capabilities that must work together in "repeatable patterns of action" (Osterwalder, 2004: 79) to design and deliver the value proposition (Eisenhardt and Martin, 2000; Teece, 2007; Wallin, 2005). The value proposition generally refers to the product or service offered (and how – through what means – it creates value for customers). Arguably, an enterprise's value proposition is the most popular business model construct. Certainly, to date scholars continue to devote considerable research effort to understanding and characterising value and value propositions. Distilling and demystifying the value proposition offers considerable room for dialogue. The conceptual quagmire around questions of how enterprises develop and innovate the products and services they offer customers (Cusumano, Kahl and Suarez, 2014; Hollensen, 2013; Zott and Amit, 2008) and the dynamics of "value" (Amit and Zott, 2001; Jolink and Niesten, 2013; Hall and Roelich, 2016) continue to occupy the minds of *academe*. In addition to the products and services offered, an enterprise's value proposition also refers to the various ways it identifies, targets and interacts with its customers (Osterwalder, 2004; Osterwalder, Pigneur and Clark, 2010). Finally, the model of revenue generation refers to the description of how the enterprise generates income and, if it is profit seeking, ultimately profits (Wustenhagen and Boehnke, 2008). As Osterwalder argued in 2004, an enterprise's model of revenue generation is most dependent and inexorably linked with all the other constructs. Specifically, an enterprise cannot generate revenue successfully and efficiently if it is unable to design and operationalise its value proposition and configuration of value creation immaculately. Thus, with this business model lens, I structured my analyses and descriptions of the REEs I studied in emerging markets.

Differences in the ranking of challenges across the four types of renewable energy enterprises can be examined closely in Table 2.1. The table shows, for example, that access to finance is a more severe challenge for the REE consultants (Type I) than the REE integrators (Type IV). It also shows that infrastructure and logistics were a bigger challenge for the Distributors than the other business types.

In the rest of this chapter, I highlight some of the business model characteristics I encountered in the research, some of which were introduced only briefly previously (*cf.* Gabriel and Kirkwood, 2016 and Gabriel et al., 2016). In addition to these characteristics, I also discuss regional implications, supported by insights about the perceived challenges faced in each emerging market.

Type I: consultants

Consultants rely on their knowledge of renewable energy sources and technologies to provide advice on every aspect of the renewable energy supply chain. Among the 43 renewable energy enterprises (REEs), consultants were the youngest and smallest (in terms of number of employees). The consultants' small size is advantageous because it lowers their enterprises' fixed costs. Table 2.2 outlines the consultant profile as identified in this research.

The defining characteristic of renewable energy consultants is a primary reliance on their own renewable energy acumen as the primary value

Table 2.1 The ranking of challenges across the four types of renewable energy enterprises**

	Overall Average Rank	Average for Consultants (Type I)	Average for Innovators (Type II)	Average for Distributors (Type III)	Average for Integrators (Type IV)
Inadequate local demand	5.0	5.5	**3.4**	5.7	4.0
Price of renewable energy technologies	4.4	4.3	**3.6**	4.9	4.5
Access to institutional finance	2.9	**2.2**	3.4	3.1	3.8
Lack of skilled labour	4.8	5.1	5.4	**4.3**	**4.4**
Physical infrastructure & logistics	5.2	6.0	4.6	**3.9**	5.4
Power of existing players on energy market	5.8	5.7	6.2	5.9	5.8
Governmental/ policy support	3.4	**3.0**	4.2	3.8	3.5
Other	4.4	4.1	5.2	4.4	4.8

** Figures **underlined in bold** indicate a ranking considerably higher (i.e. it is a bigger challenge) than the overall average.

Table 2.2 Profile of renewable energy consultants (Type I)

Configuration of Value Creation	• Reliant on own acumen • Reliant on complementary acumen from professional networks, local installers and technicians, sub-contractors and casual staff • Tender, development and management of IDO projects • Non-financial investors (e.g. start-up spaces, incubators)
Value Proposition *Service Offered*	• Knowledge and advice
Value Proposition *Customers (Who, How?)*	• Customers are typically international aid and development organisations (IDOs), non-governmental organisations (NGOs), or commercial entities, with whom Consultants have a direct relationship • Indirect relationship with RET end-users, especially BOP households • Uses word -of-mouth and tender process to reach potential customers, uses subcontractors and professional partners to reach end-users
Model of Revenue Generation	• Costs: Low fixed costs, subcontracted human capital • Revenues: Consulting fees, IDO and NGO grants and tenders

proposition offered to customers. They leverage their own knowledge, skills and experience to provide advice to renewable energy end-users. Indeed, knowledge creation and transfer and providing advice are the main services offered (Value Proposition).

To successfully achieve the aim of knowledge transfer and counsel in emerging markets, the consultant's Infrastructure Management apparatus includes leveraging the skills of other entrepreneurs and renewable energy professionals, secondarily. This enables them to fill knowledge and/or experience voids to achieve the aims of commissioned projects (see Table 2.2). Arguably a pivotal point of differentiation between consulting and distribution (Type III) enterprises, the consultants' value propositions are centred on their ability to leverage their knowledge of and networks within the renewable energy industry. Thus, the consulting REEs provide advice to customers on their anticipated renewable energy loads, system design and sizing (e.g. the number of kilowatts of solar equipment needed to meet the household's energy demands), appropriate energy sources (e.g. solar versus wind), as well as the best brands to suit their needs. Additionally, although these REEs are not directly active in the physical installation of the designed systems, they are able to utilise their networks to find the right technicians to carry out the installation of the renewable energy systems. In addition, if system development and installation require a RES or RET with which the consultant is unfamiliar, he/she will rely on sub-contracting and hiring casual staff within the enterprise to manage workload during peak project times. Therefore, the limit of the consultant's technical role in installation is in the monitoring, rather than the carrying out of installation.

The renewable energy consultant serves primarily commercial and governmental customers directly. They are hired to manage the installation of renewable energy generation systems for businesses, for example. I also found that governments, non-governmental organisations (NGOs) and international aid and development organisations (IDOs) regularly seek their advice to design renewable energy systems for communities, especially when such projects relate to the community's socioeconomic development. However, despite their involvement in designing and setting up renewable energy generation systems for communities, I found the consultants maintained an arm's length, indirect relationship with the end-users of renewable energy, especially households at the base of the pyramid (BOP) in emerging markets. Interestingly, the consultants have also reported to me that customer recurrence is relatively low because customers' energy issues are usually handled holistically so that once the problem has been solved or the system designed, they no longer require the consultant's services. Once a renewable energy system has been installed, the customer usually only requires maintenance and repairs.

I posit that running a consulting business seems to be the early life stage preference of REEs because of lower start-up costs. Later in the lifetime of their businesses, once they acquire additional capital investment, the REEs begin to incorporate import and distribution activities into their business model. In my research, the consultants frequently cited concerns about the difficulty of managing inventory, as well as the logistical challenges associated with importing a technology that changes frequently. These concerns served as a hindrance to developing their enterprises into distribution businesses (Type III).

Among the entrepreneurs I studied, both directly and indirectly, consultants were the largest group. Here, I pause to reflect on the implications of this finding. I do not claim that I studied a representative sample of REEs. I also do not claim that the majority of REEs in emerging markets are consulting enterprises. However, I argue that it is significant that the overwhelming impression from and about REEs in emerging markets is that they are, largely, generalist advisors (and retailers – see Type III (Distributors)). The popularity of the consultant business model suggests a certain ease with which renewable energy enterprises are able to engage in consulting activities in emerging markets. I explore this ease in previous publications (Gabriel and Kirkwood, 2016; Gabriel et al., 2016), linking this finding to the prevailing socioeconomic conditions in emerging markets. In sum, I reemphasise here that the business activities of REEs in emerging markets suggest a progression from consulting to distribution (Gabriel and Kirkwood, 2016). When institutional support for enterprise and renewable energy is low, consultants thrive. I surmise that this is because they are able to maintain successful consulting enterprises with fewer capital and assets than those operating under other business models. However, my conversations with these enterprises revealed that they aspire to become distributors of RETs. As their enterprises develop and institutional conditions improve (e.g. access to credit, investor attractiveness, improved distribution infrastructure), consultants found it easier with time to transition to a distribution business model (Type III). In sum I found compelling qualitative evidence, from the entrepreneurs' description of the history of their REEs and future plans for their ventures, that the consultant business model is considered temporary, early stage, low-hanging fruit. Indeed, the consultants shared passionately their aspirations to one day run a renewable energy distribution enterprise (Type III).

Type II: RES and RET innovators

> *The technology we have we have developed independently, there is no other company in the world to use [this resource] to produce energy. We create the technology applied to [this resource]. We train our own staff; there are no experts outside our company.*
>
> (Martín, operating in Chile)

Of the 43 REEs involved in this study, only four developed and were working on the commercial distribution of renewable energy technologies they invented and designed themselves: Martín, Hans, Sai and Elton, operating in Chile, Uganda, India and Tanzania, respectively. Since my first interview with Sai, I designated these REEs as innovators', and to date I continue to assign the same designation to this group of enterprises. Three of these enterprises developed new solar energy equipment, designed to meet the needs of end-users at the BOP (that is, reverse innovation, as described previously in Chapter 1). Specifically, they designed, developed and worked on the distribution of their own solar lighting technologies for household use. One enterprise, owned by Martín, invented a novel way of producing biogas from an underutilised biological resource.

At the time of initial involvement in this research, these RES and RET Innovators had been operating for an average of five years. They employ an average of 11 employees. The three solar innovators in this category received financial support from a range of providers, including angel investors and IDO grants or awards available to enterprises in emerging markets (such as the Lighting Africa programme). Martín found it more difficult to acquire funding in Chile. He reported that he attempted to acquire funds "from banks, capital, angels and other sources of money but none of them helped". I observed a clear distinction between the solar innovators (Hans, Sai and Elton) and Martín's biogas enterprise. For instance, while the solar innovators emphasised a desire to serve end-users in poor or marginalised communities at the BOP, Martín was adamant that he had no intention of targeting BOP communities. Instead, Martín focused his efforts on private commercial entities that could benefit from the use of the new kind of biogas he introduced. RES and RET Innovators reported demand for their innovations among the main challenges faced in emerging markets. This is in contrast

Table 2.3 Profile of RES and RET innovators (Type II)

Configuration of Value Creation	• Think Tanks and Incubators • Prototype manufacturers • Reliant on own acumen
Value Proposition *Products Offered*	• New renewable energy device or technology • New renewable energy resource
Value Proposition *Customers (Who, How?)*	• Anyone who benefits from the new resource or technology developed, with whom Innovators maintain a direct relationship • Innovators of non-solar technologies maintain an indirect relationship with end-users prior to installation and use, but they may establish contact for monitoring and evaluation post-installation
Model of Revenue Generation	• Costs: proof-of-concept and prototype design and production, research and development, marketing • Revenues: Sales, installation and maintenance of new RET products and equipment; consulting fees from end-users of new resource

to the key challenges identified by the 43 entrepreneurs interviewed overall, who reported demand for their products and services among the least challenging issues faced. Indeed, demand was especially challenging for Martín (Chile) and Hans (Uganda).

REEs in this category require individual consideration, as they appear to embody various aspects of technological and product innovation. For instance, for Martín, it is possible that though demand is, in general, not considered a major challenge by other participants in this study, his invention may be extremely difficult for local renewable energy stakeholders to accept. This difficulty in gaining legitimacy and acceptance is consistent with the fact that Martín's REE is the only enterprise in this category started without the financial support of NGOs or IDOs in emerging markets. This is poignant, especially in the context of Balachandra, Nathan and Reddy (2010)'s assessment of the diffusion of RETs. Indeed, Balachandra and colleagues reported in 2010 that bio-energies were still in the pre-commercial stages of diffusion. This means that the technology is not considered sufficiently mature to achieve significant market penetration. As Martín was first engaged for this research in 2013, I surmise that bio-energies remained at that time in this pre-commercial stage. Martín was also challenged by the fact that his biogas technology utilised a biological resource that has never before been used for energy. The struggle to achieve legitimacy is reflected in Martín's explanation of the difficulty he faced finding a niche within the local energy market in Chile:

> *We have plants built and operating processes. The technology shows operating normally, and even so, the experts believe it is not possible.*
>
> (Martín, operating in Chile)

Therefore, the innovators' perceptions of the challenges involved in running their enterprises appear to be related to both the type of RET or RES invented and their ability to access finance. As mentioned previously, Martín received no financial support for the start-up or running of his business. I inferred, based on my conversations with the solar innovators that his frustration is partly borne of a clear preference by investors for solar technology innovations in emerging markets, especially those innovations that provide energy poverty solutions for BOP communities. Especially in the wake of the strong institutional support for the Lighting Africa programme, solar innovators focused on the design and distribution of solar lighting equipment in emerging markets at the time (such as Hans, Sai and Elton) found the institutional environment in Africa extremely favourable for their enterprises. More so, in fact, than their counterparts, such as Martín, whose enterprises focused on other types of renewable energy technologies. Even the only non-African solar lighting innovator, Sai, was able to develop his enterprise on the basis of testing his product in an African market before bringing it to India. Although he does not manage an innovator enterprise, one Ethiopian entrepreneur, Aaron, explained why:

> *Now, this Lighting Africa programme of the World Bank – they set aside some nearly forty million dollars in a bank accessible to the private companies for any renewable energy technologies. So they can also get access to financing as a loan and at the same time, because the money is there in hard currency, they didn't have any problems getting money to import product.*

However, although the Lighting Africa programme may have created a more supportive environment for solar lighting technologies in the region, Hans and Elton were no less likely to report access to finance and governmental policy support among the main challenges faced. Notably, however, the innovators' concern with access to finance relates to their inability to get funding to maintain their enterprises (rather than to start-up an enterprise). Indeed, financial support from NGOs and IDOs (e.g. via the Lighting Africa programme) is offered largely on a project-by-project or product basis. This means that once the funded project is over, or they achieve the sales milestones stipulated by funders, REEs such as those run by Hans, Sai and Elton must seek other sources of funding and capital investment (or additional grants) to maintain their enterprises.

In essence, the common feature of this category of REEs is a value proposition centred on the design and commercialisation of their own RES or RETS (refer to supply chain in Figure 2.1), rather than the distribution of already existing, branded technologies.

Type III: distributors

Among the REEs studied, I encountered ten distributors. The central and defining feature of the distributor business model is a value proposition that focuses on the distribution and sale of renewable energy products and equipment. Table 2.4 outlines the overall renewable energy distributor profile commonly found in emerging markets.

The renewable energy distributor's Infrastructure Management apparatus is characterised by a combination of locally- or regionally-specific and international partners and collaborators. This is a necessary combination because the majority of the world's RETs are manufactured in China and other parts of Asia, including Taiwan, Malaysia and the Philippines. For instance, 70% of the world's PV modules were produced in China and Taiwan alone in 2017 (Fraunhofer Institute, 2019), while the world's largest wind turbine manufacturers are based in Europe and China (Bloomberg New Energy Finance, 2017). The majority of distributors in sub-Saharan Africa and Latin America (and some parts of Asia) must import these technologies from overseas.

Table 2.4 Profile of renewable energy distributors (Type III)

Configuration of Value Creation	• International manufacturers and suppliers as key partners to import RETs to emerging markets that do not make them themselves • Local installers and technicians as possible key partners for installation of RETs, but distributors more likely to rely on fixed staff trained in RETs in-house • May supply RETs for IDO and NGO projects, often in partnership with professional networks and consultants (Type I)
Value Proposition *Products/Services Offered*	• Knowledge/advice about the use of RETs • Sales and/or delivery of RET products and equipment
Value Proposition *Customers (Who, How?)*	• Customers are typically RET end-users (middle-to upper-class residential and commercial entities) with whom distributors maintain a direct relationship • Point of sale payment for products or on-demand procurement of bespoke products or system components • Distributors tend to avoid BOP customers, except when supplying development-oriented RETs for IDO and NGO projects (e.g. solar lights for Lighting Global) • Micro-franchising often used to reach end-users in remote areas
Model of Revenue Generation	• Costs: hiring and retaining staff; logistical and operating expenses, including cost of physical retail spaces or distribution centres; cost of RETs, plus import duties/taxes • Revenues: Sales, installation and maintenance of RET products and equipment; IDO and NGO grants and tenders

Renewable energy distributors reported that they were most challenged by the task of establishing reliable distribution channels for their products at first. However, as their enterprises progressed, they were able to design their own distribution channels, or rely on already existing ones (Gabriel et al., 2016). Distributor REEs distribute and sell either bespoke, made to order RET systems or generic products and equipment via retail shops. One participant operating in Ghana, Kofi, described the latter as a "commoditised" approach to the distribution of renewable energies in emerging markets. When the client is an established commercial entity, a bespoke approach is more useful, as the distributor can rely on the services of a consultant (Type I) to design the system according to the client's needs. Once designed, the distributor is involved in importing just the amount of equipment needed for installation (e.g. the number of solar PV panels). The commoditisation approach, however, is more common and more suitable for operating at scale, especially in BOP communities. Indeed, it is the approach used by solar lighting distributors in emerging markets, for instance, especially those supported by the Lighting Global initiative. Individual end-users could purchase solar lanterns and other apparatus from local shops in the same manner they purchase food and other household items.

Renewable energy distributors may offer a wide range of products and equipment, depending on the needs of end-users in the market. They may offer a range of solar products, including solar panels, solar water heaters, solar lights (lanterns) or solar charging equipment, for instance. I found that many distributors in emerging markets also provide a slightly more limited array of small wind turbines and biomass cooking equipment. In my research, I noted that distributor REEs distributed biomass cook stoves in greater abundance and wider variety among communities targeted by initiatives such as the Clean Cooking Alliance. Distributors also advise customers about the use and maintenance of their newly purchased products and equipment. However, few distributors using the commoditised, over-the-counter approach assist customers with installation of equipment or follow-up after the time of sale. End-users may solicit the services of local installers and technicians instead. It is distributors who offer (often larger) bespoke systems that maintain a longer relationship with end-users, monitoring system performance and providing maintenance and advisory services if needed.

I posit that the prevalence and importance of distribution business models in emerging markets is linked to the importance of the off-grid market in these regions for two reasons. First, the REEs themselves explained that the institutional and infrastructural challenges they encountered (described previously in Chapter 1) supported the distributor business model. Second, research from so-called more developed economies seldom acknowledges the distribution model of renewable energy enterprise. Indeed, much of the research from more developed markets focuses on integration approaches and models of renewable energy enterprise (i.e. Type IV; see Wustenhagen and Boehnke, 2008 for example). This is likely because there is already well-established centralised and grid-tied electricity supply infrastructure in such markets to deliver renewable energy to end-users. By contrast, the off-grid nature of renewable energy systems and installations in emerging markets means the products and services offered by the distributors include stand-alone equipment for generating light, power and heat, such as solar lights and PV, solar water heaters, micro wind turbines and biomass cookstoves, for instance.

Distributors may develop into integrators when their experience acquiring international funding and local government support allows them to develop and establish large-scale systems suitable for more than one end-user at a time.

Type IV: integrators

Having acquired and honed additional strengths under more supportive market conditions, Integrators use an even larger scale version of the renewable energy distributor model. In addition to their larger size (in terms of number of employees) and longer time in business, the Value Propositions, Key Partners and Key Resources aspects of the integrator business model, appear to be an important means of differentiating it from the other two models. The value propositions offered by integrators include a combination of consulting and distribution activities.

Integrators design, create and implement larger-scale renewable energy systems such as micro-grids, usually at the request of community leaders, NGOs or international development organisations. The integrators hire more permanent fulltime staff and have been in business longer, and their employee numbers are higher than those of the consultants and distributors in the study. Additionally, as their direct customer is usually an

Table 2.5 Profile of renewable energy integrators (Type IV)

Configuration of Value Creation	• Reliance on professional networks and networking • Local installers and technicians (only if capacity not in-house) • Manufacturers and suppliers as key international partners • Governments and community leaders • IDOS, NGOs, etc • Local businesses and utilities • IDO project development and management tenders and grants • System integration activities • Training own employees with RET skills • More likely to have fulltime staff • Private (financial) investors • Public/Government investors • IDO business grants as key resources
Value Proposition *Products/Services Offered*	• Knowledge/advice • Technology and system design • Direct contact to manufacturers/suppliers • Large scale supply of energy services
Value Proposition *Customers (Who, How?)*	• Sophisticated advertising, incl. word of mouth, company website, print and digital ads • Indirect relationship with RET end-users, but direct relationship with customers (governments, community leaders, etc) • After-sales contact with end-users (for monitoring and evaluation activities) • Direct system sales to customers, often indirectly to end-users • End-users: BOP and middle-class residential • IDOs, governments, community leaders, commercial entities (agricultural, resorts, etc) as customers
Model of Revenue Generation	• High overheads/operating expenses • Cost of hiring and retaining human capital • Import duties/taxes • Scaled-up logistics and operations • Advice/knowledge transfer • IDO project tenders • System sales and infrastructural integration

(development) organisation, their contact with end-users is indirect, except when carrying out research and development (R&D) activities. Notably, of the nine integrators identified in the study, only one was operating in Africa (i.e. Alain, operating in Senegal). Accessing finance after start-up was easier for the integrators than the consultants and distributors in the study. Additionally, there is some suggestion by participants that the possibility of a single business achieving "full vertical integration" (Hans, operating in Uganda) may be specific to RETs, given that they are governed by very specific policies that stimulate activity in all aspects of the renewable energy value chain.

The integrators and distributors described similar motivations for engaging in an integrator business model. That is, they had experienced improved institutional and infrastructural conditions in their local markets and, over time, were able to develop strong industry networks to help build their enterprises. Indeed, as shown in Table 2.1, the integrators identified the support of government as one of the least important challenges they faced. The integrators were the only REEs who reported a close relationship with government – in fact, they see government as one of their Key Partners (Infrastructure Management).

A regional perspective of the four types of renewable energy enterprises

Geographically, I categorised the REEs into three broad regions: Africa (specifically, all participants operated in sub-Saharan Africa), Asia and the Pacific and Latin America and the Caribbean. Table 2.6 shows the distribution of the four types of REEs across these regions.

On one hand, the largest cluster of REEs with consultant business models operated out of Africa (11 REEs). All of the REEs operating within African were, more specifically, operating in sub-Saharan Africa. This is worth noting because sub-Saharan Africa is the region most often characterised by the most constraining institutional conditions among the world's emerging markets (Antonites and Mungoni, 2011; Foster-Pedley and Hertzog, 2006; UNEP, 2012; World Bank and IFC, 2014). This implies that it is more difficult for REEs in this region to develop and maintain successful enterprises. Indeed, none of the 11 consulting REEs in the region received financial support (neither equity nor debt financing) to start their enterprises. Aaron, who runs a REE operating in Ethiopia, explained:

Table 2.6 Distribution of business types across regions

Regions	TYPE I Consultants	TYPE II RES and RET Innovators	TYPE III Distributors	TYPE IV Integrators
Africa	11	2	5	1
Asia and Pacific	5	2	1	6
Latin America and Caribbean	3	1	4	2

We wanted to open an improved cookstove factory. So we wanted to access funds to begin constructing the facility and that was really tough – to get funds here in Ethiopia.

The policy environment in sub-Saharan Africa was also difficult for the REEs I studied; they reported a lack of direct support not only for RETs, but also for small enterprises. REE owner, Kofi, explained the challenges associated with renewable energy policy in Ghana:

There's supposed to be tax exemptions for renewable energy systems. When they went and wrote the law, they wrote the law for solar generating sets specifically. So that is exempt. When I bring panels they are not exempt. When I bring batteries they are not exempt. When I bring inverters they are not exempt. So if I as a packager want to package systems here, I'm immediately at a disadvantage to the person who is importing full systems. Now, is the government helping me or not?

On the other hand, the largest cluster of integrators (larger, more mature enterprises) operated in Asia and the Pacific (six REEs). I surmise that this pattern may apply more broadly within emerging markets as the Asia-Pacific region is characterised by more favourable institutional conditions. Quotes from REEs operating in sub-Saharan Africa and Asia-Pacific illustrate the contrasting business environments:

A German researcher told me that he checked all the press releases for photovoltaic projects in Africa, and after 2–3 years he checked again and not one of the projects had been realised.

(Francis, operating in Zambia)

The issue is that the Tanzanian government has been dependent on the donor sector to contribute funding for too long. The donors are getting tired and the government had a wake-up call realising it needs to stop depending on this. So they introduced a tax that increases the taxes to be paid by the businesses. This affects our cash flow.

(Mark, operating in Tanzania)

Thailand, from a Southeast Asian perspective, even from a worldwide perspective, especially as an emerging market, is probably one of the most advanced renewable setups available. Access to finance, if I look at that, I would say that in Thailand it's actually not really a major issue. Generally, the government support and facilitation is quite high.

(Raphael, operating in Thailand)

Actually, [infrastructure & logistics] is not such a big problem because we have a lot of sub-contractors here.

(Ernesto, operating in The Philippines)

Inclusive business models

Along with growing interest in 'doing business with the poor' (Prahalad and Hammond, 2002; Prahalad, 2006; Yunus, 1998), came discussion about ways of doing business with the poor. Although not all REEs aimed to include socioeconomically disadvantaged communities in their business model, many did and continue to do so today. If enterprises in emerging markets include socioeconomically disadvantaged communities as partners within their business model, the enterprise is described as using an inclusive business model. Inclusive business models recognise and engage the poor as not only consumers, but as viable and effective partners in enterprise. The United National Development Programme (UNDP)'s Growing Inclusive Markets initiative describes inclusive business models as quoted here.

> Excerpt from **Creating Value for All: Strategies for Doing Business with the Poor,** July 2008:
>
> Inclusive business models include the poor on the demand side as clients and customers, and on the supply side as employees, producers and business owners at various points in the value chain. They build bridges between business and the poor for mutual benefit. The benefits from inclusive business models go beyond immediate profits and higher incomes. For business, they include driving innovations, building markets and strengthening supply chains. And for the poor, they include higher productivity, sustainable earnings and greater empowerment.

Therefore, especially because they operate within emerging markets, in addition to the four types of business models I identified, I also noted the extent to which the REEs embraced and operationalised inclusive business models in their enterprises overall. Seven approaches related to inclusive business models emerged from my conversations with REEs over the years: communal ownership, community immersion, crowdfunding, fee-for-service, indirect sales, microfinance and micro-franchising. Indeed, these seven approaches are consistent with recognised approaches commonly identified among enterprises operating in emerging markets in general, but especially in BOP communities. Table 2.7 shows the number of REEs using these elements of inclusive business models in emerging markets, by type and region.

In general, I noticed there were no discernible trends in the use of elements of inclusive business models among the four types of REEs. However, there was more evidence of communal ownership, community immersion and micro-franchising among the consultant and innovator business models. This may be because these three elements of inclusivity require the enterprise to leverage its own technical acumen; indeed, I described this previously as an important aspect of the Infrastructure Management apparatus and Value Propositions of consultant (Type I) and innovator (Type II) REEs. It is also worth noting that the majority of REEs who described elements of inclusivity in their business models were operating in the Asia-Pacific region.

Table 2.7 Number of REEs using elements of inclusive business models, by type and region

	Communal ownership	Community immersion	Crowd-funding	Fee for service – pay as you go	Indirect sales	Micro-finance	Micro-franchising
Consultants (Type I)	1	1	0	1	0	0	2
Innovators (Type II)	0	3	0	1	1	1	2
Distributors (Type III)	0	1	1	1	1	1	1
Integrators (Type IV)	0	2	0	1	0	1	1
Africa	0	1	0	1	0	0	2
Asia and the Pacific	1	4	0	2	2	2	3
Latin American and the Caribbean	0	2	1	1	0	1	1

Iwan, who manages a renewable energy consulting enterprise operating in Indonesia, identified an innovative *communal ownership* scheme as an important aspect of his enterprise's business model. Iwan's enterprise focuses on providing advice on micro hydropower technologies, which are usually owned and managed at the local government level, to communities. Together with partners and other employees of the enterprise, he works with communities to help them purchase and retain 100% ownership of the installed hydropower systems. Iwan claims that his enterprise uses communal ownership as a way to not only deepen its niche, but also to enhance its appeal among BOP communities (because individual villages prefer to have energy autonomy). For Iwan, it was also important that renewable energy technologies are used not only as a source of energy, but also as a "strategic development tool for the rural areas". He acknowledged that the major challenge he encountered was ensuring that villagers have the capacity to manage and maintain the systems themselves after they were installed. It is for this reason that he combines communal ownership with the immersion of the enterprise's staff within client communities.

Seven REEs in the study claimed to have incorporated some form of *community immersion* into their business models. This involved opting not to install a technology in a village unless at least one of the villagers is involved in the design and installation of the system (adopted by Iwan (Indonesia), Ángel (Ecuador), Luis (Guatemala) and Chris (Laos)). For this form of community immersion to be successful, employees must spend a considerable amount of time living in the village itself, to fully understand its needs (adopted by Iwan, for example). Another approach is to provide technical training to the community end-users themselves, thereby ensuring that the village is capable of managing the system on its own even after installation is completed (adopted by Ángel and Chris). A modified version of this latter approach is to perform pilot installations and onsite research before full rollout to larger portions of communities begins (adopted by Luis, Arif (Indonesia), Sai (India) and Elton (Tanzania)). Indeed, REEs may use one or all of these approaches to community immersion as a way to ensure the community is involved in the entire process, and REE staff are aware of the unique circumstances of each community. I inferred from my conversations with these REEs that these elements of inclusiveness are adopted as a way of coping with the challenges of accessing remote communities and the local shortage of technical skills.

Although three REEs attempted to use *crowdfunding*[1] as a way of financing one or more of their enterprises' projects, only one has been able to use it successfully. Luis, whose business model also includes forms of community immersion, used a crowdfunding platform to "fund a change in the business model" for extremely remote communities in Guatemala. Luis' crowdfunding campaign gained worldwide attention and was able to generate enough seed capital as an initial investment that helped the enterprise transform from a product distribution model to a pay-as-you-go (fee-for-service) model.

Four REEs (managed by Delphine (Cameroon), Luis, Sai (India) and Chris (Laos)) described their innovative *fee-for-service models* as important elements of their approach to inclusiveness in their respective emerging markets. Fee-for-service models are considered inclusive because not only are they tailored to the norms and specific circumstances of BOP end-users, but also because they maintain ongoing relationships with these end-users beyond simply selling products and equipment. For instance, instead of purchasing the equipment themselves, REEs who use this approach provide end-users with the equipment free of charge. The REE received payment for the equipment over time, as the end-user pays only for the energy generated and used by the equipment (that is, only what they need and use), when and if they need it. In the case of Luis' enterprise in Guatemala, end-users purchase energy 'credits' from local shops – they receive a code that can be entered into the installed equipment in their homes, thereby recharging the equipment so that it provides a corresponding amount of electricity. This approach is similar to established methods of purchasing prepaid mobile credit, for example, which is popular even in more developed markets. In all four REEs, the fee-for-service aspects of their business models focus on solar technologies for BOP households specifically. As they described it, the reason for the adoption of a fee-for-service strategy (or "pay-as-you-go" as it was described by Luis) is that although BOP customers are unable to afford the upfront costs of acquiring these technologies, they are able to "buy kerosene or batteries for their lighting purposes" (Delphine). Therefore, fee-for-service models are a way to mimic how BOP end-users in emerging markets would normally acquire (fossil) energy, thereby easing their transition to renewable energies.

Arif and Sam, operating in Indonesia and Fiji respectively, incorporated *indirect sales models* into their REEs. Arif leveraged the support of local banks to "sell the equipment to the banks and then the customer can do the business with the banks" instead. Sam described a scheme he hoped to deploy in partnership with IDOs: solar micro-grid systems would be sold to government, who would then collect monthly payments from end-users for the energy consumed. Thus, instead of selling products and systems directly to impoverished end-users, these models work by engaging third parties as owners who can then manage the supply of energy as a service to the end-user. Therefore, based on Arif and Sam's descriptions of this aspect of their business models, I inferred that indirect sales also incorporate elements of the fee-for-service approach described previously.

Three REEs described how they rely on *microfinance*[2] as an important and inclusive aspect of their business models. Luis (Guatemala) and Sai (India) partnered with microfinance and microcredit institutions serving their target BOP communities. Dhruv's enterprise, operating in India, offered its own micro-financial services. The aim of incorporating microfinance into one's business model is to address the challenge of affordability (usually of lighting products and equipment or solar home systems (SHSs)) for BOP end-users; I described this challenge in Chapter 1 of this volume. It is noteworthy, however, that microfinance as a strategy for inclusiveness is usually combined with other elements of inclusive business models, such as micro-franchising.

The REEs managed by Luis (Guatemala), Sai (India), Ajay (India), Chris (Laos), Liam (Somalia) and Hans (Uganda) use various forms of *microfranchising* as a strategy for reaching customers located in remote areas at the BOP and also for extending the market for their products. For instance, the model used by Sai's REE includes elements of microfinance and fee-for-service – micro-entrepreneurs in each BOP village are provided with a set of solar lamps as well as the equipment needed to charge them. These micro-entrepreneurs access microfinance to purchase the equipment. They then resell the lamps and, in addition, provide lamp recharging services to end-users within their villages. In so doing, these micro-entrepreneurs are engaged as partners of the enterprise – that is, franchisers of Sai's REE. This approach has two advantages within these villages. First, the micro-franchisees developed a livelihood for themselves and earned an income. Second, end-users at the BOP who would otherwise be unable to afford the lights themselves could now pay for and manage the *use* of them instead (that is, the use of the light produced). Similarly, Chris' solar rental (fee-for-service) system relies on micro-entrepreneurs in remote villages who are responsible for collecting payment and managing the rental of solar equipment.

All seven elements of inclusive business models are geared towards the REEs' customers and their relationships with customers. In addition, strategies such as community immersion and micro-franchising rely on leveraging and transferring the enterprise's own acumen, and indirect sales and microfinance often rely on partnerships with other organisations. Both are important features of the Infrastructure Management apparatus of the business models used by REEs in emerging markets. Indeed, these strategies are commonplace among REEs operating in emerging markets, especially those that serve customers in BOP communities (SustainAbility, 2014; UNDP, 2008).

Notes

1 Crowdfunding is a means of funding that relies on the donations/contributions of the general (local or international) public. It is usually done on the internet via crowdfunding platforms.
2 Microfinance is a type of financially inclusive service for individuals and micro-enterprises who are otherwise unable to access banking and other financial services.

References

Amit, R. and Zott, C., 2001. Value creation in e-business. *Strategic Management Journal*, 22(6/7), pp. 493–520.

Antonites, A.J. and Mungoni, E.M., 2011. Obstacles to the entrepreneurial start-up process in Zimbabwe: A dynamic market perspective. *The Business Review*, Cambridge, 18(2), p. 215.

Balachandra, P., Nathan, H.S.K. and Reddy, B.S., 2010. Commercialization of sustainable energy technologies. *Renewable Energy*, 35(8), pp. 1842–1851.

Bloombery New Energy Finance, 2017. Vestas reclaims top spot in annual ranking of wind turbine makers. *BNEF*. Retrieved from https://about.bnef.com/blog/vestas-reclaims-top-spot-annual-ranking-wind-turbine-makers/ (accessed 03 June 2019).

Casadesus-Masanell, R. and Ricart, J.E., 2010. From strategy to business models and onto tactics. *Long Range Planning*, 43(2–3), pp. 195–215.

Cusumano, M.A., Kahl, S.J. and Suarez, F.F., 2014. Services, industry evolution, and the competitive strategies of product firms. *Strategic Management Journal*, 36(4), pp. 559–575.

Eisenhardt, K.M. and Martin, J.A., 2000. Dynamic capabilities: What are they? *Strategic Management Journal*, 21(10–11), pp. 1105–1121.

Foster-Pedley, J. and Hertzog, H., 2006. Financing strategies for growth in the renewable energy industry in South Africa. *Journal of Energy in Southern Africa*, 17(4), pp. 57–64.

Fraunhofer Institute for Solar Energy Systems, ISE, 2019. Photovoltaics report. Retrieved from www.ise.fraunhofer.de/content/dam/ise/de/documents/publications/studies/Photovoltaics-Report.pdf (accessed 03 June 2019).

Gabriel, C.A. and Kirkwood, J., 2016. Business models for model businesses: Lessons from renewable energy entrepreneurs in developing countries. *Energy Policy*, 95, pp. 336–349.

Gabriel, C.A., Kirkwood, J., Walton, S. and Rose, E.L., 2016. How do developing country constraints affect renewable energy entrepreneurs? *Energy for Sustainable Development*, 35, pp. 52–66.

Hall, J. and Wagner, M., 2012. Integrating sustainability into firms' processes: Performance effects and the moderating role of business models and innovation. *Business Strategy and the Environment*, 21(3), pp. 183–196.

Hall, S. and Roelich, K., 2016. Business model innovation in electricity supply markets: The role of complex value in the United Kingdom. *Energy Policy*, 92, pp. 286–298.

Hollensen, S., 2013. The blue ocean that disappeared: The case of Nintendo Wii. *The Journal of Business Strategy*, 34(5), pp. 25–35.

Jolink, A. and Niesten, E., 2013. Sustainable development and business models of entrepreneurs in the organic food industry. *Business Strategy and the Environment*, 24(6), pp. 386–401.

Osterwalder, 2004. *The Business Model Ontology a Proposition in a Design Science Approach*. These présentée à l'Ecole des Hautes Etudes Commerciales de l'Université de Lausanne pour l'obtention du grade de Docteur en Informatique de Gestion.

Osterwalder, Pigneur, Y. and Clark, T., 2010. *Business Model Generation: A Handbook for Visionaries, Game Changers, and Challengers*. Hoboken, NJ: John Wiley & Sons Inc.

Prahalad, C.K., 2006. *The Fortune at the Bottom of the Pyramid*. New Jersey, USA: Wharton School Publishing.

Prahalad, C.K. and Hammond, A., 2002. What works: Serving the poor, profitably. A private sector strategy for global digital opportunity. World Resources Institute. Retrieved from http://web.mit.edu/sp.784/www/DOCUMENTS/serving_profitably%20-%20paper%20Jorge%20sent.pdf (accessed 02 June 2019).

SustainAbility, 2014. *Model Behaviour: 20 Business Model Innovations for Sustainability*. New York, NY: Sustainability Inc.

Teece, D.J., 2007. Explicating dynamic capabilities: The nature and microfoundations of (sustainable) enterprise performance. *Strategic Management Journal*, 28(13), pp. 1319–1350.

UNDP (United Nations Development Programme), 2008. *Creating Value for All: Strategies for Doing Business with the Poor*. New York, USA: UNDP.

UNEP (United Nations Environment Programme), 2012. Global trends in renewable energy investment 2012. U.C. Centre (Ed.). Frankfurt School, UNEP Collaborating Centre for Climate & Sustainable Energy Finance, Bloomberg New Energy Finance, German Federal Ministry for the Environment, Nature Conservation and Nuclear Safety, Germany.

Wallin, J., 2005. Operationalizing competencies. In R. Sanchez and A. Heene (Eds.), *Competence Perspective on Managing Internal Process*. Advances in Applied Business Strategy, Vol. 7. Bingley: Emerald Group Publishing Limited.

World Bank and IFC (International Finance Corporation), 2014. Doing business: Ease of doing business index. *Doing Business*. Retrieved from www.doingbusiness. org/rankings (accessed 30 June 2014).

Wustenhagen, R. and Boehnke, J., 2008. Business models for sustainable energy. In A. Tukker, M. Charter, C. Vezzoli, E. Stø and M.M. Andersen (Eds.), *System Innovation for Sustainability 1: Perspectives on Radical Changes to Sustainable Consumption and Production* (Vol.1, pp. 70–79). Routledge, UK: Abingdon.

Yunus, M., 1998. *Banker to the Poor: The Story of the Grameen Bank*. India: Penguin Books.

Zott, C. and Amit, R., 2008. The fit between product market strategy and business model: Implications for firm performance. *Strategic Management Journal*, 29, pp. 1–26.

Part II

The challenges of selling renewable energy product

'Vijay' (renewable energy entrepreneur, Fiji):

The old-style grassroots tree-hugging days of renewable energy are gone or going fast. They are disappearing really soon. They are becoming this really commercial business-driven thing. Fortunately, we are all developing nations, so there is a lot more social focus than in the western world. But it's becoming business-business now.

Renewable energy entrepreneurs, such as Vijay, often reminisce about the effects of ostensibly obvious changes in motivation for growing the market for renewable energy technologies (RETs). Indeed, they suggest that previously overwhelmingly 'green' motives for advancing RETs have waned considerably or are fading gradually. In its place is a drive for increasing profits and growing market share. While I, personally, do not advocate the relentless pursuit of profits because of its adverse effects on ecological health and social equity, thinking of increasing the uptake of renewables in emerging markets as growing market share is a potentially useful notion. Indeed, we want more RET products in the hands and households of more and more people and communities around the world and especially in emerging markets. However, the renewable energy enterprises (REEs) in the study lament that increasing this market share seems to have come at a price, at least, as Vijay put it, in "the western world". The continuing and overwhelming social and ecological challenges in emerging markets mean that the challenge facing REEs is to couple and intermingle increased market share with environmental and social advantages. However, this constant balancing act is not easy, and REEs continue to face many challenges in emerging markets.

In this section, I describe and undertake an assessment of the specific challenges REEs face while trying to distribute renewable energy products more widely in emerging markets. In Part I I provided a more general overview of different business models and the ways of doing business of REEs. In Part II and henceforth, I focus on challenges related to the distribution of RET products only for two reasons. First, the challenges described by the REEs I studied were primarily challenges related to the supply and distribution of RET products in emerging markets. I found that these challenges were faced either by the enterprises with a significant distribution component to their business models (i.e. Distributors (Type III) and Integrators (Type IV)) or by Consultants (Type I) aspiring to become distributors of RETs themselves but facing overwhelming difficulty. For instance, among the REEs I studied is the story of Thomas, who tried unsuccessfully to scale his Type I consulting enterprise to a Type III distribution enterprise. Thomas, who operates his REE in Kenya, lamented many times during our conversation that he was unable to acquire the key networks and resources necessary to gain a foothold in existing supply chains for RETs. In addition, he observed there were significant opportunities in the industry to collaborate and benefit from projects funded by international aid and development organisations (IDOs):

> The original goal was that we would try to sell equipment. But, we found that most of the opportunities that could pay for the work we wanted to do were professional high-end World Bank type.
>
> (Thomas, operating in Kenya)

Eventually, Thomas and his business partner acquiesced, closed the distribution infrastructure of the enterprise and reverted to a predominantly consulting (Type I) business model. He explained that "trying to sell equipment wouldn't work for us" (Thomas, operating in Kenya). Indeed, in this example, although he operates a consulting enterprise, he, too, was affected by logistical challenges in emerging markets.

The second reason for my focus on logistical challenges affecting distribution is much broader. I make an observation in the spirit of the pursuit of sustainable human thriving in which the REEs in this study have engaged and in the context of the global 'sustainable development' agenda so avidly pursued. My observation is that the extent of distribution and uptake of physical, tangible RET products will determine and have a significant impact on our ability to sustainably eradicate energy poverty (and its associated tribulations) in emerging markets. That is, for example, Sai's success in distributing his solar lights and the innovative power cycle that charges them more widely across remote Indian villages will affect the ability of the micro-franchisees dependent on his enterprise to maintain sustainable livelihoods. In another example, although he runs his REE under an innovator (Type II) business model, Martín's ability to distribute the new type of biomass energy he discovered more widely will enhance the diversity of renewable energy sources (RES) exploited in Chile specifically, but also potentially more broadly in emerging markets. His success could potentially relieve pressure on land and other resources used for food production in emerging markets.

Therefore, importantly, I distinguish between the challenges faced by the Distributor enterprises specifically (i.e. Type III) and distribution-related challenges more broadly. Indeed, even Consultants (Type I – who aspire to become Type III Distributors) and Integrators (Type IV – who operate scaled-up distribution enterprises) face many distribution-related challenges; I have found that these challenges are not restricted to Type III REEs only. Thus, in Part II of this volume, I focus on the main strategic and operational challenges of selling renewable energy products in emerging markets: the logistical growing pains associated with distribution, sources of competition for REEs in emerging markets, the legitimacy and power of IDOs, and identification and the use of performance measures that are appropriate in emerging markets. I conclude Part II with a summative illustration of "success" as defined by the ideals and desires of the struggling or unsuccessful enterprises in the study and as exemplified by a successful few.

However, given the likely wide reach of this volume outside the business disciplines, I first define and explain what I mean by strategic and operational challenges as they relate to REEs in emerging markets. I also elaborate on the key features of a business model, which I explained only briefly in Part I of this volume.

What is a strategic challenge?

A strategic challenge is an issue or problem with potentially negative effects on the long-term vision and planning of an enterprise. Sometimes, such challenges emanate from changes within the enterprise itself – such as a change in ownership or scarcity of key resources – and can lead to significant long-term changes to the enterprise's structure, vision and product or service offered. However, often, strategic challenges arise from a complex web of factors external to the enterprise, including institutions and establishments, competing and collaborating organisations, international and local markets and political and economic regimes. In my research, I found that it was more often the latter that presented REEs with significant strategic challenges in the running of their businesses.

In Part II of this volume, I address the two key strategic challenges, as identified by the REEs themselves, which affect the efficacy and efficiency of their RET distribution endeavours: the competitive landscape of the renewable energy industry and the legitimacy of IDOs. In Chapter 4, I describe, analyse and diagnose the competitive landscape of REEs, especially as it pertains to RET product distribution in emerging markets. Chapter 5 serves as a brief introduction to the aid landscape in emerging markets, especially as it pertains to the renewable energy industry for those unfamiliar with aid and IDOs. Chapter 5 also outlines the advantages and disadvantages of aid interventions for RET distribution in emerging markets. It offers a description and assessment of the problematic aid-centric business model, which has negative effects on the self-sufficiency of REEs in emerging markets. I conclude the crucial chapter on aid-centric business models with a proposed alternative aid-independent logic of value creation.

What is an operational challenge?

An operational challenge is an issue or problem with potentially negative effects on the day-to-day activities and interactions of an enterprise. Operational challenges may ensue solely at the pragmatic level of daily interaction. For instance, some aspects of the logistical and distribution challenges faced in emerging markets simply relate to the processes and procedures involved in transporting and selling RET products to end users. These procedures may include, for example, negotiating taxes and duties on RET products entering the country or getting products to end users via poorly maintained or undeveloped road infrastructure in remote areas. However, commonly, operational challenges trickle down from the strategic level – that is, issues with long-term consequences for the enterprise may eventually manifest themselves in smaller, incremental problems that affect the daily running of the enterprise. For instance, REEs face logistical growing pains as a matter of course in the day-to-day running and maintenance of their ventures. Although the supply chain for RETs, especially solar, is generally similar across emerging markets, each entrepreneur's experiences at different stages of the supply chain are unique.

Therefore, in Chapter 3, I take a discursive approach to relate the REEs' stories of the logistical challenges faced in emerging markets. In addition, although they are largely strategic challenges, the difficult competitive landscape and legitimacy of IDOs in the renewable energy industry also has significant implications operationally. Attentive readers will observe that I describe some of these operational implications in Chapters 4 and 5. Finally, Chapter 6 highlights suggested solutions to a significant operational challenge related to selecting the most appropriate measures and indicators of success for REEs. Indeed, I dedicated Chapter 6 to definition and measurement of success for REEs in emerging markets despite the challenges faced.

What, exactly, is a business model in this context?

As defined in Part I of this volume, a business model captures and reflects how an enterprise implements the business strategy or plans conceived by its owners and/or managers (Casadesus-Masanell and Ricart, 2010). The business model describes the logic of how enterprises create and retain value (Hall and Wagner, 2012). In a previous article, I describe inconsistencies in academic conceptions of the components of a business model (Gabriel and Kirkwood, 2016). Indeed, scholars traditionally espouse different interpretations of the business model (*cf.* (Teece, 2010; George and Bock, 2011; Trimi and Berbegal-Mirabent, 2012; Zott and Amit, 2013). Nevertheless, some aspects remain consistent. When Jodyanne Kirkwood and I published our article in 2016, we outlined three constructs that scholars define and describe in common as components of business models: the *value proposition*, the *model of revenue generation* and the *configuration of value creation* (Wüstenhagen and Boehnke, 2008). Using these constructs,

Table 0.2 outlines business model features specific to the distribution of renewable energy products in emerging markets.

The *value proposition* is the product, service or experience offered by the enterprise to its customers. Quite literally, the enterprise offers or proposes to its customers a product, service or experience that the customer considers valuable – it is a proposition to provide a specific artefact or feature of value to the end-user. However, in emerging markets there are cultural and RET industry norms that define and govern how REEs may offer and deliver sustainable value to end-users. For instance, in more developed markets research has shown that RET industry norms prioritise high quality RET products over lower quality ones (Painuly, 2001). Yet, in emerging markets some REEs defy these norms by offering lower quality products instead that are more affordable to impoverished end-users and effective in the short-term (*cf.* Gabriel et al., 2016) (see Table 0.2). I have often surmised that the value offered in such cases is the gradual facilitation of longer-term systemic de-institutionalisation of fossil energies (albeit at the expense of quality and durability), instead of the shorter-term product acceptance often pursued in these industries. Indeed, taking a longer-term view, providing services and offering lower quality products allows the enterprises to survive, potentially grow and remain relevant in emerging markets. The impact on systems and markets is the establishment and growth of sustainability enterprises that offer innovative solutions to the sustainability needs of end-users in emerging markets. In addition, REEs offer value to end-users by offering socially tiered pricing strategies (see Table 0.2), which makes their resulting business models more socially sustainable. I infer that the resulting systemic learning means the RET industry is better positioning itself for longer-lasting socially relevant enterprise. These strategies for value proposition design in emerging

Table 0.2 Business model features for RET distribution in emerging markets[1]

Value Proposition	Model of Revenue Generation	Configuration of Value Creation
• Micro-franchise with end-users in remote villages • Piece together own technology tailored to local conditions • Consulting services instead of product distribution • Socially-tiered pricing strategies • Compromise on product quality	• Alternative customer segments • Project grants/payments from international aid and development organisations (IDOs) • Independent models financial, social and environmental revenue/ value generation • Payment "migration paths"	• Repurpose competitors as partners • Employ unskilled tradesmen without renewable energy technology (RET) experience • International networks • International development and sustainability programs • Informal distribution channels • Existing fossil fuel channels and networks • Product innovations built from untapped resources

1 The author created this table based on insights from Gabriel and Kirkwood (2016).

markets offer specific advantages for the attainment of sustainable human thriving and for the enhancement of RET distribution in emerging markets. For instance, such value propositions may offer sustainable value to end-users that is scalable, accessible remotely and locally relevant. In addition, the sustainable value offered helps make RETs more widely available and accessible across social strata in emerging markets.

The *model of revenue generation* defines and governs how the enterprise generates revenue from the exchange of these valuable artefacts or features for payment from end-users. Enterprises consider the costs of producing and delivering valuable products, services and experiences to its customers and end-users and aim to generate revenues in excess of these costs – essentially, in for-profit enterprises to generate a profit (Wüstenhagen and Boehnke, 2008). Conventionally, organisational sustainability is often defined as the combined social, environmental and financial benefits for both the enterprise and its stakeholders (Stubbs and Cocklin, 2008; Schaltegger, Hansen and Lüdeke-Freund, 2016). In my research, I observed that REEs in emerging markets separate their financial value capture logic from their social and environmental logics (see Table 0.2). That is, on one hand the entrepreneurs' direct relationship and interactions with end-users across socio-economic strata are the benchmark against which their social and environmental impacts are measured. On the other hand, the entrepreneurs' ability to leverage their experience with low-income end-users to derive financial benefits from stakeholders who are not impoverished end-users themselves (e.g. IDOs, other large-scale users) determines the financial sustainability of their ventures. Despite a widely expressed desire to encourage self-sustaining sustainability enterprise in emerging markets, REEs are still reliant on IDOs to capture financial value. If they are unable to operate independently of IDOs, their dependence on these organisations could have potentially negative implications for the financial sustainability of all REEs in emerging markets. These features of revenue generation models adopted and developed by REEs in emerging markets also contribute to sustainable human thriving and the distribution of renewable energy products in emerging markets. Notably, REEs capture revenues and maximise financial value from a variety of stakeholders who are not necessarily end-users of renewable energy products. However, the human thriving impacts of these innovative models of revenue generation extend beyond financial revenues – there is also significant social and environmental value to be captured. For instance, REEs maximise the generation of social and environmental value by providing RETs to low-income households only indirectly – that is, by retrieving financial value from third parties such as IDOs. In addition, REEs often adopt and offer scalable, widely accessible payment terms and conditions, making renewable energy products more accessible by those living in poverty in emerging markets.

The supply chain and organisational infrastructures needed to produce and deliver the enterprise's products, services and experiences to its customers and end-users is its *configuration of value creation*. I remain today, as I have been engaged in this research for the past eight years, intrigued by REEs' ability to develop and maintain relationships along their supply and distribution chains in unique and innovate ways. In Part I, I describe many of the business model innovations developed and espoused by these enterprises in emerging markets in general. However, with specific relevance to the distribution of renewable energy products, I found REEs innovate and use untapped sources of labour in their relationship with competitors, their own personal international networks as well as their own customers to distribute and deliver renewable energy products in emerging markets (see Table 0.2). Indeed, in emerging markets REEs create sustainable value by managing and configuring actors outside of their organisational boundaries. In emerging markets, these co-creators of sustainable value are often international networks, local end-users or tribal leaders, for instance (see Table 0.2). I discuss the implications of this co-configuration of value creation, especially with IDOs and other international entities in Chapter 5 of this volume. REEs often co-configure and co-deliver the supply chains for renewable energy products with a variety of stakeholders in emerging markets. For instance, these stakeholders often include end-users, international networks who contribute value-adding inputs, international aid and development organisations (IDOs), purveyors of least preferred unsustainable products and distribution networks and the informal sector. REEs achieve these supply chain relationships by exploiting and addressing infrastructural and institutional voids in emerging markets. As their enterprises are designed and run on the basis of technology, entrepreneurs' ability to respond to constraints and adapt their business models accordingly is vitally important, especially in emerging markets (Günzel and Wilker, 2012; Trimi and Berbegal-Mirabent, 2012).

Thus, in this section, the concept of the business model, defined as the logic of value creation and conceptualised through these three key aspects as they relate to these unique contexts, is the basis on which I describe and assess the challenges associated with selling renewable energy products in emerging markets. However, to be conscientious I must acknowledge at this stage that those already familiar with business concepts and business models might consider a substantial proportion of the analyses in this volume overly, though arguably, simplistic. Therefore, I remind readers that this volume serves as an introductory device. Hence, simplicity (though not triviality) in the rendering of business and management concepts in this volume is necessary to introduce and orient those unfamiliar with renewable energy enterprise and/or emerging markets.

References

Casadesus-Masanell, R. and Ricart, J.E., 2010. From strategy to business models and onto tactics. *Long Range Planning*, 43(2), pp. 195–215.

Gabriel, C.A. and Kirkwood, J., 2016. Business models for model businesses: Lessons from renewable energy entrepreneurs in developing countries. *Energy Policy*, 95, pp. 336–349.

Gabriel, C.A., Kirkwood, J., Walton, S. and Rose, E.L., 2016. How do developing country constraints affect renewable energy entrepreneurs? *Energy for Sustainable Development*, 35, pp. 52–66.

George, G. and Bock, A.J., 2011. The business model in practice and its implications for entrepreneurship research. *Entrepreneurship: Theory and Practice*, 35(1), pp. 83–111.

Günzel, F. and Wilker, H., 2012. Beyond high tech: The pivotal role of technology in start-up business model design. *International Journal of Entrepreneurship and Small Business*, 15(1), pp. 3–22.

Hall, J. and Wagner, M., 2012. Integrating sustainability into firms' processes: Performance effects and the moderating role of business models and innovation. *Business Strategy and the Environment*, 21(3), pp. 183–196.

Painuly, J.P., 2001. Barriers to renewable energy penetration: A framework for analysis. *Renewable Energy*, 24(1), pp. 73–89.

Schaltegger, S., Hansen, E.G. and Lüdeke-Freund, F., 2016. Business models for sustainability: Origins, present research, and future avenues. *Organization & Environment*, 29(1), pp. 3–10.

Stubbs, W. and Cocklin, C., 2008. Conceptualizing a "sustainability business model". *Organization & Environment*, 21(2), pp. 103–127.

Teece, D.J., 2010. Business models, business strategy and innovation. *Long Range Planning*, 43(2), pp. 172–194.

Trimi, S. and Berbegal-Mirabent, J., 2012. Business model innovation in entrepreneurship. *International Entrepreneurship and Management Journal*, 8(4), pp. 449–465.

Wüstenhagen, R. and Boehnke, J., 2008. Business models for sustainable energy. In A. Tukker, M. Charter, C. Vezzoli, E. Sto and M.M. Andersen (Eds.), *System Innovation for Sustainability: Perspectives on Radical Changes to Sustainable Consumption and Production* (pp. 253–258). Sheffield: Greenleaf Publishing Ltd.

Zott, C. and Amit, R., 2013. The business model: A theoretically anchored robust construct for strategic analysis. *Strategic Organization*, 11(4), pp. 403–411.

3   Logistical growing pains

Getting renewable energy products to end-users

Logistical considerations associated with the supply chains for renewable energy product were ranked as the most significant challenge faced by renewable energy enterprises (REEs) aiming to distribute renewable energy technology (RET) products in emerging markets. Five years later, upon reflection and assessment of the enterprises no longer in business, I surmised that logistical complications and supply chain challenges in general could be one of the main reasons distributors of RET products fail in emerging markets. The logistical challenges are those factors – institutional, procedural, geographical, socio-cultural and financial – that hinder the smooth transition of RET products from one stage of the supply chain to another. Indeed, these challenges are related to simply getting renewable energy products into the hands of the end-users that need them most. The REEs face an enormous task, which because of its challenging and mercurial nature, may be described by some as "dirty work":

> Our work is a lot of travel, a lot of going to uncomfortable places and staying. It is a lot of quote unquote 'dirty work'. It is a lot of engaging with an extremely diverse set of people. From the grassroots entrepreneur to talking to the operations head of a state or of a bank. That's the kind of diversity of people that we need to engage with.
>
> (Ajay, operating in India)

The REEs I studied spent a considerable proportion of the time I spent interviewing them describing the logistical challenges they faced. Indeed, many of the challenges might be the same for almost any enterprise operating within emerging markets. Some, however, such as procedural and cost-related barriers, might be peculiar to RETs in certain markets. Nevertheless, to maintain fidelity to the entrepreneurs' experiences as entrusted to me, and because this particular challenge is so important, I opted to take a more grounded, discursive approach to this chapter than I did for preceding and most of the subsequent chapters. So rich are the REEs' experiences and stories that sharing them in good faith requires a discursive approach.

Researchers who embrace discursive approaches see value in the richness and depth of discourse – that is, value in the use of language and words, whether spoken, written or otherwise conveyed. Indeed, words convey meaning and reveal the entrepreneurs' own perceptions of the challenges they face. In a sense, while the challenging reality of renewable energy enterprise in emerging markets undoubtedly influenced the way they speak about their businesses, in turn, the way the entrepreneurs speak about their businesses simultaneously constructs and constitutes their reality within the contexts in which they operate. Semi-structured interviews allowed the entrepreneurs to verbally recount and reflect upon their actions and experiences, and thus make sense of them retrospectively. By engaging in this process of retrospective recounting and reporting of their actions and experiences, the entrepreneurs simultaneously verbalised and made sense of the challenges they faced in emerging markets.

Thus, in this chapter, I intend to "let the data speak for itself" (Easterby-Smith, Thorpe and Jackson, 2012: 163). That is, I will introduce the broad supply chain categories of the logistical challenges the REEs face and then provide quotes from the interviews – examples of the exact words spoken by the REEs when describing each challenge. I selected quotes that illustrate each challenge clearly and that speak directly to the specific problems at hand at each stage of the supply chain.

Stories from the supply chain for renewable energy products

RET products travel considerable distances through several stages of the supply chain before reaching end-users in emerging markets. Figure 3.1 highlights a segment of the RET supply chain I illustrated previously in Figure 2.1 (Chapter 2).

Figure 3.1 represents an admittedly generalised and intentionally simplified illustration of the supply chain for RET products in emerging markets. Indeed, it is perhaps arguably more broadly generalizable to solar RETs. For instance, RETs for generating wind power are imported in parts and components then assembled in the country where it will be installed and used. Furthermore, this same supply chain gains perhaps a few additional steps when RETs must be delivered to remote communities. Chea, who runs a REE operating in Cambodia, explained:

> We have to import some technologies and products because it is hard to find the stuff for these technologies, for the job, based on technology capacity and technical skill here. So people who have the idea to sell products, they buy technologies and products outside. And solar, some kind of biodigester accessory, and especially microhydro and picohydro, we don't know any local suppliers in Cambodia.
>
> (Chea, operating in Cambodia)

Thus, the supply chain for RET products can be complex and unique to individual RET market environments. My aim, therefore, is to illustrate this

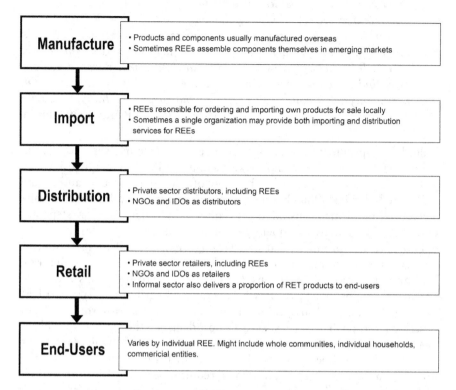

Figure 3.1 A typical supply chain for RET products in emerging markets

complexity through the stories of the REEs as they navigate processes and challenges at each stage of the supply chain. Therefore, I divided this section according to the main operational challenges faced at each stage of the supply chain. Within each of these sections, readers can expect to find and hear the voices of the REEs as they grapple with these logistical challenges in emerging markets.

Trade barriers to importing RET products

From an emerging market perspective, the first stage of the supply chain usually involves a series of processes to get the RET products into the country where it will be distributed. David, an entrepreneur operating a REE in Papua New Guinea, explained that REEs are particularly dependent on trade with other countries (often, more developed markets, China and India) to access and import RETs for hydropower generation. He explained:

Nepal is also a rugged country and they have a lot of hydro systems all over the country. The terrain is similar to Papua New Guinea. In

Papua New Guinea we do not have industries where the equipment is manufactured locally. Hydro equipment is site-specific. You will never find turbine equipment sold in the hardware. You do the measurements, and then you give it to the turbine manufacturer who will make the turbine. But, picohydro turbines you can find some. Because you can easily find the components to make some. But all the other renewable energy equipment you have to get from outside, so Australia, Germany.

(David, operating in Papua New Guinea)

Indeed, site specificity is a major challenge REEs face in their quest to distribute RETs more widely and make them accessible in emerging markets. Often, REEs can only meet the challenge of addressing specific and unique local needs by installing bespoke power generation or lighting systems. Therefore, tailor-made installations require additional logistical steps and considerations, and they frequently incur compounding logistical challenges.

However, the products that can be imported, as well as the countries or regions one can import them from, are often dependent upon the trade laws and institutional regulations that govern trade relationships with other countries. For instance, Arthur, who operates a distribution (Type III) REE in Barbados, an English-speaking island nation in the eastern Caribbean, described the challenge of selling his products in the French Caribbean islands. Arthur's enterprise began making its own RETs, which are tailor-made for the Caribbean market, but to export his products to islands that are overseas territories of France would require special certification to trade with European markets. Therefore, in response, Arthur aims to try to boost domestic sales to enhance his enterprise's ability to manage and navigate trade barriers in the region. He explained:

We hope to be the only UN-certified European manufacturer, so we can sell the product into Martinique and Guadeloupe, which is French territory. They have some trade barriers, and right now just exporting to CARICOM[1] is a challenge. But because our net profit is so marginal, we cannot afford to employ fulltime export managers. So, it comes back to how many sales dollars you are earning from your domestic market.

(Arthur, operating in Barbados)

REEs operating in landlocked territories also face significant challenges during the import phase of the RET supply chain. For instance, Francis, an entrepreneur operating a REE in Zambia, describes the implications of this challenge for his enterprise: You need a lot of permissions, and so we have that. We have sent in the containers of photovoltaics and batteries. They are on their way to Africa. Zambia has a big transport problem because they have no sea access and everything you have to land in Dar es Salaam and then bring it over in trucks to Zambia for 1000km. This makes a lot of costs for us. It only makes sense if you send material containers and that means a lot of money because you have to invest 60–90 days on the ship. This can kill you if you are not careful.

(Francis, operating in Zambia)

Procedural barriers to importing RET products

Once RET products enter their destination country, REEs aiming to make distribution a core component of their business model are likely to face the challenge of navigating country-specific procedural barriers. In particular, these barriers appear most potent at the stage of customs and border administration. Entrepreneurs Chiagozie and Delphine, operating REEs in Nigeria and Cameroon respectively, described the issue as such:

The other problem about the infrastructure is I could say clearing of the goods at sea and at the airports. We get our goods into Nigeria within 3 days from our warehouse in Houston. It flies over the weekend and in 2 or 3 days, it is in Lagos. But sometimes it can take 3 weeks for us to clear our goods and have it in our warehouse. Sometimes 6 weeks! So moving goods from different parts of the world takes about 3 days to reach Nigeria, but then again sometimes customs takes 6 weeks, so it's crazy really.

(Chiagozie, operating in Nigeria)

The policies are not really good. If you buy solar components, you have to declare it at very high costs.

(Delphine, operating in Cameroon)

Likewise, two entrepreneurs, Tim and Günther, who operate REEs in Central America – Costa Rica and Belize respectively – described a similar challenge related to customs and border administration for RET products in particular:

It is not very efficient here in customs how you get equipment in. We have a licence here where we get things in tax-free. All solar is tax-free. But it's very, very difficult to process and time-consuming, where it just eats up our resources.

(Tim, operating in Costa Rica)

Now we are suffering because my client calls and asks why my battery is costing $8,000 and if they buy it in the United States, it costs $5,000. We have to explain it is our import duties. And Belize has an import duty on the renewable stuff.

(Günther, operating in Belize)

Unfortunately, these logistical challenges are not easily resolved once RET products clear customs and border administration. Indeed, it appears that while many of the challenges associated with getting RETs into emerging markets are largely political and administrative, based on my conversations with the entrepreneurs themselves, I surmise that the most challenging physical infrastructural and logistical issues arise when REEs need to design or develop processes to deliver RET products to end-users. For instance, one entrepreneur, Liam, who co-founded a REE that operates in Somalia, explained:

> *There is no mail system here. There is no one that delivers it to your home. The only way to get something delivered here is to use DHL, which is really expensive. I mean we have been carrying books in when we make trips, and we'll bring in containers ourselves when we do workshops.*

(Liam, operating in Somalia)

Corruption further complicates the already-complex procedural challenges experienced while navigating customs and border administration. One REE reported as recently as 2017 that the solar lamps he imported to be distributed to end-users were confiscated by customs without explanation. The entrepreneur explained that customs asked for thrice the regular fee associated with importing solar lamps into the country. Corruption, not only in government but also in several local and regional organisations, was the most popular "Other" challenge identified by the entrepreneurs I interviewed. Kenneth, who runs a REE in Trinidad and Tobago, clarified this challenge. He explained that it related to nepotism and the lack of transparency in the awarding of renewable energy projects. Interestingly, whenever the entrepreneurs described procedural challenges and issues related to bureaucracy, they invariably also raised the issue of corruption. For instance, Vicente, Mark and Francis, operating in Chile, Tanzania and Zambia, respectively, lamented the high levels of bureaucracy in government and other public offices – they describe it as "demotivating", as it makes starting and running "an above-board business" difficult. Francis, in particular, mentioned that corruption has the unintended effect of penalising, and therefore discouraging, law-abiding renewable energy businesspeople. Both Francis and Joshua, whose REE operates out of Uganda, claimed the only way to run a successful REE is to develop networks and partnerships with individuals "willing to make administrative exceptions". Worryingly, the REEs' experiences with corruption are not limited to institutions within the countries in which they operate. For example, Sam, who operates a REE in Fiji, acknowledged that there are many discrepancies in the tender processes administered by IDOs and other international organisations as well. He indicated that the tender process for projects in the Pacific islands in particular is biased, and only a select few enterprises constantly win international contracts. Thus, corruption emerged as an important factor as REEs navigate the procedural requirements embedded in the process of moving RET products along the supply chain to end-users in emerging markets.

Based on my interviews, I inferred there are two key challenges to delivering RET products to end-users in emerging markets: cost-related and geographical barriers.

Cost-related barriers to delivering RET products to end-users

REEs face significant challenges related to the cost of delivering RET products to end-users in emerging markets. This challenge is especially jarring because the high costs of delivery translate to high costs for the end-users themselves. Indeed, cost-related barriers can be prohibitive. This challenge is felt especially strongly by entrepreneurs such as consultants like Jean, who operates a REE in Cameroon, and described costs as an important barrier to his ability to grow his enterprise into a distribution business. He explained that his enterprise is not yet able to import RET components itself, because "we do not have enough money until now to import, but that is our objective" (Jean, operating in Cameroon). In another example, Ángel, who operates a REE in Ecuador, echoed the same experience. He explained during his 2013 interview, "it is quite costly because we are entering by plane, and the flight one way will be $400."

In fact, many REEs lamented the costs of manoeuvring logistical challenges, often concluding that, inevitably, it may not be economically feasible to continue operation of their enterprises:

> *If you need like turbine, the cost is so expensive. And combined with the transportation and other costs along the way, it's more than buying solar or solar panels. Like if you do an economic analysis for that, it's sometimes not possible. That is also a challenge.*
>
> (Chea, operating in Cambodia)

Indeed, REEs often identify emotional and financial frustration as a specific point of failure for their enterprises. These costs appear insurmountable because of the legitimised processes (or lack thereof) in emerging markets.

Delphine and Tim, operating in Cameroon and Costa Rica, respectively, introduced and explained the knock-on effects of the cost of navigating these logistical challenges. Specifically, they revealed they face a consistent operational balancing act, continuously reconciling their own operational costs and the final price of the product for the end-users. Arguably, this challenge is familiar to all entrepreneurs and business owner-managers in general, who must decide on a price point for their products that customers are willing to pay but that also produces a sustainable profit margin for the enterprise. However, the market for RET products in emerging markets compounds this issue because REEs design and offer value propositions to customers considered among some of the world's most disadvantaged and impoverished. Yet, their logistical costs and associated challenges are the same for conventional enterprises. Delphine and Tim explained the issue of affordability for end-users in emerging markets:

> *We're buying in small quantities. And when you're buying in small quantities you have to bring them by air. And when you fly it by air, by DHL or UPS, the cost goes up. And the cost of duty here is the same as the value of the products themselves. And you cannot sell these products. Because most of the people who need solar are the poor people in the rural areas.*
>
> (Delphine, operating in Cameroon)

> *And then getting financing here is very very expensive for our company, for cash flow, for investment, all that is very expensive. There are also very little financing options available for customers to purchase the systems.*
>
> (Tim, operating in Costa Rica)

These logistical challenges seem insurmountable for REEs operating on the world's island nations, such as those in the Caribbean and Pacific, for example. Vijay, who operates his REE on the islands of Fiji in the Pacific, explained this issue. He described not only the geographical challenges associated with delivering RET products to the remote islands of Fiji, but also the financial implications of the costs of delivering to these islands:

> *Logistics is always an issue in the islands. Issue One is the cost. And the second is reliability of the services, and also the scheduling of the services. Some places may not have transport access for weeks on end. So that is always a big challenge. Logistics in Fiji is actually very good compared to the rest of the region. We have worked in other parts of the region and it is very challenging – it can be a real make or break on your profitability. It is very easy to lose a lot of money with all your technicians stuck out somewhere on the islands and they are missing a part or cannot come back. For instance, you can charter a plane or a helicopter or a boat, but then you're into the thousands of dollars. So it depends on the situation. Whether it is better to bite the bullet and pay that to get the job done, or whether you have to leave them out there.*
>
> (Vijay, operating in Fiji)

Yet, despite the resulting financial hardship of engaging with logistical challenges, and the negative implications for the affordability of RETs for impoverished end-users in emerging markets, many of the REEs I interviewed remained positive and shared their strategies for overcoming or coping with these challenges.[2] For instance Thomas, whose REE operates in Kenya, explained that a well-organised and competent logistical team and effective logistical expertise are key factors in overcoming these cost-related logistical challenges:

Because the focus is on off-grid, of course everyone who does solar has
to have a pretty well organised logistical team.

(Thomas, operating in Kenya)

Kofi, operating in Ghana, also suggested that they key is in "volume". He
suggested the quicker a consulting REE (Type I) can scale their enterprise
to larger scale distribution, the quicker they reap the advantages of economies of scale. However, scaling RET business is the ostensibly insurmountable overarching challenge many nascent REEs face in emerging markets.[3]
Indeed, many avoid scaling too rapidly to the point where they need to
maintain and manage large amounts of inventory. REEs often choose to
continue to deliver RET products and systems to customers and end-users
just in time or, admittedly, considerably late, after they have been purchased.
Jean, from Cameroon, explained, "I do not have stock. It is only when we
agree with the customer and he gives a little money to start the work."

The implications of this particular challenge are that in order to maintain
the affordability of their products, REEs must either abandon the usual,
formal distribution channels in favour of informal distribution channels,
or offer the products at almost no margin, with negative effects on profitability. There is a need to develop more efficient distribution networks in
emerging markets. However, once work has started on delivery of purchased
RET products and systems, REEs' next challenge is the installation of RET
systems and getting RET products into the possession of end-users. Here,
REEs must surmount the significant challenge of the sometimes-difficult terrain, weather and other geographical conditions that accompanies delivery
of RET products to remote regions in emerging markets.

Geographical barriers to delivering RET products to end-users

Indeed, remoteness is a significant challenge. It presents a considerable barrier to the delivery of RET products to end-users in emerging markets, especially those whose lives and livelihoods endure at the Base of the Pyramid
(BOP). For the entrepreneurs who prefer to serve only end-users in urban
regions in emerging markets, this is not a significant challenge. However,
for those with a clear mission (and, for many, a clear moral incentive) to
serve those most in need, travelling and delivering RET products to the most
remote regions is unavoidable. Below, and in the endnotes for this Chapter,[4]
I provide several excerpts from the REEs' own descriptions of the challenge,
some of which include descriptive accounts of the difficult routes RET products must travel to reach end-users in remote areas:

In the capital, the infrastructure is not so much a challenge. But if you
want to work outside Accra (the capital city of Ghana), it is a challenge
because there are some areas that are not so accessible.

(Abeiku, operating in Ghana)

Guatemala is divided up into 22 departments or regions. And at the moment we've been selling solar kits in 18 of the 22 departments. 20% of the population in Guatemala do not have access to electricity and their villages are really, really remote. I went to one recently. And from Cobán we drove for 3 hours. 1 hour was by road, and then for 2 hours it is just on a track and at the end of that, somebody met us and we walked for another 2 hours through hidden Mayan paths that you wouldn't even know were there. And it was really hard. It is all hidden in the mountains. You walk for 2 hours and eventually you reach the community. So that means that the electricity grid would never reach there. It is not worth the investment. And I think the landscape in Guatemala is such a massive obstacle to overcome. The journey is such a hard job for the sales teams.

(Luis, operating in Guatemala)

Laos is a very interesting challenge or kind of a battleground infrastructure-wise, just based on geography. It is a very mountainous, hilly, geographically dispersed country. So, villages are very spread out and there might be a road and then you have to take a boat for half a day and then you have to go down a dirt road for another 20km. Very hard to reach. So doing that, just logistically, bringing solar panels, batteries and every other component that matters to build an off-grid project, we built up a lot of experience figuring out how to do that in Laos. And a lot of those lessons learned have helped us in our work whether it's in the Marshall Islands or in Sierra Leone.

(Chris, operating in Laos)

The roads is an issue because they do not have access to good roads, especially during the rainy period like now: it's very difficult to access the villages. Even if you have a 4-wheel drive vehicle, you will not find it easy to go through. So most of our interventions are planned for during the dry season. It is only during the dry season you can get access to those villages.

(Delphine, operating in Cameroon)

Physically, the natural geographic features of many regions pose obvious but significant logistical obstacles. Regions characterised by high or steep mountains, unnavigable rivers or islands make the actual physical transportation and delivery of RET products to end-users increasingly difficult in emerging markets:

Moving goods especially in the riverine areas and the mountainous areas could really be challenging. Most of the money goes into transporting goods. If only we could get that aspect sorted out because the price of fuel is high and then you have to move these things by trucks and the

further away you are from the central government, the more expensive
fuel is. So really, logistics is crazy.

(Chiagozie, operating in Nigeria)

Several of our projects are high in the mountains, and it is not easy to get
all the logistics and infrastructure there. Sometimes it is really a constraint.

(Vicente, operating in Chile)

It is so difficult to go to these islands, and that is why (off-grid) renew-
able energy products are a good idea. A boat goes to these islands maybe
once every 6 months. it takes a week to go there and the project might
take only a few weeks to complete, but if you have to wait for transport,
in most of the Pacific Islands logistics is one of the most challenging, and
it is very costly to go from Point A to Point B.

(Sam, operating in Fiji)

The implications of these logistical challenges are the difficulty of expanding
existing electricity grid infrastructure into remote regions. Often, the terrain
is so difficult and communities in the direst need are so remote that grid-tied
electricity supply may never be a viable option.

If you go to the homes, you will see a lot of people still using firewood.
Electricity is very slowly spreading. It is very rugged, Papua New Guinea.
The communities are very scattered. It is very expensive to extend the
grid to a few houses. PNG Power they have to make money, so they just
look at government buildings and a few plantations."

(David, operating in Papua New Guinea)

Thus, off-grid installations, especially solar-powered electricity and lighting,
are the most feasible solutions. However, the REEs need to get these solutions delivered to the communities that need them most. Unpacking this
issue, there are several important sub-issues one must consider before deciding to pursue a distribution business model for RET products in emerging
markets. One crucial sub-theme of the entrepreneurs' descriptions of the
geographical challenges they face is the inadequacy, poor maintenance or
lack thereof of road and other transport infrastructure in many territories:

Transportation, yes roads to access rural communities now, especially in
this season, the wet season, it is very, very difficult. A lot of road prob-
lems. So, we cannot access the communities that we target.

(Chea, operating in Cambodia)

Roads in Costa Rica are terrible. A lot of the installations we go to the
electrical systems are not up to scale, so we end up having to do a lot
more work to implement our systems.

(Tim, operating in Costa Rica)

The thing is, when it comes to providing logistics to these remote areas, it has become a really difficult issue in Indonesia because the infrastructure is not that good. The road access in these places sometimes they have like airports etcetera, but when it comes to getting things from the airport to the site itself, sometimes it is really difficult for us. Dealing with the local logistical companies is quite a big support for us but the thing is, even working with them, we still need to rely on the existing infrastructure. The time of delivery is not satisfactory at the moment because we need sometimes quite a lot of time to send our wind turbine to these places.

(Arif, operating in Indonesia)

Another important geographical sub-theme and concern of international significance is safety. One entrepreneur, operating in Nigeria – Chiagozie – articulated this particular concern clearly:

These border communities, the one we just did, sometimes we have to get reliable protection from because they are in remote places and this is where kidnappings are so rampant. So we have to get police protection.

(Chiagozie, operating in Nigeria)

The remote location of the communities in need is also a concern for REEs who need to collect payment for their products and services in cash from the villagers who purchased them. In 2013, Chris, who operates a REE in Laos, described this challenge to me:

When you are working in remote hard to reach areas, there are plenty of other challenges too. For example, payment collection. How do we go and collect those payments when it costs more to pay for the petrol or pay for the boat or pay for the trip to go collect the payment? It is just not sustainable when it costs more to do that than what all the payments are – it is only a few dollars as villages are very poor areas.

(Chris, operating in Laos)

Despite the geographical challenges of delivering RET products to end-users in remote regions, some entrepreneurs offered solutions that are worth sharing. In one example, Sai, operating in India, also recommended a focus on the type and relevance of the products and services offered for the end-users in emerging markets. He believes that if REEs design and offer only products that are suitable for the climate and geography in their targeted emerging markets, then logistics will become less challenging. Indeed, RET products designed with the physical environment in end-user communities in mind should be more durable and adaptable to conditions of their usage in such markets.[5]

There were challenges around distribution, but we've definitely done a lot in the last six months to get past them. And I think we strongly believe that once we have the right products in our portfolio, distribution will no longer be a challenge.

(Sai, operating in India)

In another example, entrepreneurs operating in Laos and Indonesia describe the benefit of community participation. Indeed, getting the community involved in the logistical planning and delivery of RET products and systems seems to have helped these REEs out of difficult logistical situations:

I would not say it is a problem as far as us getting a project done. That is one of our strengths actually, is that we can figure out ways to get a huge load of batteries down a hill or get a box of solar panels on a boat and get them to the village. It is just that when you have to deal with all these things on a scaled-up basis, I think that is where it becomes a challenge. To overcome that, you just have to work through it. On a previous project in Laos, dozens of villagers came out to help us. They had to get the hydro turbine down this really steep hill. We had these ropes and pulleys. It is things like that where you just have to be resourceful and be patient. A really common thing that I've seen and heard from some of the different projects is that the villagers and the community members seem to always be eager to take part and participate. They help dig the foundation for the powerhouse or help move the solar panels or help setup the power lines – the things that would be very hard to do. So that is definitely a big factor, just the community assistance.

(Chris, operating in Laos)

For the hydro projects, usually it is located in the more remote areas. So we must disassemble the equipment so that we can carry it one-by-one on foot to the site. That is why we need the cooperation of the villagers. The other type of hydro, the 1MW, which is usually the hydro social business, we cannot disassemble the equipment, so usually we must make a new road in order to take the equipment to the power plants. So there are many considerations – how to deliver it safely without any damage, and electrically for installation. We have electrical engineers and we train the villagers for installation and maintenance. Actually, the villagers have low levels of education so we only teach them the logics of the equipment, what is the rule of thumb of the equipment. If something goes wrong, what are the logics of this equipment, what are the logics of this situation? By teaching them about the logics and the rule of thumb. And the other thing is they must be involved in the construction so they also know about the equipment since it was constructed.

(Arif, operating in Indonesia)

In the latter example, Arif enlisted the help of the end-users themselves in remote villages to ensure that the installed RET systems are well maintained. Indeed, REEs also worry about the maintenance of the systems they install after they have left the remote villages and the REE's technicians are no longer available to provide on-site support.

Providing after-sales service for RET products

At the final stage of the supply chain, after RET products have finally been delivered to end-users, the main challenge REEs face is providing after-sales service. Indeed, the same geographical challenges that limit access for distribution also limit re-access when things go wrong or installed RET systems require maintenance. In addition, it appears that even when geographical factors are not a major barrier, the costs associated with re-accessing end-users in remote locations can be prohibitive. As the REEs explained, the costs associated with maintenance and repairs (for example, in the form of warranties) are not currently included in the price of the small-scale RET products sold in emerging markets, especially to customers at the BOP:

> After-sales services are not effectively provided for rural households who are spending something like 50 or 60 dollars for a lantern. And if some difficulty emerges, unless they get a warranty or some kind of maintenance at a cost, then that would be really difficult. This has been popular in mainly rural areas.
>
> (Aaron, operating in Ethiopia)

> One of the difficulties in creating a distribution channel is that you need after-sales service and all the technical stuff. But if you're installing a solar array on someone's roof and it is costing them a lot of money, then there's a lot of support services required thereafter in your sales channel. We did not want to do that, so our target market is very much composed of the lowest rung of the energy ladder.
>
> (Elton, operating in Tanzania)

The challenge of providing after-sales support is not limited to solar energy technologies. As Adamu explained, some REEs who provide larger biogas plants in Kenya appear to be doing so without offering after-sales support and advice:

> People have been building biogas plants without going back and seeing whether the biogas plant has been working or not. Too many people are doing business that does not include follow-up because that is cheaper. If you give the client a price that includes follow-up, they would not

choose you because you will be too expensive. They will go instead for
the cheaper guys who do not do follow-up.

(Adamu, operating in Kenya)

Success in the supply chain for renewable energy products

Indeed, REEs face numerous frustrating and often-crippling challenges
while trying to navigate the supply chains for RET products in emerging
markets. However, when they discuss the implications of these challenges, it
is also evident that the REEs I studied have devised effective and sometimes
innovative solutions.[6] For instance, Jean, an entrepreneur running a REE in
Cameroon, explained that REEs could attain logistical success if they are
able to choose trading partners in specific countries. Indeed, while there are
challenges associated with trade with some markets, trading with some of
the world's largest manufacturers and suppliers of RETs in China appears
to be no problem for Jean:

Normally if you buy something in China to Cameroon, it is not a prob-
lem of logistics because there is already logistics enterprises that work
between China and Cameroon. There is also logistics between USA,
Europe, France and Belgium. To get it to Cameroon there is no problem.
We know there are some logistics firms. They do everything and then
you just receive your product. They will charge you something and then
you will receive your product. But there are specific countries where risk
and costs are high.

(Jean, operating in Cameroon)

In fact, Sai (India) and Ernesto (Philippines) also relieved some logistical
angst by selecting and enlisting the assistance of logistics partners in China:

We actually have a logistics partner that brings the product in from
China to India. And then we have a logistics partner in India to help us
distribute the product here. So, logistics itself is not really a challenge.
But there's some government bureaucracy around logistics where there
are a lot of forms to be filled out and permits you need etcetera, but
we've streamlined that process, so I wouldn't say logistics is a problem.

(Sai, operating in India)

Actually, it is not such a big problem because we have a lot of sub-
contractors here. We get the project and, if it is a challenge, the contractor
can do it for you.

(Ernesto, operating in The Philippines)

Like Ernesto above, another entrepreneur, Raphael, runs his Type IV integrator REE in a large highly industrial emerging market: The Philippines.

Raphael, too, described only minor issues related to traffic, and described generally favourable logistical infrastructures, comparable to Europe. Another owner-manager of a large Type IV integrator, Alain, operates out of West Africa (Senegal). He explained his enterprise had grown successfully and enjoyed strong partnerships internationally and therefore experienced very few logistical challenges:

> *I have very honestly no issue at all. In regards to logistics support, to shipments, to custom clearance and everything and sending stuff, Thailand is comparable almost to Europe. We are probably importing this year I would say 300–400 containers of equipment for solar projects, probably a little bit more because we're doing quite large numbers. So it is quite well organised. The only problem is that everything goes via the road here and one of the main problems from a business perspective on a day-to-day basis is just traffic in Bangkok honestly. So it is very difficult for meetings and planning your day-to-day activities based on traffic, same like in Jakarta or other countries, which can be actually a challenge on a day-to-day basis.*

(Raphael, operating in Thailand)

> *With mini-grids, logistics are quite easy – you just bring the system to the site once and then it works and then sometimes as we use some 10 to 20% of diesel fuel to cover our peak power demands, we are to bring diesel to these sites every now and then. Then there are some maintenance services required with some spare parts and that's it. Logistical challenges are not that much, and we can handle them quite easily together with our joint venture company, which is setup quite well in that regard.*

(Alain, operating in Senegal)

In response to challenges related to after-sales service, the REEs look inward to their products and value propositions offered and to the standards and norms within the industry:

> *In terms of repairs, we try to avoid buying solar systems that can easily break down. So what we are doing is we'll make sure that we buy quality products. And this time around we've added a kind of innovation on the product by putting a sticker – a quality assurance sticker, that has possibility of the end-user communicating in case there is a system failure in the rural areas. In case there is a problem with this product, the end-user can SMS us and we can intervene immediately through our distribution network. So these are some of the ways we would try to see how we can better serve the rural areas.*

(Delphine, operating in Cameroon)

What we try to do is create a product that does not need any after-sales service and is easy to operate. So, you buy it like you would buy a torch. So that, in terms of where we're headed strategically, opens up a lot more distribution channels so anywhere that sells washing detergents could sell our lights or anything like that. Because that is what I see a lot of people doing – new channels for renewable energy – that's great, and that's a long difficult thing to do as far as someone doing it, but for us we want to keep our product more like fast-moving consumer goods and a more customer-specific energy product.

(Elton, operating in Tanzania)

So, we are trying to work on biogas standards, and hoping that if we can have biogas standards in place, then it will actually force our colleagues in the sector to play to the rules. So that's what we're trying to do to counter this cheap way of doing the business.

(Adamu, operating in Kenya)

Successful REEs also empower and include end-users in the maintenance of RET products and systems:

We try to train persons, the villagers. It is likely that every eight out of ten villagers, we need to train them to see how they can install these systems and do the basic maintenance.

(Delphine, operating in Cameroon)

Consistent with the effort by many REEs to design and develop inclusive business models (see Chapter 2), entrepreneurs consider community owner-ship of RET installations a viable solution to the challenges associated with providing after-sales services to remote communities in emerging markets. Related to this solution is the need to ensure that the technologies and solu-tions offered are suitable to the needs of end-users. According to Luis (Gua-temala), Aaron (Ethiopia) and David (Papua New Guinea), to be successful and sustainable, RETs must be adaptable to the heterogeneous cultures, needs, languages and peoples of emerging markets. For instance, Vicente (Chile) explained that legal bureaucracy and enterprise's social license to operate influence the design and implementation of renewable energy projects on the lands of the indigenous people of Chile. Iwan (Indonesia) emphasised the importance of offering only highly suitable technologies for rural villages, which must require minimal maintenance – it is pivotal that end-users are able to operate and maintain the installed technologies themselves. Although these challenges are locally specific, they are impor-tant to all of the REEs I studied to varying degrees. REEs, governments, non-government organisations (NGOs) and IDOs alike must consider them carefully when establishing RET projects and systems in emerging markets. I surmise that RET projects, and the REEs that deliver them, cannot effectively enhance the well-being of their end-users and contribute to sustainable human thriving in their markets unless they contribute to the independence of end-user communities. Achieving this requires the distribution and use of RETs tailored to the specific geographical, financial and institutional conditions of end-users. RETs must be locally appropriate and *adaptable* to the cultures and needs of different locales in different parts of the world (Bidwell, 2013; Blenkinsopp, Coles and Kirwan, 2013; Kolk and Buuse, 2012; Lenzen et al., 2014; Pierce, Steel and Warner, 2009). It is for this reason that the literature on RETs in emerging markets emphasises the importance of locally-relevant and socio-culturally appropriate installations (*cf.* Wüstenhagen, Wolsink and Buerer, 2007 Retnanestri and Outhred, 2013), as well as the development and use of inclusive business models (SustainAbility, 2014; UNDP, 2008; Kolk and Buuse, 2012) in emerging markets (see Chapter 2).

Notes

1 CARICOM, or "Caribbean Community", refers to an organisation of Caribbean territories that aim to achieve economic and foreign policy integration and cooperation among its members. There are fifteen full members of CARICOM: Antigua and Barbuda, Bahamas, Barbados, Belize, Dominica, Grenada, Guyana, Haiti, Jamaica, Montserrat, Saint Kitts and Nevis, Saint Lucia, Saint Vincent and the Grenadines, Suriname and Trinidad and Tobago.
2 Refer to my article, "How do developing country constraints affect renewable energy entrepreneurs?" (Gabriel et al., 2016) for a description and discussion of how emerging market constraints directly affect renewable energy enterprises.
3 Refer to my article, "What is challenging renewable energy entrepreneurs in developing countries?" (Gabriel, 2016).
4 Here are two additional descriptions of the geographical barriers to delivering RET products to end-users in emerging markets:

> *Sometimes the road that we have in several provinces is only 2 lanes, and that is the provincial road, and some of them are being used for carrying heavy equipment vehicles. So the road gets destroyed quite easily. Actually, I recently experienced this thing where a part of a wind turbine got damaged. For 3 days I demonstrated this technology in one remote place in Sumatra, and we have to carry the product by land. We cannot send it through air because of the size problem. Thus, the product has to travel 1200 km by land and when it comes to the site, the product is quite damaged! It was not really functioning properly. In several areas, the road is really bad, so it gets really bumpy and that's why the product we had was destroyed. So, we need to come up with a new solution on how we can actually package our products so it can sustain road infrastructures which are not really in the best condition. We are working right now on how to get claims from the logistics company.*
>
> (Arif, operating in Indonesia)

> *The market channel is not well developed for renewable energy products. This includes solar products and the improved cookstove products.*

Especially when it comes to solar technology, most of the major suppliers are in Addis Ababa. They might have recently developed or formed some link to some major regional capitals. But even that, at the district level and at the village level where the real demand is, there is no market channel. And that is one of the difficulties of getting the products or making products accessible to finance institutions. Secondly, you know because the market channel is not well developed, the physical infrastructure is not very good in rural areas. Even in areas where physical infrastructure is available, the market is not well developed.

(Aaron, operating in Ethiopia)

5 I published a chapter of a recent book, *Encyclopaedia of the UN Sustainable Development Goals: Affordable and Clean Energy.* The chapter is titled, "Reverse Innovation" (Gabriel, 2022) and addresses the affordability and local appropriateness of renewable energy technologies for end-users at the Base of the Pyramid in emerging markets. I encourage readers to consult this chapter for further guidance around the adaptability and appropriateness of RETs for impoverished end-users.

6 I describe which solutions relate to specific challenges faced in an article published in *Energy for Sustainable Development,* titled "How do developing country constraints affect renewable energy entrepreneurs?" (Gabriel et al., 2016).

References

Bidwell, D., 2013. The role of values in public beliefs and attitudes towards commercial wind energy. *Energy Policy,* 58, p. 189.

Blenkinsopp, T., Coles, S.R. and Kirwan, K., 2013. Renewable energy for rural communities in Maharashtra, India. *Energy Policy,* 60, p. 192.

Easterby-Smith, M., Thorpe, R. and Jackson, P., 2012. *Management Research.* London: Sage Publications.

Gabriel, C.A., 2016. What is challenging renewable energy entrepreneurs in developing countries? *Renewable and Sustainable Energy Reviews,* 64, pp. 362–371.

Gabriel, C.A., 2022. Reverse innovation. In W. Leal Filho, L. Brandli, P. Özuyar and T. Wall (Eds.), *Encyclopaedia of the UN Sustainable Development Goals: Affordable and Clean Energy.* Switzerland: Springer.

Gabriel, C.A., Kirkwood, J., Walton, S. and Rose, E.L., 2016. How do developing country constraints affect renewable energy entrepreneurs? *Energy for Sustainable Development,* 35, pp. 52–66.

Kolk, A. and Buuse, D.V.D., 2012. In search of viable business models for development: Sustainable energy in developing countries. *Corporate Governance,* 12(4), pp. 551–567.

Lenzen, M., Krishnapillai, M., Talagi, D., Quintal, J., Quintal, D., Grant, R. and Murray, J., 2014. Cultural and socio-economic determinants of energy consumption on small remote islands. *Natural Resources Forum,* 38(1), pp. 27–46.

Pierce, J.C., Steel, B.S. and Warner, R.L., 2009. Knowledge, culture, and public support for renewable-energy policy. *Comparative Technology Transfer and Society,* 7(3), pp. 270–286, 346.

Retnanestri, M. and Outhred, H., 2013. Acculturation of renewable energy technology into remote communities: Lessons from Dobrov, Bourdieu, and Rogers and an Indonesian case study. *Energy, Sustainability and Society,* 3, pp. 1–13.

SustainAbility, 2014. *Model Behaviour: 20 Business Model Innovations for Sustainability*. New York, NY: Sustainability Inc.

UNDP (United Nations Development Programme), 2008. *Creating Value for All: Strategies for Doing Business with the Poor*. New York, USA: United Nations Development Programme.

Wüstenhagen, R., Wolsink, M. and Buerer, M.J., 2007. Social acceptance of renewable energy innovation: An introduction to the concept. *Energy Policy*, 35(5), pp. 2683–2691.

4 How renewable energy enterprises compete

What it means to 'compete'

In everyday parlance and especially in the business disciplines, our use of the word 'compete' usually refers to rivalry between individuals or organisations. However, 'compete' traces its origins to the Latin *competere*, which is the confluence of *com* ('together') and *petere* ('to aim at or seek'). Literally, to compete means 'to strive together' or seek after some aim or end goal in company with each other. Arguably, as scholars in business, there is a tendency to emphasise the negativity and aggressiveness of competing forces, ostensibly at the expense of the potentially positive implications of 'togetherness' implied in the literal origins of competition. For instance, while firms might rival each other on price, the net positive outcome could be a more affordable product for impoverished end-users. In addition, rivalry based on differentiation (or uniqueness of products or services offered) could enhance innovation and the development of more locally appropriate products and services. Similarly, I argue that whether deliberately or unintentionally, it is the combined efforts of renewable energy enterprises (REEs) as well as their complex strategic interactions with other organisations, on aggregate that could eventually fulfil the aim of a sustainable energy transition in emerging markets. In short, I believe competition defined simply as 'striving together' is an important and necessary experience for successful REEs in emerging markets.

Therefore, in the context of striving together in pursuit of a sustainable energy transition, I noted that REEs pursue two clear aims in emerging markets. The first is to increase their market share (that is, the availability and popularity of their products to end-users). The second is to become economically self-sufficient (although not necessarily financially profitable in the traditional sense – I discuss this in Chapter 6 of this book). However, the global sustainable development agenda cannot realise the aim of sustainable human thriving unless there is a levelling of the field within the renewable energy industry. Levelling the field is pivotal to ensure equity of access to and participation in renewable energy technology (RET) markets for REEs. Interestingly, considerable development effort has been dedicated to seemingly provide equity of opportunity for these enterprises: RET support schemes, non-government organisation (NGO) and aid grants, and supply chain and logistical support, for example. However, paradoxically, these same development organisations have also contributed to the inequitably low influence of many REEs in emerging markets. In addition, REEs compete daily with larger multinational enterprises (MNEs) whose supply chain integration and international legitimacy give them a significant advantage over REEs in emerging markets. Thus, REEs do not have a fair chance to contribute their significant experience and expertise to the collective efforts to facilitate the sustainable energy transition in these markets.

In this chapter, I address some of these challenges specifically. I framed these challenges as competitive forces deliberately to reflect their significant influence on the market positioning, customer relationships and overall success of the REEs I studied in emerging markets. Like entrepreneurs in other sectors and contexts, REEs also grapple with the challenge of survival in a competitive landscape. This chapter addresses two aspects of this landscape. First, I highlight the main sources of competition in emerging markets and why ignoring and underestimating them could lead to failure for nascent REEs. Second, I characterise the main market niches in which REEs operate in emerging markets in response to the competitive challenges endured. My aim is to not only highlight the often-contradictory interests of REEs and their key stakeholders and contemporaries in emerging markets, but also the ways that competitors within the industry strive together to collectively enhance the state of sustainable human thriving on these markets.

Thus, this chapter does not constitute an objective strategic assessment of the competitive positioning of renewable energy enterprises (REEs) *per se*. Instead, I present and infer from the perspectives of the entrepreneurs themselves as they operate within and navigate the competitive landscape of the industry. I have taken the entrepreneurs' own observations and perspectives and placed them within the context of RET distribution, using competition and competitive forces as an organising frame.

Competing in the renewable energy industry in emerging markets

As REEs in emerging markets operate within an industry environment that is unique and challenging (see Chapter 1), their strategic concerns are equally unique and challenging. In particular, many of the REEs I interviewed lamented operating in an industry where other REEs are not their only or major source of competition. Each aspect of the REEs' business models, from their value propositions to configurations of value creation, must be crafted to gain a competitive edge despite unfair access to supporting resources and institutions. A SWOT assessment of REEs' enterprises and the markets in which they operate unveils two clear conclusions (Figure 4.1).

First, and strikingly, I surmise that REEs' core competence, the inimitable aspect of their business that they do best, is their embeddedness within and

STRENGTHS	WEAKNESSES	OPPORTUNITIES	THREATS
• REEs are embedded socio-culturally and socio-economically in emerging markets	• Unless collaborating on aid project, distributing enterprises have a tendency to avoid end-users at the Base of the Pyramid as customers, which makes them vulnerable to competition from international aid and development organisations (IDOs) and larger multinational enterprises	• After some time, infrastructure and distribution channels become more established and reliable	• Cheaper products available in the value propositions of competing REEs
• Experienced REEs have existing relationships with suppliers, installers and key technical partners		• Opportunity to include cheaper products in Value Propositions, as overall quality increases in the industry	• Lighting Africa certified products on the market
• REEs focused solely on distribution serve as 'networking hub' for other REEs, including consultants and integrators	• High costs of operation versus unstable and/or uncertain revenues	• Opportunity to receive endorsement / certification from Lighting Africa	• Low product differentiation
• When collaborating on aid projects distributing REEs may develop close ties with end-users in remote areas (especially at the Base of Pyramid)	• Fiscal dependence on NGOs, IDOs / aid organisations	• Growing demand (need) for RETs	• Low cost to end-users of switching brands
• Distributing REEs develop close ties and brand recognition with middle- to upper-class residential and commercial end-users		• Opportunity to lead or collaborate on IDO/aid-funded distribution projects	• Ease of entering the RET market for new enterprises means increasing number of competitors
			• Potential for RET suppliers and multinational enterprises to integrate forward into local renewable energy distribution (especially when funded by IDOs and/or aid projects)

Figure 4.1 Strengths, weaknesses, opportunities and threats (SWOT) of RET product distribution in emerging markets

knowledge of local sociocultural and socioeconomic conditions. I argue that all other strengths are imitable by other entities in the renewable energy industry. For instance, although the logistical challenges of delivering solar lighting and power generation technologies may act as a barrier to entry for nascent REEs, I argue any competent enterprise can obtain and sell these RETs. Likewise, the opportunities available to REEs in emerging markets, namely those associated with international aid and development organisations (IDOs), are also exploitable by others in the industry. Thus, I believe the knowledge and deep connections with communities developed by REEs in emerging markets are core strengths that REEs must leverage to level the field in the renewable energy industry.

Second, I noted the threats to REEs' self-sufficiency and therefore survival is significant. Indeed, the REEs describe the challenge of grappling with threats from an increasing number of players in the industry, not all of whom are local entities. I discuss this particular stressor in the section on 'Competition from Local and International Public Sector Organisations'. In Study I, the REEs also described purveyors of traditional fossil energy technologies and solutions as key competitors within the market. However, in general, most reports indicate the transition to sustainable energy seems well underway in emerging markets. For several years now, experts and policymakers have considered renewable energy a mainstream source for electricity generation. For instance, REN21, the Renewable Energy Policy Network for the 21st Century, reported that all around the world renewable energy installation and uptake continues to increase steadily. REN21 reports that "net capacity additions for renewable power were higher than for fossil fuels and nuclear combined for a fourth consecutive year, and renewables now make up more than one-third of global installed power capacity" (REN21, 2019: 29). Indeed, RET products continue to spread in noticeable quantities globally. Specifically, as of 2017, renewable energy sources (RES) comprised an estimated 18.1 percent of total final energy consumption (TFEC) – demand for these RES grew 4.4 percent (REN21, 2019). Therefore, I am optimistic that, as the transition materialises, the ubiquity and increasing attractiveness of RETs will neutralise any perception among REEs of competitive threat from fossil energies.

However, other threats persist that have potentially negative effects on the enterprise's ability to compete. If one consulted Michael Porter in the 1970s and early 2000s (Porter, 1979, 2008) and any mainstream business and management textbook ever since (*cf.* Schermerhorn et al., 2017 and Samson, Donnet and Daft, 2018), one would conclude that the main concern is the overall intensity of rivalry among competitors in the industry. This rivalry is affected by what Porter and other leading strategy scholars describe as the bargaining power of suppliers and end-users, the threat of new entrants, and the threat of substitutes. As educators in business and management, we teach our students to undertake strategic analyses by understanding where enterprises fit within their field and amongst the other players in their industry. Figure 4.2 outlines these so-called 'threats' generally,

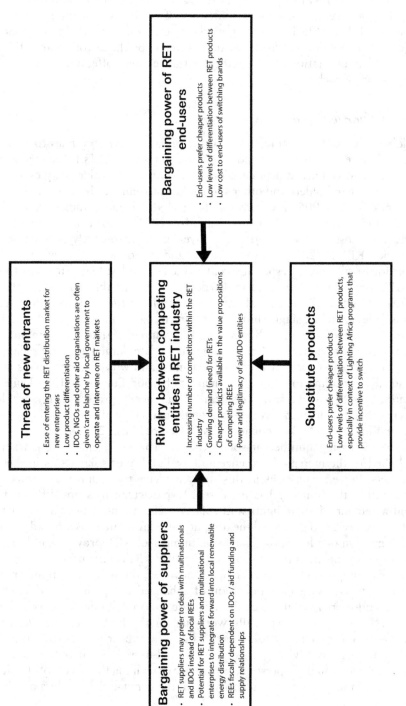

Threat of new entrants

· Ease of entering the RET distribution market for new enterprises
· Low product differentiation
· IDOs, NGOs and other aid organisations are often given 'carte blanche' by local government to operate and intervene on RET markets

Bargaining power of suppliers

· RET suppliers may prefer to deal with multinationals and IDOs instead of local REEs
· Potential for RET suppliers and multinational enterprises to integrate forward into local renewable energy distribution
· REEs fiscally dependent on IDOs / aid funding and supply relationships

Rivalry between competing entities in RET industry

· Increasing number of competitors within the RET industry
· Growing demand (need) for RETs
· Cheaper products available in the value propositions of competing REEs
· Power and legitimacy of aid/IDO entities

Bargaining power of RET end-users

· End-users prefer cheaper products
· Low levels of differentiation between RET products
· Low cost to end-users of switching brands

Substitute products

· End-users prefer cheaper products
· Low levels of differentiation between RET products, especially in context of Lighting Africa programs that provide incentive to switch

Figure 4.2 Competitive analysis of RET product distribution in emerging markets

as they relate to REEs operating in the RET industry in emerging markets. In my assessment of the overall intensity of rivalry within the industry, I concluded that REEs in emerging markets face rivalry from two broad categories of competitors: private entities, as well as public sector organisations locally and internationally. Therefore, in this section I offer a more detailed discussion of each factor.

Competition within the private sector

Globally, REN21 (2019) reports that the private sector continues to play a key role in enhancing the deployment and uptake of RETs by engaging in procurement and investment decisions in favour of renewable energies. Pressure from shareholders and other stakeholders to enhance both value-driven (Carbon Trust, 2005; Richardson, 2011; UNEP Finance Initiative, 2005) and values-driven (UNEP Finance Initiative, 2005) investment has now led even large fossil fuel corporations to invest more aggressively in renewable energies (REN21, 2019). As sociocultural and economic legitimacy and support for fossil energies, especially coal, waned in the last few years (Morton, 2017), fiscal support for coal has also decreased remarkably (Morton, 2019). With the withdrawal of fiscal support, notably in the insurance industry, companies are increasingly shifting away from coal. Noticeably, much of this growth has been supported by the over 175 companies that have committed to 100 percent renewable electricity targets to date (largely to more reliably and cheaply meet their own energy demands) and whose commitments are gradually spreading to regions and markets beyond Europe and the United States. Specifically, we saw considerable and steady growth in renewable energy investment in the world's emerging markets, which increased by 20 percent in 2018 (Frankfurt School-UNEP Centre/BNEF, 2018).

The increasing number of solar RET enterprises in emerging markets is linked to the increased presence and availability of solar RETs in these markets. Indeed, the REEs in this study perceive the number of competitors within the industry has increased. In particular, it is not difficult to find a retailer of solar lights and solar panels in emerging markets. The REEs I interviewed described the ubiquity of solar retailers as a paradoxical dilemma. On one hand, the increasing number of RET providers indicates the industry has matured, which bodes well for REE institutional recognition and support. On the other hand, however, the increasing number of RET providers is also an indication of enhanced competition in the market as end-users have more choice and, thus, more bargaining power (Figure 4.2). This seemed especially worrying for the REEs I interviewed, as they observed that many solar retailers do not appear to have the technical knowledge to advise and support the end-users of their products. For instance, I have had the personal experience of walking the streets of the city of Port Vila in Vanuatu and identifying all the commercial retailers of RET products. Some were professionals specialising in RET products. However, for most retailers on the streets of Port Vila, it was clear that RET products were simply one of the wide array of household products offered. Supermarkets, convenience shops, a telecommunications provider and a hair and beauty supplies store – within each of the shops I found solar lights and lanterns, solar chargers and small solar photovoltaic (PV) panels on offer. It is difficult to believe that such a disparate and undifferentiated array of retailers possessed the specific technical knowledge needed to advise end-users who purchased RET products from their shop. However, this technical expertise is not required for simply getting RETs into the hands and homes of end-users. Indeed, this is one of the major challenges faced by RET distributors in emerging markets.

To compete, RET distributors must do more than simply distribute RET products. Indeed, these products are available virtually everywhere, especially in urban centres in emerging markets. Successful distributors differentiate themselves by their skillset and expertise, often offering complete RET systems and the full range of services to accompany them. However, when distributors differentiate themselves and their products in this way, they must offer their products and services at a premium, at a higher price, to RET end-users in emerging markets who are notoriously price sensitive. This means that end-users easily fall prey to low-price, low-quality alternatives in the market.

Aaron, operating in Ethiopia, once remarked, "About 80 percent of products in the market are of questionable quality". Like many other entrepreneurs I studied, he lamented losing contracts to competitors offering low price substitute products. He described these products as "knock-offs". These knock-offs have had the effect of forcing RET distributors to attempt the seemingly impossible task of developing low-cost distribution systems for high quality RET products that are able to compete with the low-quality products entering their local markets (as described in Chapter 3). The task is insurmountable, especially for pico-solar products such as lights, lanterns and chargers. Such products are in demand largely by the most economically deprived segments of emerging markets, for whom the high price of better quality products is usually prohibitive. Within the context of striving together towards the sustainable energy transition in emerging markets, price remains an important hindrance for many REEs. As Sai explained, for example:

> [There is a] lack of control on the black market. The entry of black market products from China into India distorts the market – they come very, very cheap and they do not last very long. So, they do create a completely different perception about electronics and lighting devices.
>
> (Sai, operating in India)

Others simply added the reportedly lower quality items to their value proposition, in order to match end-users' (in)ability to afford the technology.

Such REEs explained that it was the customer's choice what quality RET system they wanted:

> *So many people have bias to Chinese products. But Chinese products it all depends on how much you can afford to buy.*
>
> (Delphine, operating in Cameroon)

> *We ask the client whether they want it cheaper, then we can buy it separately from China. But, then you have low efficiency. If you want good efficiency then the price is different. But it's up to them.*
>
> (Ernesto, operating in The Philippines)

However, unwilling to compromise on quality, some REEs respond by maintaining relationships with suppliers of high quality solar RETs, to ensure the best possible outcome for end-users:

> *These days I think price of the solar modules has not been so much of an issue because there's excess capacity suddenly in the market. Modules from China have flooded the market so prices are really falling down. The landed cost per watt peak from China is as low as $0.25 US which is really shocking. But still one of the things that we have done is we have not gone to the Chinese panels and all, so we still go with the slightly more expensive modules, primarily because the supplier is in the local area. The office is located less than 20 km from supplier and we believe that that has a certain value – that if there are any issues, if there are any failures, we can easily talk to them. And so it's not quite a long-term arrangement, I mean there are medium-term arrangements on price and so on. But we are still dependent on a couple of suppliers of PV panels who are located in the local area and we have seen the value of that and continued with that. So we are so far not switched to much lower cost options mainly because of the quality concerns.*
>
> (Dhruv, operating in India)

Nonetheless, price volatility and impoverished end-users' inability to afford RET products and services may have a crippling effect if REEs are unable to respond, and thus compete, effectively and appropriately (Arinaitwe, 2006; Aslani and Mohaghar, 2013; Kirchgeorg and Winn, 2006). However, REN21 reports that power generation from RETs is becoming increasingly cost competitive – importantly, more so than power plants and technologies fired with fossil fuels (REN21, 2019). This is especially true for newly built solar PV and wind power plants, which are now cheaper to build than to continue running existing fossil power plants (REN21, 2019). There is already evidence to suggest this leads eventually to a net reduction in price for solar RETs overall, hopefully to the point of enhancing affordability for impoverished end-users in emerging markets.

The REEs I studied perceived fewer competitive threats in the market for solar home systems (SHSs). As I explained in Chapter 1 of this volume, SHSs are larger solar products than pico-solar devices, that rely on PV technology. They are small systems designed and installed to generate distributed power for use in households and other small structures. After speaking with the REEs over the last 8 years, I inferred that the larger the system offered the less REEs perceived intense rivalry within the industry. It is plausible that this might be because SHSs require more technical skill and involvement by the REE for installation. In addition, I have seen larger internationally established enterprises, such as Illumination Solar, differentiate based on affordability and individual market needs and preferences. For instance, Illumination Solar also offers its pico-solar lights and lanterns to the outdoor adventure industry within Australia – they are an extremely convenient source of light for camping, hiking and other outdoor activities (Gabriel, Stanley and Thatcher, 2018). Other distributors have resolved to adapt the products in their value proposition to the peculiar needs and challenges in emerging markets:

> What we are looking to do right now is still tweak and adapt the products for the market. So there is a lot of product development work taking place at the moment. We will enhance the product to compete. I would say the biggest challenge for us is that we are not geared to make 'cheap cheap' product. As a small company and with the kind of manufacturing setup we have, we cannot really make cheap product. But what we can make is very, very inexpensive high quality products. We are not 100% sure how many lights we will be able to sell or what sort of play we'll be able to have in that segment which is extremely poor, which is on less than $2 a day. So our main challenge right now is designing the world's first cheap solar light for that market. And that's something we're currently working on and we hope to produce it by the end of the year. So overall the challenges are product development. There were challenges around distribution, but we have definitely done a lot in the last six months to get past them.
>
> (Sai, operating in India)

Efforts such as those described by Sai reflect his deep understanding of needs and possibilities within the market. In addition, his intentions demonstrate the potential for actions taken in response to perceived competitive threats to have an overall effect of enhancing innovation within the industry. Responding to the specific challenges of emerging markets over the years is an important source of competitive advantage for REEs as they develop and leverage their locally embedded core competencies. An REE operating in Laos described the competitive advantage gained by specialising in off-grid RET distribution in remote areas:

> Actually, it should be a challenge and has been a challenge, but it has really turned into something that has become a strength for us. When you start to look at the nitty-gritty of a big project, for example say you have to do 6000 solar home systems in Laos. You have to bring in

kilometers and kilometers and kilometers of different cable, you have to ship in batteries from Singapore and solar panels from Germany. How do you bring in all these pieces of the puzzle together to a place like Laos? And then disperse them to villages? All those upfront project management skills that i think would be much easier in a place like Germany or really any developed country where those things, they would be tough to do but a whole lot easier to do in the developed world. I think we have learned through all of those challenges over the last decade and now, at this point it has become really a strength for us. One of the things that sets us apart from other off-grid renewable energy practitioners is we figured out how to do it in Laos and if we can do it here, that really helps our efforts in other places around the developing world.

(Chris, operating in Laos)

In some emerging regions, where the market for RETs is larger, REEs compete against each other. One solution described by entrepreneurs operating in Fiji is to specialise in the supply of specific brands and technologies. Vijay and Henry described the nature of the relationship among competing REEs in Fiji and South Africa, respectively:

Interestingly, we have tried several times to see if we can sort of wholesale if you like to competition. So what you'll find here, say the three bigger companies all have distribution rights for various brands of components to some extent. So each one of them has good buying rights or buying price on certain components. But interestingly, we hardly ever purchase from each other. It is usually the brand manufacturers or some of the larger renewable wholesaling companies, either in Australia or New Zealand or in America. So in general you'll find we'll be associated with one supplier and then our competitors will be associated with another supplier. So generally the larger wholesaling suppliers will usually supply just one of the companies, they will not do all of them. Generally, that's what it appears to be. Most bring their own equipment in and the only time that the three big businesses buy from each other is if you're short a component and it's urgent that you need something. Then you tend to sell to them. But other than that everyone brings it in themselves.

(Vijay, operating in Fiji)

Instead of competing against each other, we partnered up with other entrepreneurs, to add value.

(Henry, operating in South Africa)

Indeed, competition from the international private sector is difficult for the REEs to cope with. However, as Sam, who runs his enterprise from Fiji, explained there are advantages and disadvantages to the involvement of MNEs in the local renewable energy industry:

In Fiji, we face difficulties competing with the big players from Europe. It puts a lot of pressure on us to do the projects in the best way, as there is so much competition. We used to get preference in the past where they used to give preference to regional companies. But they don't give this preference anymore. For example, people come from Denmark, they do the project and they go back. And that is when failures happen because there is nobody in the Pacific to look after these projects.

(Sam, operating in Fiji)

The disadvantage of the renewable energy industries in emerging markets remaining ostensibly reliant upon and entrusting the sustainable energy transition to MNEs and other international private sector actors is there is little incentive for follow-up and monitoring post-delivery. In fact, in Chapter 3 I highlighted the logistical and financial challenges of providing after-sales service and support in emerging markets, especially in remote locations such as some parts of the Pacific Islands. However, the issue extends far beyond simply logistics and finances. According to REEs, many aid-funded tenders and programmes do not include support and monitoring for periods well after the end of the project. More local REEs must be included in such projects. Furthermore, more profoundly than simply inclusion, REEs should be empowered, hired and entrusted to monitor and follow-up on these projects after completion. I surmise this could assuage some concerns about competition from international private sector entities, as REEs will have the opportunity to leverage their considerable strength and core competency in understanding the sociocultural environment in which are embedded. However, in the spirit of striving together, I have also noted with interest that, like Sam, many REEs admit that this competition from international private sector entities enhances the quality of the products and services they offer daily. It encourages them to develop and offer their best work, towards the aim of transitioning to sustainable energy technologies.

Competition from local and international public sector organisations

Many of the organisations operating within the renewable energy industry with the intention to facilitate and accelerate the sustainable energy transition in emerging markets are public sector organisations. That is, those organisations that exist to serve some need of interest to the general populace of a society. Typically, the public goods and services provided include, for example, education (e.g. schools), transportation and infrastructure (e.g. roads and postal services), healthcare (e.g. hospitals) and security (e.g. military). Thus, these public sector organisations may include locally run institutions such as governments, and their ministries and other subsidiaries, as well as non-government organisations who provide or enhance public services not offered by government. Intuitively, such organisations generally provide electricity and lighting infrastructure, support for the logistical challenges associated with bringing RETs into a country to establish and develop these infrastructures (see Chapter 3), as well as support for access to these services such as subsidies, feed-in-tariffs[1] and other financial support schemes for end-users.

For instance, sometimes REEs described incumbent utility providers as a major hurdle to the sustainable energy transition in emerging markets. The reason for this perception, I surmised, was that, compared to small REEs, these utilities had better access to funding and better ability to lobby for (or create) institutional support (Brunnschweiler, 2010; Richter, 2012; Smink, Hekkert and Negro, 2013; Wüstenhagen and Boehnke, 2008). However, because utility providers generally only operate within the electrified, centralised grid-tied market, and are notoriously slow, resistant or unable to change (Christensen, Wells and Cipcigan, 2012; Smink, Hekkert and Negro, 2013), I do not believe they are a strong contender in the market for renewables. REEs' strength and experience in the off-grid market give them a significant competitive edge over utility providers. Moreover, growing international concern and influence means public sector organisations, including state-owned utility providers, face mounting pressure to provide effective solutions to energy poverty within their jurisdictions (OECD/IEA, 2018). Targets towards enhanced renewable energy uptake and energy poverty alleviation have been developed and written in most countries, with a growing proportion of them enforced locally (REN21, 2019). Specifically, at the time of the Study I interviews, there were an average of ten renewable energy policies in force in the Asia-Pacific countries represented by the REEs in my research – this, notably in contrast to an average of five in Latin America and the Caribbean (IEA and IRENA, 2014).[2] Indeed, the International Energy Agency (IEA) quoted its Executive Director, Dr Faith Birol:

> *Over 70% of global energy investments will be government-driven and as such the message is clear – the world's energy destiny lies with decision and policies made by governments.*

Thus, with consistent sentiment globally that governments have the largest share of responsibility for the sustainable energy transition, it is not surprising that many jurisdictions have also made their targets more ambitious (OECD/IEA, 2018; REN21, 2019). It is also logical, therefore, that public sector organisations actively and, sometimes, aggressively, concern themselves with the tasks of transition. However, this raises a core question of concern in emerging markets: Is there also a place for private sector entities such as REEs to contribute to this transition, in ways that will support the overall self-sufficiency of their enterprises?

Scholars argue that civil society and entrepreneurial private sector actors fill the voids in society left by ineffective or misdirected government efforts (*cf.* Mair and Marti, 2009; Santos, 2012 and Pathak and Muralidharan,

2017). For instance, because governments traditionally design and provide basic networks of electricity generation and distribution grid infrastructure, it is difficult for them to meet the needs of communities located in remote locations quickly and effectively. To do so requires governments to adopt new business models, technologies, skills and knowledge about areas and challenges within their jurisdictions that may previously have gone undetected and/or unaddressed. While some governments around the world meet this challenge competently in some communities, the onus has largely befallen local private sector enterprises (such as REEs), as well as social enterprises and NGOs that provide goods and services to meet the needs of the public, to take on the task of energy access in emerging markets.

If social enterprises involved in solar energy distribution in emerging markets played a more consistent role in the industry, REEs could adapt quickly and perceive less intense rivalry. However, social enterprises learn and adapt quickly, and this has become a challenge as REEs report that many adapt their business models to local conditions in the industry:

> *A big number of social enterprises have been converted into commercial enterprises. Like solar has got quite a number of players in the sector*
> (Adamu, operating in Kenya)

Another key challenge is that many public sector organisations operating within the renewable energy industry in emerging markets are not local entities. Instead, they may be managed internationally or by foreign governments. These include international NGOs (who might be funded by private sector entities and interests) and IDOs (funded by international governments), for instance.[3] The rivalry REEs perceive with these international public sector organisations relates, in part, to the immense support and legitimacy these organisations enjoy from local governments. REEs perceive these public sector organisations to benefit inequitably from this support, seemingly at the expense of support for and investment in local enterprise:

> *Incumbents is a challenge because the majority of them are actually international organisations. They are the ones we are supposed to compete against and they have all the financing.*
> (Adamu, operating in Kenya)

Another dimension of the perceived rivalry between REEs and international public sector organisations such as IDOs is the 'warping' effect these international organisations could have on the market. That is, because they offer RET products as a form of aid, end-users are not generally expected to pay for these products. In addition, aid-funded social enterprise programs that do require end-users to pay a fee for RET products usually offer these products at rates far below market prices. This means REEs who offer the same or comparable products at market prices face an unlevelled playing field;

that is unfair comparison, and therefore competition, in their respective markets. The competitive threat from IDOs is unfair because while REEs generally need to recover their costs to sustain their enterprises, IDOs do not:

> *This is a problem for local business as well, because you cannot compete against aid. If end-users are getting free solar panels from aid projects, then you are not going to be able to sell it to them because their idea of how much that is worth goes out the door.*
>
> (Tane, operating in Tonga)

> *So the other side of the story is biogas. To make biogas suitable for the poorest of the poor, they have to reduce the price. To reduce the price they need to create a number of players in the sector. These players have not been properly trained. So the biogas plants they construct they work for maybe one or two months and then they fail. That sector now has a number of foreign players from China, Uganda, South Africa and other places. So at the end of the day the only players who seem to be making any headway in this sector are the international organisations like GIZ, because these are people who get money from outside of Kenya. And at the end of the day they are able to run a business because they have manpower and so forth. They just spend the money they have been given and the only condition is that they have to spend the money within a certain period of time . . . .But most of them are not going at it in a commercial way.*
>
> (Adamu, operating in Kenya)

However, there is a potential opportunity inherent in this perceived rivalry. As local knowledge and sociocultural competence constitute an important strength of REEs in emerging markets, governments (both local and international) might see the benefit of consulting with them on projects within communities with which they are familiar. In addition, as Joshua, who operates a REE in Uganda, explained, his enterprise's success rate in local tenders increased by about 30 percent when he started collaborating with large international partners. Prior to engaging with these international entities, he had very little success winning projects and acquiring work from the local government. Therefore, on aggregate, despite perceptions of rivalry within the industry, I argue REEs who work together with but do not depend solely upon their international public sector rivals might enjoy more success in emerging markets. Therefore, in response to their perceived rivalry with IDOs, NGOs and other public sector entities, many REEs have simply opted to avoid the market niches in which they predominantly operate:

> *It does not matter too much for me. Because most of the time, they get money or funds from abroad to implement those projects. I also come from a different angle where I look for clients who have money and want my services. So I don't interface with them at all.*
>
> (Abeiku, operating in Ghana)

Market niches for renewable energy enterprise in emerging markets

My assessment of these factors over the last eight years suggests that, in response to these competitive challenges, REEs commonly occupy five specific niches in emerging markets: picosolar products and devices, Solar Home Systems (SHSs), Clean Cookstoves, Micro-and Mini-grids, and Micro Turbine Generation. I characterise each niche in Figure 4.3, and I describe the competitive forces that make them attractive and advantageous for some REEs.

The difficulty of reaching remote communities in emerging markets and establishing off-grid, distributed renewable energy installations is well documented. In fact, I address the logistical and financial aspects of these challenges in Chapter 3 of this volume and the market and competitive aspects in the current chapter. I believe REEs' development of core competencies around distributed renewables for energy access (DREA) is a direct response not only to the obvious demand for power and lighting in such communities, but also to the competitive forces within the industry in emerging markets. DREA systems allow the generation and distribution of energy independently of centralised electricity grid infrastructure. In emerging markets, they are characterised by either stand-alone and off-grid systems or micro-or mini-grids (REN21, 2019), which can be found in both urban and rural areas. The International Energy Agency (IEA) (2018) reports, "an estimated 5% of the population in Africa and 2% of the population in Asia – or nearly 150 million people across these two regions – benefit from energy access through off-grid solar systems" (REN21, 2019).

Those involved in facilitating the sustainable energy transition in these markets have had considerable success, as the number of people without access to electricity in remote areas fell below one billion in 2017 (REN21, 2019; OECD/IEA, 2018). Similarly, the number of households without

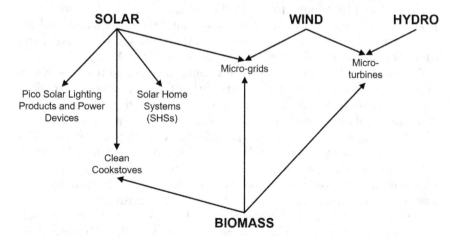

Figure 4.3 Market niches for renewable energy enterprise in emerging markets

access to clean cooking facilities has also dropped considerably (REN21, 2019). Nevertheless, there is still room for improvement, as private sector enterprises such as REEs are expected to play a crucial role as innovators, as well as providers of technical and cultural support and collaborators for public sector programs targeting energy access in remote areas. Indeed, DREA solutions are considered most suitable for end-users at the BOP, and therefore an important technological complement to activities towards the sustainable energy transition. DREA systems necessarily substitute traditional centralised electricity grid infrastructure and are the most cost-efficient and reliable means of delivering power to communities in remote areas. Thus, DREA is not only necessary to meet energy access needs and targets, but also competitively advantageous for REEs who understand the unique sociocultural environment in their locales. Therefore, the following five market niches are all characterised by features of DREA.

Pico solar lighting products and power devices

In remote locations across all emerging markets, households, communities and businesses are becoming increasingly reliant on solar PV powered products to power their lives and livelihoods. In addition to electricity to power home appliances, the demand for energy also includes other uses such as "lighting, mobile phone charging, entertainment and other income-generating uses" (Albi and Lieberman, 2013: 144). I consider pico solar devices an important form of reverse innovation[4] for DREA in emerging markets (Gabriel, 2022). Pico solar devices are PV-powered. They are extremely small and portable and end-users throughout the world use them to provide light and other basic energy services, including mobile phone charging and radio. Although largely designed for emerging markets, specifically for use in remote areas and by communities at the Base of the Pyramid (BOP), the use of pico solar devices is broader ranging today. As they range in size from about 1 Watt peak (Wp) to 10 Wp (Lysen, 2013), pico solar devices are also useful for users in more developed markets for outdoor activities, such as hiking and camping, for instance (Gabriel, Stanley and Thatcher, 2018).

Pico solar devices offer several advantages in emerging markets, which assist with the acceleration of the transition to sustainable and modern energy at the BOP. Indeed, the documented benefits of these devices include enhanced availability and better quality lighting for use in households. Simply enhancing access to lighting has had additional flow-on effects. Children in remote areas are now able to complete homework at night, which enhances their school attendance and performance. Their parents and other members of their community also increase their income because they are able to perform and develop marketable trades and crafts at night. Women feel more empowered and are able to contribute to the livelihoods of their communities if they wish. There is a negative side as well. In Vanuatu, there was concern that the enhanced earning power of women put them at odds with local customs and culture in some remote villages, which could lead to higher rates of domestic violence in some cases.

Thankfully, these advantages and potential negative side effects are well known and understood by the REEs operating in these markets, many of whom were raised in or have worked closely with these communities over several years. Indeed, the geographical and socioeconomic challenges associated with working with remote communities (see Chapter 3) mean REEs are ideally positioned to address these challenges. More so, in fact, than public sector organisations (both local and international), who grapple with the costs associated with extending electricity grid infrastructure to rural or remote areas (government) or the challenge of monitoring and evaluating aid-commissioned projects in these areas (e.g. IDOs and NGOs). REEs who operate within this niche design, develop and offer pico solar products tailored to the unique needs of end-users in the communities that need these devices most. They offer lower prices or effective microcredit options and operate using inclusive business models (see Chapter 2 and Chapter 5 for additional information on inclusive business models). In sum, the pico solar market offers the opportunity for REEs to leverage their embeddedness within and specialised tacit knowledge and experience with sociocultural conditions in remote communities in emerging markets.

Solar Home Systems (SHSs) for distributed energy use

Geographical remoteness is not the only criterion for adopting distributed, off-grid renewable energy systems in emerging markets. In many countries, the supply of electricity even to urban centres can be unreliable. Reliability of power supply is an issue raised frequently by REEs in some West African regions, for instance, who lament the almost universal need for backup generators for urban households. Solar PV technology integrated into SHSs offer a solution to this challenge, as they are stand-alone systems that generate electricity independently of electric grids. SHSs are therefore an important solution to the challenges faced in both urban and rural areas in emerging markets. REN21 reported that SHSs have played a significant role in enhancing electricity access for individuals in emerging markets. As the artefacts of modernity spread in emerging markets, the demand for power has also increased, which led to a 77 percent increase in sales of these larger solar systems in 2018 (REN21, 2019).

SHSs consist of one or more PV modules, at least one battery and a charge controller to regulate and protect the batteries and any appliances connected to the SHS. The batteries are used to store energy to be used when there is inadequate sunlight. SHSs usually generate power for a single household or building, which may or may not be connected to established electricity grid infrastructure. When connected to an electricity grid, the SHS supplies power to the connected building and appliances first, and then to the larger electricity grid only if the system has generated surplus electricity. SHSs are therefore potential building blocks for micro-grids, where various members of a single community might contribute to sharing electricity over a small area. SHS users in emerging markets use them to power larger home appliances, such as refrigerators (not only charge phones and power small appliances, as with pico solar). Therefore, SHSs are also popular sources of power for remote clinics, schools and providers of essential care and services in remote areas.

As with pico solar products, REEs are also well aware of the technical advantages and socioeconomic appropriateness of SHSs for end-users in emerging markets. REEs who design and establish mini-grids in communities are also aware of the scalability of SHSs. REEs who offer and install SHSs in emerging markets also manage its affordability for end-users. Indeed, SHSs are usually installed using some form of microcredit or prepaid pay-as-you-go (PAYG) system, which mimics prepaid mobile phone models. With PAYG, the REE retains ownership of the SHS, and the end-user pays for a specific amount of electricity upfront. When they run out of prepaid electricity 'credit', end-users simply purchase more from the REE. PAYG enhances the affordability of SHSs for impoverished end-users at the BOP in remote communities. It is yet another niche occupied by REEs, as well as some social enterprises, but rarely by governments and other public sector organisations. Once more, the REEs' embeddedness and knowledge of these communities, as well as their relative business model and logistical flexibility, put them at a significant competitive advantage over perceived rivals in the public sector. In addition, the REEs' considerable knowledge and experience of these technologies and the business models and credit systems that work in these communities make them attractive local partners and collaborators for the MNEs who benefit directly from aid funding internationally.

Clean cookstoves for distributed cooking facilities

Clean cookstoves are "solar-powered or fuel-burning household stoves that reduce greenhouse gas emissions by either increasing thermal efficiency, reducing specific emissions, or increasing ventilation" (Project Drawdown, 2019). Clean cookstove technologies replace traditional household cooking stoves operated by burning traditional unprocessed and processed solid biomass. These traditional cookstoves produce emissions harmful to the environment and human health. Generally, clean cookstoves are also a technical solution to the problem of inadequate ventilation in impoverished households in emerging markets. Both issues underline the complex web of challenges associated with the use of traditional biomass cookstoves, which normally run on charcoal or firewood, but also on unprocessed solid biomass fuels such as dung and crop residues. These challenges include the increased deforestation that results from the use of firewood as well as the greenhouse gas emissions associated with burning charcoal. In addition, when households and communities use traditional cooking methods indoors within poorly ventilated houses, families become increasingly susceptible to harmful smoke containing carbon monoxide (CO) and particulate matter (PM). The Differ Group (2012) estimates these respiratory diseases lead to around 1.6 million deaths each year. The advantages of clean cookstoves in emerging markets, therefore, are that they perform the same function for households, but in a manner that improves overall health and cooking efficiency and reduces fuel consumption in the process (Differ Group, 2012; REN21, 2019). Therefore, as a form of DREA, the use of clean cookstoves is an important criterion for a successful and rapid sustainable energy transition in emerging markets. In remote communities in particular, clean cookstoves also lead to enhanced socioeconomic and health outcomes, reducing the effects of chronic and acute respiratory illnesses. These illnesses are especially common among women and children in emerging markets, particularly in communities where they take on the responsibilities of preparing family meals (REN21, 2019).

For REEs, clean cookstoves represent a significant opportunity in these markets, especially at the BOP. In the past, the predominant strategy to enhance uptake of clean cookstoves among communities that need them most was to donate them, free of charge in the form of aid, by IDOs and NGOs. While this approach addressed the need in the short-term, once aid funding ceased, so did the supply of these important and necessary technologies. Indeed, there was risk of fewer established and enduring supply and distribution channels. In addition, support for using clean cookstoves and adapting them to the local sociocultural and socioeconomic conditions of each community waned once IDO and NGO support was taken away. Thus, in 2012 the Differ Group concluded that "giving away the stoves for free, which previously was the strategy of development and aid agencies, is proven not to be a viable path" (p. 1) (I discuss this challenge in more detail in Chapter 5). Therefore, REEs have a significant opportunity to carve out a niche for themselves in the clean cookstoves market (see Figure 4.3).

REEs may offer a variety of cookstove solutions, powered by solar or biomass technologies. REEs successfully competing in this market understand the unique perceptions and operationalisation of value within the BOP communities in the direst need of clean cookstoves. For instance, the clean cookstove distributors I interviewed demonstrated a deep and complex understanding of the cooking norms and habits within the communities in which they operate: Who does the cooking in each household? When? What is the most important meal of the day in each culture? What are the most popular meals, and how are they prepared? Does the technology used affect the taste of the meal, and how?

Indeed, REEs' knowledge, experience, sociocultural embeddedness and competence, as well as their intention to stay within these contexts, give them a significant competitive advantage over IDOs and NGOs in emerging markets. Dymhna van der Lans, CEO of the Clean Cooking Alliance, remarked, "There's no single stove, fuel, or business model capable of solving this complex issue. Businesses and entrepreneurs must have the right tools, resources, and policies in place to produce high quality products, reduce costs, and improve margins" (Clean Cooking Alliance, 2019). In emerging markets, locally embedded REEs are better placed to meet these conditions than their perceived rivals.

Micro-grids for distributed electricity generation

Micro-grids are "independent electricity delivery systems, in which the power is produced near the point of consumption" (Numminen and Lund, 2019: 34). In emerging markets, micro-grids powered by RETs are widely considered an important solution for remote distributed electricity generation (REN21, 2019). Small-scale micro-grids of less than 5kW are usually developed to meet the energy needs of groups of households, while larger ones up to 100kW may also be used for productive purposes such as agricultural processing (Booth et al., 2018). Indeed, they offer a more efficient solution to the challenges associated with centralised power generation and distribution, as well as the challenges associated with the reliability of electricity supply in the urban regions of emerging markets (see Chapter 3). Therefore, reports of RET progress in emerging markets – especially those that emphasise energy access and the overall sustainable energy transition – applaud the increasing pace of growth and uptake of micro-grid systems across emerging regions. This is especially the case in Africa and Asia (REN21, 2019). The growing interest in micro-grids has led to enhanced financial support in the form of increased aid funding or better access to credit. The enhanced funding options enable the development of not only the micro-grids themselves, but also the productive uses to which they are committed in emerging markets around the world (REN21, 2019).

The REEs I interviewed explained that micro-grids were often commissioned by local governments or NGOs and IDOs, as a means to bring modern energy services to rural or remote areas. In my research, I interviewed REEs who designed, developed and established RET-powered micro-grids (usually using Type IV Integrator business models). Generally, they were solar PV powered systems, but occasionally the systems also integrated some wind and biomass generation. However, noticeably, entrepreneurs from more developed markets started the majority of these REEs. Indeed, although they were private sector and relatively small enterprises registered locally, I found that REEs involved in the micro-grid niche leveraged the international networks of their founders, owners and managers to access financial and institutional support. Indeed, much of this support was aid-sponsored (see Chapter 5). Since micro-grids are technically, financially and socio-culturally difficult to establish and generate support for, REEs who design and build them have the support of IDOs, governments in more developed markets and local governments. Therefore, this sub-group of REEs leverage their own knowledge to collaborate effectively with perceived rival forces in emerging markets. They do so by connecting and scaling up renewable energy systems in emerging markets.

Micro-turbines for standalone distributed electricity generation

Micro-turbines are no longer just gas-fired technologies. As interest and uptake of RETs spread, many REEs offer standalone installations of micro-turbines, which generally produce electricity for a small remotely located community or to power small agricultural activities in emerging markets. In addition, they are generally put to productive uses that contribute to enhanced income for small-scale livelihood and commercial activities, such as farming. In my research, the REEs who offer standalone micro-turbine installations operated in the Asia-Pacific and Latin American and Caribbean regions. They used business models with characteristics akin to either Type III Distributor and/or Type IV Integrator models. As the supply chain for these technologies are more difficult to access and understand for the REEs I interviewed, renewable energy powered micro-turbines represented another niche within which REEs could thrive with few rivals. Indeed, when combined with the right technical knowledge, the REEs' embeddedness enables them to design, suggest and install suitable and locally-relevant micro-turbine solutions in emerging markets.

Notes

1 A Feed-in-Tariff (FIT) is a policy instrument used to encourage generation of electricity using renewable energy sources. Households or businesses who generate renewable electricity can give any surplus energy generated to the central electricity grid (literally, 'feeding' their surplus electricity into the grid). The utility that manages the electricity grid infrastructure will pay the household or business for the electricity supplied based on contractually agreed rates or tariffs.

2 Based on the IEA/IRENA joint database, here are the numbers of renewable energy policies in force (in parentheses) in each of the countries represented by the REEs interviewed at the start of the research:

> Barbados (3); Belize (2); Cambodia (no data); Cameroon (no data); Chile (10); Costa Rica (no data); Ecuador (3); Ethiopia (no data); Fiji (2); Ghana (6); Guatemala (no data); India (19); Indonesia (10); Kenya (5); Laos (no data); Nigeria (1); Panama (no data); Papua New Guinea (no data); Philippines (13); Senegal (4); Somalia (no data); South Africa (13); Tanzania (2); Thailand (7); Tonga (no data); Trinidad and Tobago (no data); Uganda (5) and Zambia (no data).

3 In Chapter 5 (The aid-centric business model), I discuss the role of IDOs and international governments in more detail.

4 In my chapter on Reverse Innovation, available in the Encyclopaedia for the UN SDGs on Affordable and Clean Energy, I define reverse innovation as follows:

> *The term 'reverse innovation' describes an innovation first developed, tested and used successfully in developing countries before it is adopted (intentionally or otherwise) in more developed countries. 'Reverse' innovation is so-called to reflect a reversal of the traditional and more widely acknowledged*

approach to innovation, which relies on the mainstream markets, infrastructure and creativity of western countries as innovation loci.

(Gabriel, 2022)

References

Albi, E. and Lieberman, A.E., 2013. Bringing clean energy to the base of the pyramid: The interplay of business models, technology, and local context. *Journal of Management for Global Sustainability*, 1(2), pp. 141–156.

Arinaitwe, S.K., 2006. Factors constraining growth and survival of small-scale businesses: A developing countries analysis. *Journal of American Academy of Business*, 8(2), pp. 167–178.

Aslani, A. and Mohaghar, A., 2013. Business structure in renewable energy industry: Key areas. *Renewable and Sustainable Energy Reviews*, 27, pp. 569–575.

Booth, S., Li, Xiangkun, Baring-Gould, I., Kollanyi, D., Bharadwaj, A. and Weston, P., 2018. Productive use of energy in African micro-grids: Technical and business considerations. August. USAID-NREL Partnership.

Brunnschweiler, C.N., 2010. Finance for renewable energy: An empirical analysis of developing and transition economies. *Environment and Development Economics*, 15(3), pp. 241–274.

Carbon Trust, 2005. A climate for change: A trustee's guide to understanding and addressing climate risk. Retrieved from www.iigcc.org/files/publicationfiles/A_climate_for_change_a_trustees_guide.pdf (accessed 08 December 2018).

Christensen, T.B., Wells, P. and Cipcigan, L., 2012. Can innovative business models overcome resistance to electric vehicles? Better place and battery electric cars in Denmark. *Energy Policy*, 48(2012), pp. 498–505.

Clean Cooking Alliance, 2019. *2018 Annual Report*. Investment, Innovation and Impact.

Differ Group, 2012. A rough guide to clean cookstoves. 23 March.

Frankfurt School-UNEP Centre/BNEF, 2018. Global trends in renewable energy investment 2018. Frankfurt am Main. Retrieved from www.fs-unep-centre.org (accessed 07 September 2019).

Gabriel, C., 2022. Reverse innovation. In W. Leal Filho, L. Brandli, P. Özuyar and T. Wall (Ed.), *Encyclopedia of the UN Sustainable Development Goals*. Affordable and Clean Energy. Switzerland: Springer.

Gabriel, C., Stanley, M. and Thatcher, S., 2018. *Illumination Solar: Delivering Energy Poverty Solutions*. Case Study, Ivey Publishing.

IEA (International Energy Agency), 2018. Chapter 2: Electrification. In *Tracking SDG7: The Energy Poverty Progress Report 2018* (pp. 28–30). Washington, DC: World Bank. Retrieved from https://trackingsdg7.esmap.org/data/files/download-documents/chapter_2_electrification.pdf. (accessed 08 September 2019).

IEA (International Energy Agency) and IRENA (International Renewable Energy Agency), 2014. *IEA/IRENA Joint Policies and Measures Database*. Retrieved from www.iea.org/policiesandmeasures/renewableenergy/ (accessed 08 September 2019).

Kirchgeorg, M. and Winn, M.I., 2006. Sustainability marketing for the poorest of the poor. *Business Strategy and the Environment*, 15(3), pp. 171–184.

Lysen, E.H., 2013. Pico solar PV systems for remote homes: A new generation of small PV systems for lighting and communication. International Energy Agency (IEA) Photovoltaic Power Systems Programme. Report IEA-PVPS T9–12, 2012.

Mair, J. and Marti, I., 2009. Entrepreneurship in and around institutional voids: A case study from Bangladesh. *Journal of Business Venturing*, 24(5), pp. 419–435.

Morton, A., 2017. Coal in decline: An energy industry on life support. *The Guardian*, Thursday, 24 August.

Morton, A., 2019. Insurance giant Suncorp says it will no longer cover new thermal coal projects. *The Guardian*, Friday, 26 July.

Numminen, S. and Lund, P.D., 2019. Evaluation of the reliability of solar micro-grids in emerging markets: Issues and solutions. *Energy for Sustainable Development*, 48, pp. 34–42.

OECD/IEA, 2018. *World Energy Outlook 2018*. International Energy Agency (IEA).

Pathak, S. and Muralidharan, E., 2017. Economic inequality and social entrepreneurship. *Business & Society*, 57(6), pp. 1150–1190.

Porter, M.E., 1979. How competitive forces shape strategy. *Harvard Business Review*, March, pp. 137–145.

Porter, M.E., 2008. The five competitive forces that shape strategy. *Harvard Business Review*, January, pp. 57–71.

Project Drawdown, 2019. Clean cookstoves: Technical summary. Retrieved from www.drawdown.org/solutions/food/clean-cookstoves (accessed 02 June 2019).

REN21, 2019. *Renewables 2019 Global Status Report*. Paris: REN21 Secretariat. ISBN: 978-3-9818911-7-1.

Richardson, B.J., 2011. Fiduciary relationships for socially responsible investing: A multinational perspective. *American Business Law Journal*, 48(3), pp. 597–640.

Richter, M., 2012. Utilities' business models for renewable energy: A review. *Renewable and Sustainable Energy Reviews*, 16(5), pp. 2483–2493.

Samson, D., Donnet, T. and Daft, R.L., 2018. *Management*, 6th Asia-Pacific edition. Melbourne, Australia: Cengage Learning.

Santos, F.M., 2012. A positive theory of social entrepreneurship. *Journal of Business Ethics*, 111(3), pp. 335–351.

Schermerhorn, J.R., Davidson, P., Woods, P., Factor, A., Simon, A. and McBarron, E., 2017. *Management*, 6th Asia-Pacific edition. Milton, Australia: John Wiley and Sons.

Smink, M.M., Hekkert, M.P. and Negro, S.O., 2013. Keeping sustainable innovation on a leash? Exploring incumbents' institutional strategies. *Business Strategy and the Environment*, 24(2), pp. 86–101.

UNEP Finance Initiative, 2005. A legal framework for the integration of environmental, social and governance issues into institutional investment. Produced for the Assessment Management Working Group of the UNEP Finance Initiative, October.

Wüstenhagen, R. and Boehnke, J., 2008. Business models for sustainable energy. In A. Tukker, M. Charter, C. Vezzoli, E. Sto and M.M. Andersen (Eds.), *System Innovation for Sustainability: Perspectives on Radical Changes to Sustainable Consumption and Production* (pp. 253–258). Sheffield: Greenleaf Publishing Ltd.

5 The aid-centric business model

What is aid?

'Aid' or 'foreign aid' refers broadly to public resources given voluntarily to a government or international aid and development organisation (IDO) for the purpose to enhance living conditions in a particular country or region. There are several types of aid and approaches to disbursing aid to emerging markets. Generally, aid is disbursed with a significant grant component, and it may be transferred bilaterally from individual governments of more developed markets directly to emerging market governments and organisations. However, governments also disburse aid multilaterally. Multilateral aid refers to disbursements given by multiple governments to IDOs such as the World Bank and the United Nations to be used at the IDOs' discretion for the purpose of reducing poverty and improving living conditions in emerging markets more generally. Non-government aid, from non-government organisations (NGOs) funded directly by donations from individual members of the public, is also significant and widely disbursed directly to development organisations in emerging markets. In addition, some aid is given as project aid with the purpose to finance a specific project of the donor country's choosing. This type of aid is especially popular in the renewable energy industry in emerging markets as many IDOs target energy poverty and its associated challenges at the Base of the Pyramid (BOP) in emerging markets.

However, there are a few caveats to the disbursement of aid of which one should be aware. For instance, aid disbursements may not actually arrive until much later after they were pledged by the donor country or organisation. In addition, pledged aid is rarely given directly to emerging market governments in cash to be used at their complete discretion. In 2016, Matt Kennard and Claire Provost explained that this kind of direct budgetary support accounted for only $9.5 billion of the $165 billion spent on aid globally in 2014 – less than six percent. Indeed, donor governments generally give aid multilaterally through NGOs or through private contractors in their own countries. In the United States (US), the United States Agency for International Development (USAID) is the major spender of aid money from the US (Kennard and Provost, 2016). It is comparable to the United

Kingdom (UK)'s Department for International Development (DfID). Aid is also channelled through Development Finance Institutions (DFIs) such as the International Finance Corporation (IFC). DFIs are government-supported organisations that lend money to private sector corporations and other actors (that is, *not* governments) to develop and implement projects in emerging markets. The IFC is a branch of the World Bank. Finally, donor governments often provide 'tied aid'. Tied aid is aid given with the restriction to be spent in the donor country or in a group of countries specified by the donor government. For instance, tied aid may stipulate that the receiving government must spend the funds on products and services produced and provided in the donor country only. Indeed, definitions, characterisations and appropriations of aid vary across jurisdictions.

The most widely used measure of aid flows to emerging markets is *Official Development Assistance* (ODA). The Organisation for Economic Co-operation and Development (OECD)'s Development Assistance Committee (DAC) offers its own definition of ODA flows:

> *Official development assistance flows are defined as those flows to countries and territories on the DAC List of ODA Recipients and to multilateral development institutions which are*
>
> i   *provided by official agencies, including state and local governments, or by their executive agencies; and*
> ii *each transaction of which:*
>
>   a   *is administered with the promotion of the economic development and welfare of developing countries as its main objective; and*
>   b   *is concessional in character.*[1]
>
> (OECD/DAC, 2019)

At the time of writing, the OECD/DAC's last available year for ODA data was 2017. Net bilateral ODA remained relatively consistent between 2016 and 2017, increasing at a rate of 1.5 percent in that year (OECD/DAC, 2018). According to the OECD/DAC (2019), where ODA recipients were specified, in that same year the largest proportion of ODA flows went to jurisdictions south of the Sahara (22.4 percent), South and Central Asia (11.7 percent) and Middle East and North Africa (11.7 percent). 34.4% of the aid disbursed was to an unspecified recipient country. The majority of ODA disbursements comes from the members of the OECD DAC.[2] Total bilateral ODA amounted to in excess of USD 147 billion in 2017. Of this, the EU gave more than USD 16 billion, while non-DAC member countries gave over USD 62 billion. The REEs I interviewed during my research did not identify specific individual donors, but instead refer in general to IDOs (such as the World Bank and United Nations) and specific IDO programs that influence their enterprises in emerging markets. Therefore, in this chapter I refer only to aid relationships in general, without identifying the type or source, unless specified by the REEs themselves.

How individual enterprises receive and use aid

States-and business-men in the world's developed markets have long considered that there are hundreds of billions of dollars' worth of business opportunities in emerging markets. In particular, many countries in Asia and Africa constitute some of the world's fastest growing economies. In fact, the UK government provides considerable support to assist UK businesses to trade with emerging markets. This support aims to help UK businesses profit from contracts funded by international aid (Kennard and Provost, 2016). In their article published in 2016, Matt Kennard and Claire Provost reported that Nigel Peters, Head of the Aid-Funded Business Service at UK Trade and Investment, once said to a room full of businesspeople:

> *The development and humanitarian aid business is there, it's significant business, and we're here to help you win some of that. Welcome to the world of aid-funded business. We see a lot of business opportunities around the work the UN does in peacekeeping, famine relief, disaster relief, emergency aid. We see a lot of good opportunities for those of you in products in terms of famine and disaster relief related to both man-made disasters, which today we're seeing in countries like Syria and Iraq with refugee camps, and of course natural disasters.*

Indeed, for many companies, in both emerging and more developed markets, aid is an important income stream. For a large number of enterprises all around the world, however, aid is more than simply an income stream – it is the entire business model. Indeed, even in the developed markets of the US, UK and Europe, many companies are founded and continue to thrive today on the basis of a model of growth and profitability that is dependent on the international development aid intended to address and eradicate world poverty. For instance, especially in developed markets, such businesses might market and sell their products – from mosquito nets to staple grains – to IDOs with billions of aid dollars to spend in the name of international development. They may also benefit enormously from tied aid arrangements. In developed markets and major donor countries such as the US and the UK, well-known multinationals operate on a market protected and preserved specifically for them by their government. Indeed, a large proportion of the profits of such multinational corporations are generated from preferential access to contracts to provide commodities and services to emerging markets. Many donor countries now offer larger proportions of untied aid in response to criticism from numerous sources in civil society. However, in the UK, although tied aid has been officially discontinued,[3] domestic UK businesses continue to win the considerable share of aid contracts (OECD, 2014).[4]

The lines between aid for socioeconomic development and the private sector have blurred even further with the active involvement of multinational enterprises (MNEs) on the boards and special advisory panels of aid and non-government organisations. Relationships such as those between Oxfam and Unilever, and Save the Children and GlaxoSmithKline (GSK), are key examples (Smith and Crawford, 2008; Molina-Gallart, 2014). As flows of ODA decline (Molina-Gallart, 2014), emerging market governments and development organisations rely increasingly on private sector involvement to assist with enterprise functions such as product and supply chain development. Therefore, the issue of concern for REEs in emerging markets is not simply the co-financing of energy access and sustainability endeavours by the private sector, but also the private sector's involvement in their local supply chains and distribution channels. Large MNEs bring with them the political support of governments and IDOs, as well as their own economic power, which enables them to influence policy and the renewable energy agenda in emerging markets. Indeed, together with considerable support and incentive from IDOs, private sector support and involvement in the renewable energy industry and the overall transition in emerging markets has improved considerably. In Africa, for example, REEs consistently identified the efforts of the Lighting Africa program as a key contributor to improvements in private sector engagement and support in the region. Specifically, Lighting Africa has helped make financing and foreign currency available to companies committed to importing Lighting Africa approved products. In another example, one entrepreneur who ran a REE in Ethiopia explained that the World Bank played a significant role to reduce the duty tax on solar products in the country. The combined efforts of IDOs and large MNEs are an important feature of aid for sustainable energy access and transition in emerging markets.

Many of the REEs I studied in emerging markets over the last seven years are no different than those in developed markets. Indeed, they also aim to market their products and services to IDOs and share the goal of winning more aid-funded business contracts. However, they find it difficult to compete with large multinationals and have their interests too represented on IDO panels and boards. Therefore, they have found ways to build their business models around aid to benefit from some of the significant advantages potentially available to their enterprises. In particular, REEs' familiarity with socio-economic and – cultural conditions locally in emerging markets gives them a significant competitive advantage (I explain this in more detail in Chapter 4 of this volume). This competitive edge makes them attractive subcontractors to multinationals, as well as corporate beneficiaries of tied aid in developed markets, with aid-funded contracts and a mandate to deliver in emerging markets. Thus, many of the REEs I studied embraced aid-centric business models, where they engage IDOs and their agents and contractors as not only potential funders, but also as customers and collaborators. When asked if it were possible to build a successful REE business model based entirely on aid, Tane, who owned and ran a REE in Tonga in the Pacific, responded:

> *It is definitely possible, especially in a place like Tonga. There is so much aid going in there, and they need local capacity to be able to get the projects on the way. They need that local input, and there is not that many people qualified to give it. So, in terms of a consultancy, I actually had a lot of projects going on at the same time, or that I could have applied for on top of that. So, I think you definitely can in that sort of aid-based market.*

(Tane, operating in Tonga)

However, the REEs I studied explained that this dependency on aid also poses significant strategic and operational challenges for them personally and for their enterprises. Thirty-five of the 43 enterprises studied reported working with IDOs or applying to IDO tenders as a means to cope with many of the challenges they face. Yet, their discussion of their interactions with such organisations suggests they are conflicted about their acceptance of the role IDOs play on their respective markets. Indeed, they view IDOs as rivals in emerging markets (Chapter 4), but they also understand and accept that their best chance of competing and effectively facilitating sustainable energy transition is often to cooperate and collaborate with such organisations.

At this juncture and before proceeding, I pause to acknowledge reflexivity in my approach as a researcher. Indeed, I endeavoured as always to present an unbiased account of aid and its benefits and effects on REEs in emerging markets. However, it is plausible that, despite these efforts, attentive readers will perceive my own personal reservations about international aid. Thus, with this caveat, my aim is to ensure I present my findings, implications and opinions clearly, alongside their accompanying assumptions. For instance, I note that the underlying rationale for the increasing involvement of multinational private sector entities in aid is one of profitability. Indeed, the logic is that if the endeavour is not profitable, then the impacts cannot be sustainable. The entire international system of aid is based upon an ideology, indeed a widely held belief, that unhindered economic growth is the only solution to the world's development challenges, and that this economic growth can only be realised through the private sector. There is a larger distributional justice question to be answered here— for whom, exactly, does aid ensure profitability and sustainability? I discuss these implications in the depictions of aid-centric business models provided later in this chapter. First, however, I consider the question: is aid good for business?

Is aid good for business?

> *I think with all the aid it kind of warps the industry in a big way. The governments are accepting it openly – with arms opened wide to take all this aid. But the industry is getting suffocated a little bit, with no incentives going for those sort of entrepreneurs.*

(Tane, operating in Tonga)

I completed my research interview with Tane in 2013. Several other participants shared the same viewpoint and experience. By 2015, after completing several other interviews that included the same theme of aid-centricity and its influence on the markets in which REEs operate, in a moment of considerable perplexity, I wandered into the office of a colleague at the University of Otago in an effort to make sense of what I heard. I conveyed the experiences of the REEs in my study to Associate Professor Adam Doering who, at the time of writing, was based at Wakayama University in Japan. He considered the dilemma for a moment, and then asked, "*So, is aid good for business?*"

I put aid flows allocated to the sustainable energy transition aside. I considered the issue more broadly instead, and the possibility that aid could be, objectively, beneficial for individual enterprises in emerging markets. Aid flows to the private sectors of emerging markets aim to help enterprises such as those included in my research develop and maintain successful businesses. However, relatively little is known about whether these business-specific aid interventions truly enhance local business capacity and performance. This is because a considerable portion of the research on aid supply and effectiveness focuses only on macroeconomic influences and effects, such as on economic growth (GDP) for instance (*cf.* Cook and Uchida, 2003; Easterly, 2003 and Jones, 2015). Does business aid really improve business performance? Does aid truly enhance the lives and livelihoods of small enterprises, such as REEs in emerging markets? On the macro level, for a long time the literature suggested that where aid is present, emerging markets did experience lower levels of poverty (McGillivray, 2005). In addition, we have seen that individual, targeted aid projects may be good for improving health and well-being, women's socio-economic position, education levels, trade, transparency and access to information, for example (Easterly, 2003; McGillivray, 2005; Oxfam, 2016). However, on the micro-level for individual enterprises, little empirical work exists that provides insight into the effectiveness of aid for enterprises. Does aid make it easier to setup and run a business if incorporated into the enterprise's business model as the REEs I studied have done?

The World Bank highlights the eleven aspects and influencers of the process of doing business that it measures and reports in its *Doing Business* database: starting a business, labour market regulation, dealing with construction permits, getting electricity, registering property, getting credit, protecting minority investors, trading across borders, paying taxes, enforcing contracts, and resolving insolvency (World Bank, 2019). In Table 5.1, I identify how each might translate to the process of starting and running a renewable energy enterprise in emerging markets. I also provide some perspective on the potential advantages and disadvantages of aid – that is, its potential to improve each of these eleven aspects and influencers of the process of doing business in the renewable energy industry in emerging markets. The table itself was inspired by Cali and Te Velde (2011)'s, who assessed the effectiveness of aid for trade purposes.

Table 5.1 Advantages and disadvantages of aid for the distribution of RET products in emerging markets

Challenges of Doing Business[1]	Implications for REEs Distributing RET Products	Advantages of Aid	Disadvantages of Aid
Starting a business	• Need to understand supply chain and distribution channels • Need to assess the need for physical retail space	• Project-specific aid could decrease the time, logistics and institutional requirements to start the business. • Project-specific aid could fund entrepreneurial incubators and/or idea hubs.	• The initial start-up phase is developmentally and strategically important for enterprises. Aid intervention at this stage may lead to co-opted missions and compromised self-sufficiency, especially later, when aid funding ends. • Artificial aid protection in the start-up phase may give REEs unrealistic expectations of the market and misconceived understandings of the industry.
Labour market regulation	• Need to assess availability and appropriateness of skills for installation of RET products on labour market • Appropriateness and legality of wages to be paid to employees	• Project-specific aid can target and ensure fair wages in specific sectors. • Project-specific aid can target skills development and training.	• Aid that targets skills development and training might be 'tied' to training providers in donor countries. • Internationally taught skills may not be (directly) transferable and/ or appropriate in certain emerging markets' contexts.
Dealing with construction permits	• Need permits to establish micro-grids and other micro-generation infrastructure (applicable to REEs using Integrator (Type IV) business models)	• Project-specific aid could decrease the time, logistics and institutional requirements to acquire permits, especially when the aid is specific to business and institutions.	• Aid intervention may give REEs unrealistic expectations and understanding of the market and processes involved in acquiring permits.

Getting electricity	• Electricity to establish and run retail shops • Electricity availability and reliability in households affect demand for RET products. • Electricity to power test sites and prototypes (applicable to Type II REEs)	• Project-specific aid can fund electrification/energy access projects. • Development aid can fund initiatives to modernise electricity grids, eradicate urban poverty and enhance urban living conditions, thereby improving electricity access and reliability.	• Rural electrification and energy access projects that rely on tied aid are implemented using technology and expertise from donor countries, potentially at the expense of development of potentially more locally appropriate technology and expertise. • Urban electrification and grid modernisation Schemes may decrease need for RETs overall.
Registering property	• Property and ownership rights after RET products and/or micro-grids are delivered and established (especially applicable to Type II and Type IV REEs).	• Aid money can clarify institutions and institutional processes involved in registering property. • Skills and training provided by aid funds can help REEs better understand their property rights and available options.	• Aid influenced property registration institutions might not be suited to local needs and conditions and might overlook traditional or aboriginal definitions and approaches to ownership. • Aid intervention might oversimplify communal models of ownership (especially for the establishment of micro-grids).
Getting credit	• Need financing to establish and build inventory • Need access to credit for end-users, including end-users at the Base of Pyramid (BOP) in emerging markets	• Project aid can provide direct credit or grants to REEs (especially during the start-up phase). • Subcontracting to aid-contracted MNEs reduces the need for credit as REEs can focus on simply delivering RET products to end-users. • Development Finance Institutions (DFIs) as source of direct financing/credit for REEs, as well as impoverished end-users (e.g. microfinance and microcredit schemes)	• Previous aid funding makes REEs less self-sufficient and therefore less attractive to private investors.

(Continued)

Table 5.1 (Continued)

Challenges of Doing Business[1]	Implications for REEs Distributing RET Products	Advantages of Aid	Disadvantages of Aid
Protecting minority investors	• Attractiveness of enterprises (and the wider market, country and industry) to investors is important. With inclusive business models, poor end-users or micro-franchisees may be minority investors and would require extra care, consideration and protection. • Few REEs have private investors (attracting investors was a reported challenge).	• Aid can provide stability and reputation, which might enhance investor attractiveness and protection. • Project and multilateral aid aimed to support inclusive business models and provide microfinance for micro-franchisees.	• Decision to accept aid/be involved in aid-funded business is taken at the highest strategic levels of a business and therefore rarely involves minority investors (mostly applicable to larger REEs, such as Type IV Integrators).
Trading across borders	• Taxes and duties on imported RET products and components • Geopolitical and trade relationship with neighbouring countries can affect supply to landlocked territories (especially in regions with a history of geopolitical conflict). • Exchange rates and currencies can affect price and affordability of RETs for the entrepreneurs and limit with whom REEs establish supply relationships.	• Aid can help establish geopolitical stability. • IDO interventions may stabilise trade standards and conditions artificially, including exchange rates and acceptable currencies.	• Aid interventions in trade are temporary and superficial and do not address root causes of trade problems.
Paying taxes	• Understanding and paying taxes and duties on imported RET products • Understanding and paying various or undifferentiated business taxes, including income tax	• Aid projects and interventions may lead to targeted reductions in taxes and duties on RET products.	• Leads to perception that aid money is 'free money'

Enforcing contracts	• REEs may be contracted to distribute and deliver RET products to end-users in emerging markets. • When subcontracted buy MNEs, REEs need protection to ensure MNEs honour the agreed payment, operational and delivery terms.	• Aid can provide finance and expertise to help develop strong and transparent legal institutions. • Aid donors monitor and enforce their own contracts.	• As they are subcontractors (not direct contractors), there is no oversight and monitoring by donors to ensure REEs get a fair deal. • MNEs and businesses from donor countries still benefit disproportionately more from aid contracts, than REEs on the ground in emerging markets. • Although contracts may be enforced in the short-term and until the time of delivery of project outcomes, there can be limited longer-term monitoring to ensure continued benefits to REEs and end-users in emerging markets.
Resolving insolvency	• Inability to repay creditors when the enterprise is at end of life • Some REEs may receive start-up support, but no assistance or 'bailouts' are available to resolve insolvency.	• Aid offers opportunities for partnerships with MNEs. • Aid could be redirected in the form of 'bailout' schemes for REEs (however, at time of writing, no evidence of such programs existing).	• Inability to repay creditors due to dependence on revenue streams from aid-granted subcontracting work (i.e. no profits or additional revenue generated to sustain enterprise without aid)

1 These challenges identified from the World Bank's 'Doing Business' database and website, available here (www.doingbusiness.org/en/data) and discussed in the 2019 report available for download here: www.worldbank.org/content/dam/doingBusiness/media/Annual-Reports/English/DB2019-report_web-version.pdf

During my research, I noted that the REEs operating in the Africa and Asia-Pacific regions clearly identified the presence and influence of IDOs in emerging markets as a significant challenge. Indeed, this appeared to be a greater challenge for the entrepreneurs in these regions than those operating in Latin America and the Caribbean. In addition, it seemed that none of the REEs I interviewed from Latin America and the Caribbean had failed by the time I engaged in Study II. I spent a considerable amount of time speculating about the possible reasons for this. Perhaps the Latin American and Caribbean entrepreneurs have matured enough to fully embrace and routinise IDOs into their business models (i.e. they are mostly Distributors (Type III) and Integrators (Type IV)). I compared OECD data on the quantity of ODA provided between 2008 and 2012 (that is, in the years immediately prior to the start of the research interviews) to the Latin American and Caribbean countries represented in this study to data for the Asia-Pacific and African countries represented. I found that aid disbursements to the African and Asia-Pacific territories represented in the study remained consistently and considerably higher than those to the Latin American and Caribbean territories represented (see Figure 5.1). Indeed, the region receiving the least amount of aid had the largest proportion of successful REEs.

Also, the 2013 Global Trends in Renewable Energy Investment report states that although investment in renewable energy declined significantly in the previous year, gains were observed in emerging markets: the Americas experienced an increase of 14 percent, Asia-Pacific (excluding China and

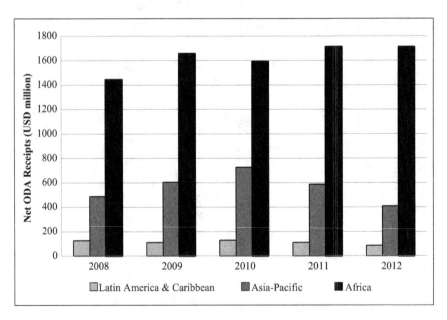

Figure 5.1 ODA Disbursements by Region (2008–2012)

India) experienced an increase of 22 percent, and Africa experienced an increase of 228 percent (UNEP, 2013). The largest percentage increase was in Africa, where REEs experienced the least success. This contrasts with what seems to be the general sentiment that increasing development assistance and investment to developing and emerging countries makes the market environment more conducive to entrepreneurship (see WorldBank and IFC, 2013 and Acs and Virgill, 2010 for example). On the contrary, entrepreneurs from the region receiving the highest amounts of IDO assistance (Africa) not only identify IDOs as a challenge, but also had the largest cluster of Consultants (Type I) whose businesses are less mature. It is therefore possible that increasing IDO presence on emerging markets will have negative longer-term effects on the growth and self-sufficiency of REEs in emerging markets. Economists like Dambisa Moyo (2009) once argued the region needs to decrease its reliance on aid in order to ensure autonomous growth, especially for small, local enterprises. Indeed, some suggest that IDOs fail to address peculiar but important features locally in emerging markets – features potentially better addressed by locally embedded enterprises.

There is, however, an alternative interpretation. Indeed, the African region might receive more aid precisely because its enterprises face the harshest conditions and lowest chances of survival. Therefore, it is possible that aid flows invested in 2012 (when the OECD/DAC ODA data were collected) will have positive effects on enterprise success in the long-term. However, by the time I started Study II 5 years later in 2017, the situation had not improved and the REEs did not perceive an improvement in aid-related markets conditions locally.

In addition, I am by both profession and personal identity a qualitative researcher. Thus, given my own persistent appetite for understanding, and being understood, through lived and recounted or observed experiences, I turned to my own research participants for an answer to Adam's question: Indeed, is aid good for business? I have since concluded that the question begets an enigmatic response. On one hand, aid and relationships with IDOs have their advantages, especially for large multinational corporations. Certainly, the influx of aid money and development of aid partnerships with REEs in emerging markets helps these enterprises develop and grow initially. On the other hand, aid and relationships with IDOs also pose considerable disadvantages. Indeed, many REEs in emerging markets fail because they are not financially self-sufficient. Often, this is because they are overly dependent on grants and other funding from NGOs, government and IDOs. When the project is finished, the aid funding subsides and the REE loses an entire revenue stream. In particular, it is difficult for the REEs to distribute their own RET products when tied aid protects and prefers products developed and originating in donor countries instead. Therefore, based on the recounted experiences of the REEs I studied (and the quotes presented in the subsequent sections of this chapter), it appears aid can have detrimental effects on the survival and efficacy of REEs in emerging markets.

Thus, my research so far has led me to the conclusion that while international aid in general has had considerable positive outcomes (especially, it must be said, in times of natural and manmade disaster), large MNEs benefitted most. Indeed, numerous scholars worldwide have called the effectiveness of aid into question (*cf.* Kosack, 2003; Cali and Te Velde, 2011; and Bigsten and Tengstam, 2015). Aid, it seems, offers a 'bandaid solution' for communities plagued by the symptoms of energy poverty. It remains, I contend, the responsibility and task of local entities, such as REEs, to develop and provide long-term, more sustainable solutions in emerging markets. Indeed, I espouse the view that an economy-wide transformation is needed, especially in many of the world's emerging markets. However, this view is beyond the scope of this particular volume. Certainly, it is not the explicit aim of the aid-centric business models widely used by REEs in emerging markets. These business models, I argue, are a coping mechanism – a strategic response – to conditions in the renewable energy industry in which REEs operate in emerging markets (I described some of these conditions in the preceding chapters of this book).

The aid-centric business model

> *The renewable energy industry is aid-driven. The people really active in the industry are all on aid projects.*
>
> (Tane, operating in Tonga)

In the aid-centric business model, IDOs are the central figures within the ways of doing business – the logics of value creation – of REEs in emerging markets. IDOs strongly influence every facet of REEs' value creation processes. REEs interact with them on a daily basis, as their key clients, influencers of the distribution channels for their products and as a major competing force within these markets as well. The influence of IDOs also resonates at the government and policy levels in emerging markets, further enhancing their power over the institutions and legal-political infrastructures on which REEs depend. This section offers a description and characterisation of the key features of what I will henceforth refer to as the *aid-centric business model*. This model exhibits the context-specific set of features as I discussed and observed them within the business models used by REEs in emerging markets. The aid-centric business model exhibits an aid-centric configuration of value creation, value proposition and model of revenue generation,[5] as illustrated in Table 5.2.

Aid-centric configurations of value creation

Importantly, successful REEs in emerging markets create value for their enterprises and customers by embedding their enterprises within an eco-system of aid or aid-funded organisations. REEs collaborate with such

Table 5.2 The aid-centric business model

Configuration of Value Creation	• IDOs are a major donor, grantor and/or creditor. • IDO influence and aid transfers influence investor attractiveness. • IDOs are a major client and key partner. • Small REEs compete for tenders against IDO-sanctioned larger corporations. • International and intra-regional relations influence taxes, duties and subsidies on RET products in emerging markets. • REEs depend on IDO support to establish distribution channels.
Value Proposition: *Products/Services Offered*	• IDOs influence product/market directly (e.g. Lighting Africa). • IDOs influence product/market indirectly (e.g. products offered by larger corporations have more market visibility/recognition).
Value Proposition: *Customers (Who, How?)*	• IDOs are primary customer. • IDOs as main competitor (free vs paid products; 'sanctioned' vs unsanctioned products) • Aid-influenced market segmentation often means REEs focus on BOP and ignore the middle class urban market.
Model of Revenue Generation	IDOs influence: • Revenue Streams (grants, loans with strict and irrelevant reporting requirements) • Costs (e.g. import procedures, taxes, cost of goods acquired) and therefore • Profits (and how REEs define profitability)

organisations as key partners to deliver RET projects and depend on IDO support to establish distribution channels, for instance (Table 5.2) (Martinot, Cabraal and Mathur, 2001; Martinot, 2001; Frankfurt School-UNEP Centre/BNEF, 2018). Facing conditions of inadequate availability or hindered access to private financing for their RET products and projects (Monroy and Hernández, 2008; Gabriel, 2016; Gabriel et al., 2016), REEs rely on aid money usually as grants. These value creation activities and partnerships enhance the REEs' chances of survival overall, at least, importantly, as long as aid funding persists (Monroy and Hernández, 2008; Gabriel and Kirkwood, 2016).

REEs Elton, Ajay and Kenneth, operating in Tanzania, India and Trinidad and Tobago, respectively, described the different forms of aid partnerships and aid organisations they integrated into their business models:

> *Well, in the aid area, when we do aid work, they are either government or NGOs in general and when we do studies we work with foreign NGOs. We do a fair bit of interaction with the NGOs but in most of the countries we work in, there is a bit of a blurred line between NGO*

*and non-NGO because most people that work in NGOs also have busi-
nesses. They usually act through their business. So if say UK Aid wanted
to do a project on the ground in Pakistan, they don't physically do the
project. What they do is quite often they use an organisation called
IOM – the International Organisation for Migration – and quite often
they say to the IOM, go buy 20,000 lights from a specific company, like
us, and put them on over here. Or they will have the licences through
other NGOs and things like that as well. But it is the actual transaction
that occurs between us and the actual organisations on the ground. All
we do here is we have access through some government departments,
as some developing countries have their own kind of disaster and aid
relief department (like Indonesia and those sort of people). So, in those
circumstances we go directly to those department,s and they'll have
their own people on the ground.*

(Elton, operating in Tanzania)

*It is usually a combination of a financial institution and a local develop-
ment organisation, which already has grassroots outreach and grassroots
engagement. It is going to be a combination of this. And there's typically also, very technically, a group that has an understanding of both
financing and technology, but financing and technology in a kind of
development context.*

(Ajay, operating in India)

*There is one I am partnering with to enter another competition called
SustainTT. So they hosted a Green Film Festival and I actually had a
film at the festival. And there is another one called GreeningTnT, there's
another one called Green Warriors, there's another one called Regreening
T&T, there's another one called PlasticKeep. And there is an organisation called Eurocham T&T. They are non-profit but they specialise in
increasing investment from Europe in Trinidad. People in Trinidad who
represent European brands, they assist them. They help get products to
Trinidad as well. They do different markets – food industry, tourism, as
well as renewable energy.*

(Kenneth, operating in Trinidad and Tobago)

In addition, Alain, at the time operating mainly in Senegal, explained how
aid finance and support enabled him to run a successful REE in multiple
emerging markets, while Dhruv, in India, explained partnering with the
Deutsche Gesellschaft für Internationale Zusammenarbeit (GIZ) to provide
RET skills and training:

*Let's take Senegal – we've got more experience in Senegal. Yeah Philip-
pines, we have worked in the Philippines together with the power source
group and the Asian Development Bank. So this is one of the countries*

where we supply knowledge, consultancy work and maybe the plug-and-play systems.

(Alain, operating in Senegal)

So with some support from GIZ, we actually tied up with what are called 'industrial training institutes', which basically offer the technician's level diploma, so you could train in various trades. You could be an electrician, you could be a plumber – you know, all those very technical training is provided through government-run institutions. Within that, we are trying to include coursework and solar technicians training today. But over a period of time, we want to spread it to more broad-based renewable energy sector training, which would include cookstoves, biogas, mini-grids and so on.

(Dhruv, operating in India)

Entrepreneurs such as Abeiku and David, with REEs operating in Ghana and Papua New Guinea, respectively, explained how they welcome partnerships with international organisations as their local partners, or 'counterparts'. In particular, David described how he used his networks in donor countries to his advantage on renewable energy projects:

Some of the projects that come are international projects, and the clients that come are international clients. Sometimes you have a client from outside who wants to put up a local project. And sometimes a project is designed abroad, and they want a local counterpart. So I avail myself as that local counterpart.

(Abeiku, operating in Ghana)

I did everything myself, with support from technical guys. Started with site assessment, feasibility study, project proposal, then we get financing, then once we get financing we will appropriate materials. I also did some renewable energy training at the university in microhydro and also solar power. I got a company from Wellington to come out and help me. But if I feel the work is beyond my capabilities, I have a lot of contacts, so I can always invite them to come and work with me. I have contacts in Australia and New Zealand and also in Nepal. I am really lucky because I already have these connections, so I can always contact them for renewable energy systems, for support or for financing. The only thing stopping implementing renewable energy projects is financing. Getting technical support from outside is no problem. Only the funding is the main problem in Papua New Guinea.

(David, operating in Papua New Guinea)

Indeed, successful REEs develop networks with IDOs to their advantage. For instance, I heard reports from the Nigerian entrepreneurs I studied that their government was on a campaign to design and implement micro-grids in Nigeria in partnership with the UK's DFID. This gave them the opportunity to become involved in and thus benefit from such projects. IDOs provide funding, project opportunities and distribution channel support that are unavailable locally:

> *To set up a distribution network is another issue. You know serving people who are far off in remote communities. There is no accessible transporting product to those areas, then there's the cost implication. We need to set up a kind of distribution network. And what we are trying to do now is network with NGOs that have presence in those grassroots areas we want to impact. So that through the NGOs we can be able to reach the grassroots. So we are setting up that kind of network, and we hope that if we succeed in setting up this network it will facilitate the distribution or the sales of our product down to the grassroots.*
>
> (Delphine, operating in CMN01)

Working with IDOs and other aid institutions also gives REEs the advantage of enhancing their negotiating power, visibility and legitimacy to their own local governments. Simply by their association with IDOs and other aid partners, REEs are able to enhance their networks and therefore their ability to co-create value with local governments and other local entities:

> *And the policy that we have at the moment from the government I think it comes from our own development partner who funds these kinds of technologies. It means we have more power to negotiate with the government for more policies for this technology. So in our case we have to use this. That, so far, that is mainly our solution.*
>
> (Chea, operating in Cambodia)

> *We are part of a couple of groups that do work with some international non-governmental organisations to present proposals to the government from time to time on what suppliers and market areas are saying about challenges and the policy framework that is put in place.*
>
> (Sai, operating in India)

In particular, REEs who specialise in remote regions are attractive partners for MNEs and other aid-funded international organisations because of their extensive local knowledge and embeddedness within such communities (Chapter 4). While local governments are more likely to manage and award contracts within more easily accessible regions (albeit also, potentially, in partnership with IDOs), REEs find a significant competitive advantage in forming direct partnerships and collaborative endeavours with IDOs for delivery of RET projects in remote communities. A Fijian REE explained this difference in the nature of aid-funded partnerships:

The Department of Energy here, they run solar home system projects every year. I think it is maybe about a thousand odd systems a year that go out to tender. And then they also have smaller projects that they do. And we do work for them installing wind monitoring stations, things like that. And then regional governments, sometimes we do consulting work for regional governments. But they're funded usually by UNDP or EU or someone on like a technical assistance type of project.

(Vijay, operating in Fiji)

In essence, the competitive and logistical relationships between REEs and IDOs described previously in Chapters Three and Four constitute the basis of the REEs' configurations of value creation. Within an aid-centric business model, REEs rely on IDOs and other aid-funded organisations as key partners in their processes of designing and offering value for end-users in emerging markets. Aid-centric value propositions tell a similar story.

Aid-centric value propositions and customer segments

In emerging markets, where aid or aid-funded organisations influence competitive forces and provide financial and other resource support for REEs, successful REEs perceive IDOs as not only rivals in the industry, but also as the major customer segment they serve:

For example, we were currently doing a project with a French NGO that focuses on rural renewable energy. They are focused on rural renewable energy and so they came to us and partnered with us. They are our client and we are establishing a mini-grid up in Northern Laos for a village of 82 households – a solar mini-grid. We did the same for a different village of I think about 100 houses a couple years ago with the same NGO.

(Chris, operating in Laos)

Within the emerging markets to which aid is disbursed, IDOs have specific targets they must achieve, including spending targets and specific socio-economic impacts. Indeed, the aim of ODA is to influence and stimulate improved living conditions in emerging markets and support the achievement of the international Sustainable Development Goals (SDGs) through locally-and regionally-specific action and activities. Often, regarding RETs, IDOs' targets may focus on the distribution of specified products or technologies. As impoverished end-users of RET products are generally unable to afford these products themselves, IDOs either give the products away free of charge, subsidise them heavily or design and implement programmes to improve end-users' ability to afford them in emerging markets. Therefore, in order to distribute their products to impoverished end-users, REEs often work directly with IDOs as clients, closing the gap between aid policy and assistance, and actual distribution on the ground.

However, depending on the type of aid disbursed, there can be considerable negative consequences for REEs. For instance, if an REE is dependent on project aid, they are bound by the requirements and specifications of the project, which are predetermined by donors and their MNE partners. The same challenges might arise when aid is disbursed in the form of tied aid. In such cases, the project can only be delivered using a specific product or technology produced or distributed in the donor's own country. In such cases, even if REEs consider the selected technology inappropriate for the local context, they are not empowered to suggest alternatives. Iwan, who ran a REE in Indonesia, described his frustration with the lack of care shown by international developers towards the local social needs of end-users:

> *You need to decide how you can build a foundation on the social aspects. Usually the other developers do not care about this, and they just sell the equipment and then move on to the next customer.*
>
> (Iwan, operating in Indonesia)

For instance, in 2013 I learned that an IDO once funded an aid program to reduce energy poverty and enhance energy access in rural and remote regions of Vanuatu. Its funding heavily subsidised and prescribed the RET products provided to impoverished end-users, which included some community centres and other buildings of communal and cultural importance. However, the IDO needed the logistical and supply chain support of REEs on the ground to help distribute its products. The local entrepreneurs who worked with the IDO to implement the project experienced significant advantages such as an improved public profile, enhanced legitimacy and better developed networks and contacts within the Vanuatu government. However, the REEs had no say about the brand or type of technology to be installed in the communities, even if they were aware of options that were more locally appropriate. Indeed, in this example, the REE's primary client and key partner was the IDO, not the end-users themselves. This means that the REE must accept and meet the IDO's demands and needs primarily. Indeed, aid contractors are bound by the rules and limitations that accompany the funding, which usually restrict not only the products and technologies to be used, but also the resources and expertise the project should rely upon:

> *And the way they work as well – you've got your local electrical suppliers that could supply a lot of these things if you gave them a contract. And some of the aid does do it that way so that they get a piece of the action: so you can have civil works for the solar plant and you know foundations and that sort of stuff done. And that was all done locally. But it is aid money so they still need their engineers and their own project managers to make sure it gets ticked off. So, on that side of things,*

that's part of the game. But then I guess the government is not putting any incentives on it either.

(Tane, operating in Tonga)

Another feature of aid-centric value propositions is the limited range of products offered by REEs in emerging markets. I take the Lighting Africa (and subsequent sister programs) as an example. Lighting Africa is a program under the World Bank-IFC's wider Lighting Global initiative, which aims to facilitate and enhance the uptake of off-grid lighting solutions to improve energy access in sub-Saharan Africa. Specifically, the program's aim is to enable "more than 250 million people across sub-Saharan Africa currently living without electricity to gain access to clean, affordable, quality-verified off-grid lighting and energy products by 2030" (Lighting Global, 2019). Lighting Africa provided its own quality certificate for off-grid lighting products. As a result, the REEs I studied reported that the general perception in the region's renewable energy industry was that only those products certified by Lighting Africa were of acceptable quality for off-grid end-users in sub-Saharan Africa. Indeed, Lighting Africa certified products gained greater visibility and better reputation on the market, narrowing the overall variety of products available. Despite their own perceptions about the high quality of the lighting products they offered to customers, REEs experienced some resistance if the lights they sold were not certified by Lighting Africa. Therefore, to survive, REEs needed to procure and distribute only those lighting products approved by Lighting Africa.

IDOs also have a strong influence on REEs' customer segmentation in emerging markets. Primarily, IDOs aim to improve the lives and livelihoods of people living in emerging markets. Those concerned with the challenge of energy access often focus on remote, impoverished communities or segments of the urban poor. Indeed, I have found that energy access aid programs generally do not target middle and upper income communities and households in emerging markets. When IDOs are the primary customer, this means that many REEs also choose to ignore the urban or middle and upper income households in emerging markets. Aid-centric value propositions also largely ignore potential commercial customers. When one is as dependent on ODA as the enterprises I studied have been, the main focus of one's customer relations is, generally, the BOP in emerging markets:

It has to do with the access to finance. What I joke about in my articles when you read them is that in Africa we sell systems to the poorest people, and we have to take these systems to the most remote areas. This is a crazy way to do business. So you have to rely on donors to do that. So the joke is you have to cross 3 rivers full of crocodiles to sell a solar panel to a person living on a dollar a day. And this is a ridiculous business model. And I'm looking out my window in Nairobi right now – there's thousands of roofs, and there's thousands of offices using hundreds of megawatts and none of them are solar-powered. So why is it that all of the policy support for renewables is for people in the far-thest villages? And to get the equipment to them is very expensive. And then to ensure that that equipment is going to last a long time requires education and requires logistics and infrastructure. So that's part of the finance problem. If the policies change so that solar was attractive for people, the middle class who live in towns, then it would be easier for the solar industries to develop. So that's my argument, instead of just trying to help the rural poor, let's invest in solar for the middle class. And by developing solar for the middle class and the huge commercial class you develop the industry as a whole and then you are not relying on this system, which is always subsidised and which is always NGO and donor-led, to get it to the rural people.

(Thomas, operating in Kenya)

David, who operates a REE in Papua New Guinea, explained that in his country part of the reason aid organisations and projects target rural remote communities at the BOP is because the aid missions themselves are located in these areas:

The aid missions are placed in many remote areas of Papua New Guinea. So they need to have electricity to run their laptops and lighting, and if they set up a health centre, then they need power.

(David, operating in Papua New Guinea)

Certainly, the aid-centric value proposition is a proposition and guarantee of value retrieved for and by IDOs in emerging markets. The products and services offered and customers served are those relevant to the achievement of international development goals. This is not necessarily a negative observation, however. Indeed, many of the aims of international development more broadly, in particular, energy distribution and access, are consistent with the aims of sustainable human thriving so avidly pursued by the REEs I studied. The challenge and the enigma are the self-sufficiency, growth and longevity of the enterprise itself.

RET products, like so many of the goods we consume, do not last forever. Indeed, though some are made more durable and context-appropriate than others, the technology itself will eventually reach the end of its functional lifetime. Thus, while IDO intervention provides a necessary jumpstart to introduce such products to the market, what happens when the aid flows cease? At the end of life of RET products, end-users at the BOP will require either further IDO intervention and assistance or to simply purchase or renovate a new device from a local REE. However, why purchase such products when one has received it for free previously? Indeed, as aid organisations usually subsidise the products distributed, end-users develop unrealistic expectations of the price, and therefore value, of these technologies. Thus, end-users at the BOP are likely to reject REEs' value proposition if they offer

RET replacements at regular market rates, instead of at the subsidised rates at which IDOs offered them initially.

In sum, IDOs influence the REEs' products and markets both directly and indirectly (Table 5.2), affecting the types and affordability of the RET products and services needed by end-users in emerging markets. Working within the parameters of these aid-designed markets, REEs have experienced some success. However, they expressed concern about the future of the renewable energy industry in emerging markets, especially their ability to survive long-term, even without IDO intervention.

Aid-centric models of revenue generation

When I interviewed him in 2013, Chris, whose REE operates in Laos, described the moment he realised aid was an important source of revenue for his business:

> *Right around 2009 or 2010, the company stumbled across – we didn't purposely seek it out – but our attention was drawn to international tenders. Just an open bid for a project and there was one here in Laos, and so naturally, we were an experienced renewable energy company in Laos. So we applied to this tender it was a large success for us. And that really opened our eyes to a whole other profit stream. That was separate from the rental model and that is essentially today what has helped our profit stream, our revenue stream a lot and that is a big part of our company – our international tenders division – which is dedicated to responding to tenders around the world. Whether it is from the World Bank, UN or Asian Development Bank or the European Commission. So, we really have several different ways that we make money to put it plainly. Tenders are a part of that.*
>
> (Chris, operating in Laos)

Other REEs actively sought the support of IDOs and international corporations in their respective regions, recognising the significant revenue generating potential of integrating these entities into their business models:

> *So I'm also working quite closely with them, and we try to develop several projects in several remote areas in Indonesia and we try to get our funds from several resources. We are trying to do some fundraising in Japan, through Japanese companies, who have CSR budgets and then we tried to get some ODA support from the Japanese embassy or Japanese government. And there's also a possibility that we are trying to seek also from international development agencies from outside Japan such as from US, such as USAID.*
>
> (Arif, operating in Indonesia)

The REEs I studied claimed they seldom received grants from IDOs as the lead contractor. Often, they must collaborate with large MNEs to enhance their own legitimacy, and thus their chances of winning substantive contracts. Aid funding for RET product distribution is disbursed through energy access and poverty alleviation projects in emerging markets, and REEs are usually sub-contracted by MNEs to distribute their products on the ground:

> *Right now there is one company that can build large projects because they have the funds. That's just one. The other is really a partnership. It is a really big project and they make partners with the multinational companies. Mostly they are Japanese companies – the big companies are partners with the local renewable energy projects.*
>
> (Ernesto, operating in Philippines)

The REEs lamented that this is often the only stable or guaranteed source of income for their enterprises. However, as the funds are usually just enough to cover their costs, they generally have little surplus available to reinvest in the further development of their business models. In addition, because emerging market governments generally have little control over the taxation procedures and regulations for MNEs, there is little opportunity for local REEs to receive tax concessions and other benefits on the import and distribution of RET products. Thus, with higher costs and stable but aid-dependent revenues (Table 5.2), REEs' entire model of revenue generation is dependent upon the processes and infrastructures that bring aid resources into their countries of operation.

An aid-centric logic of value creation

Overall, aid-centric business models are aid-centric logics of value creation, and they generally demonstrate linear flows of value to and through the enterprise. Indeed, IDOs, NGOs and other aid providers inject financial, social and logistical value into the business models of REEs by offering grants, loans or simply partnership and payment for services rendered in emerging markets. In essence, REEs may simply combine the value created through their networks and partnerships with IDOs with IDO-sanctioned products and IDO-prioritised end-users to enjoy consistent generation of revenues for their businesses (Figure 5.2).

However, prevailing sentiment towards aid, as well as concern for the long-term sustainability of REEs and the sustainable energy transition overall in emerging markets, suggests a need to consider and develop alternative ways of being for successful REEs. That is, there is the need to find alternatives to aid dependence as a core and pivotal aspect of REEs' business models in emerging markets.

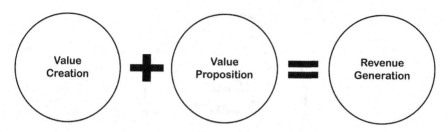

Figure 5.2 An aid-centric logic of value creation

When I considered alternatives to these aid-centric logics of value creation, several questions came to mind: How can REEs ensure sustained achievement of energy access outcomes over time, even after IDO programs are completed? How might they sustain themselves, independent of development aid, so they might continue to pursue sustainable human thriving authentically and in ways appropriate to the contexts in which they operate? Although aid is likely to continue for the near future, in what ways might the value propositions of REEs in emerging markets develop independence from ODA? Should REEs design and produce their own products? Should they target customer segments that will generate revenues to enhance their ability to deliver RET products to the poor? I incorporate some of these ideas in a proposed aid-independent logic of value creation.

A proposed aid-independent logic of value creation

To conclude this chapter, I propose a comprehensive alternative business model for REEs in emerging markets. Drawing on perceived and realised opportunities to co-create value, co-generate revenue and operationalise self-sustaining models of revenue generation, as described in the literature on the subject (*cf.* Gabriel and Kirkwood, 2016; Schaltegger, Lüdeke-Freund and Hansen, 2012 and Stubbs and Cocklin, 2008), I propose an aid-independent logic of value creation. The past seven years of research have taught me that successful REEs want to continue creating value in emerging markets, but in ways that enable them to escape the cycle of dependency on IDO funding. The complexity of their relationship with these organisations has dire consequences for survival: unless they are large, well-connected Integrators (Type IV), those who remain dependent on frequent injections of IDO funds will ostensibly struggle to survive in emerging markets. In contrast, those who use the funding acquired from such organisations to develop more sustainable business models will survive. I offer the following illustration of this proposed aid-independent logic of value creation (Figure 5.3) in contrast to the linear logic illustrated previously in Figure 5.2.

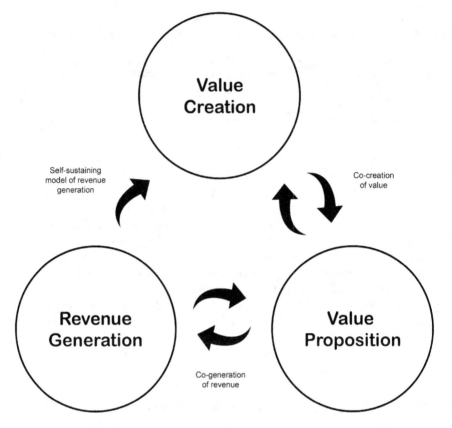

Figure 5.3 A proposed aid-independent logic of value creation

First, while in the aid-dependent logic of value creation, value flows between 'creation' and 'proposition' are linear; aid-independence would require REEs to imagine and realise more cyclical flows of value (Figure 5.3). Examples I discussed previously in this book include reverse innovation and inclusive business models. For instance, REEs who use inclusive business models involve the end-users themselves in the design and delivery of products and services. In addition, they utilise micro-franchising as a way to engage end-users as business partners and not just as customers. In this way, REEs co-create value with impoverished end-users, ensuring that the solutions devised for beneficiary communities are appropriate to their needs. In another example, reverse innovation gives REEs the opportunity to co-create value not only with end-users for whom RET products are specifically designed, but also with the local or international corporations that design or supply them. Second, I propose more circular value flows between 'propositions' and 'revenue generation' (Figure 5.3). Indeed, co-creation of value with end-user communities must be accompanied by appropriate co-generation of revenue with these communities. In this sense, not only are RET products made more relevant to the communities that need them most, but the REEs' distribution and delivery of these products also provide financial benefits, or at least, financial independence, to the end-users themselves. For instance, REEs that offer pay-as-you-go (PAYG) solar home systems (SHSs) share the financial rewards with micro-franchisees and offer end-users payment options that are manageable within their own financial means. In addition, REEs redefine returns beyond the traditional sense and measure their success by the social and ecological returns generated by their products and enterprises as well (I discuss this in more detail in Chapter 6 – *Defining and Measuring Success*). Third, I propose that REEs who successfully achieve these co-creation and co-generation flows and collaborative approaches with end-users and other stakeholders considerably enhance their chances of achieving a self-sustaining model of revenue generation (Figure 5.3). That is, the partnerships, products and distribution channels developed, as well as the revenues and enhanced values generated for all involved, should enable REEs to survive longer in emerging markets. The social, ecological and financial value generated can be re-invested into value creating activities for enhanced benefits and continued success in their respective industries.

Indeed, co-creation and co-generation of value with communities, end-users and international networks have different and more positive implications than co-creation and co-generation with IDOs in emerging markets. To remain independent of aid funding, REEs must develop and integrate the former approach. In the former case, the REE will retain control over what he or she defines and accepts as truly sustainable value, while in the latter case IDO partners define what forms of value are acceptable. For instance, REEs can develop and leverage their own distribution networks in emerging markets to achieve sustainability goals. In the latter case, however, where value is co-created with IDOs, definitional and normative control over the REEs' value configurations lies with the IDOs themselves. A defining feature of business models that prioritise sustainability outcomes is that such enterprises effectively communicate and clearly demonstrate how they create sustainable value within the context and priorities of their own end-users (Boons and Lüdeke-Freund, 2013; Schaltegger, Hansen and Lüdeke-Freund, 2016a). However, when using aid-centric approaches, the REEs' reliance on IDO programmes is the key feature of their business models, and thus the central focus of its communication with end-users. Ideally, the needs of IDOs should align with those of end-users. However, the cognitive and experiential distance between the two and layers of international protocol make this alignment seemingly impossible. Therefore, independence from IDOs could improve the effectiveness and responsiveness of the REEs' activities towards the creation of societal and natural capital value in end-user communities in emerging markets.

There are two caveats implied in this proposed aid-independent logic of value creation. First, I intended this proposed alternative logic to become a business modelling approach that REEs can adopt themselves in emerging markets. Considerable institutional change is needed in emerging markets to regulate the role of the international private sector in aid projects, as well as to optimise outcomes for beneficiary communities from aid projects. Indeed, arguably, emerging markets require closer attention to how (or, more fundamentally, *if*) large international MNEs become involved in the business of aid. However, this proposed logic does not address this need directly – I focus instead on the empowerment and self-sufficiency of individual REEs themselves, even within the existing difficult aid context in emerging markets. Second, I acknowledge that the private sector as we know it today, including REEs more broadly defined, is not a panacea for the transition to sustainable energy in emerging markets. Indeed, the work of REEs alone will not provide adequate and sustainable solutions. However, if small enterprises perceive they have greater agency and opportunity within the renewable energy industry in emerging markets, we could address one of the important factors needed to experience more tangible and sustainable transition in emerging markets.

Notes

1 In DAC statistics, "concessional" implies a grant element of at least:

> **45 per cent** in the case of bilateral loans to the official sector of LDCs and other LICs (calculated at a rate of discount of 9 per cent).
>
> **15 per cent** in the case of bilateral loans to the official sector of LMICs (calculated at a rate of discount of 7 per cent).
>
> **10 per cent** in the case of bilateral loans to the official sector of UMICs (calculated at a rate of discount of 6 per cent).
>
> **10 per cent in** the case of loans to multilateral institutions (calculated at a rate of discount of 5 per cent for global institutions and multilateral development banks, and 6 per cent for other organisations, including sub-regional organisations).
>
> (OECD/DAC, 2019)

2 There are 30 members of the OECD's Development Assistance Committee (DAC), including the European Union (EU): Australia, Austria, Belgium, Canada, Czech Republic, Denmark, EU, Finland, France, Germany, Greece, Hungary, Iceland, Ireland, Italy, Japan, Luxembourg, Netherlands, New Zealand, Norway, Poland, Portugal, Slovakia, Slovenia, South Korea, Spain, Sweden, Switzerland, United Kingdom and the United States.

3 The United Kingdom's aid is now 'untied'; tied aid is now illegal in the UK because of pressure from UK civil society organisations, as well as mounting international criticism of tied aid more generally. When aid is untied, it ensures that funds allocated to solve challenges related to poverty and quality of life in emerging markets are used more effectively by cutting out the 'middle man' corporations in donor countries. It also helps governments and others involved in delivering aid on the ground in emerging markets ensure that the best solutions for local social, cultural, geographical and economic conditions are offered. These are preferred over solutions designed by international corporations not usually familiar with needs in emerging market communities.

4 An OECD review of the UK's aid disbursements reported, "The UK reports its aid as 100% untied and the government has committed to keeping UK aid separate from national commercial interests. However, the UK reports that over 90% of centrally managed contracts – which represent the vast majority of the contract value – go to UK suppliers" (OECD, 2014: 68).

5 These terms are defined and discussed in detail in Chapter 2 of this book. However, in brief, I define them broadly as follows: the configuration of value creation refers to the physical and human infrastructure needed to produce a product or service; the value proposition generally refers to the product or service offered; the model of revenue generation refers to the description of how the enterprise generates income.

References

Acs, Z. and Virgill, N., 2010. Entrepreneurship in developing countries: Foundations and trends in entrepreneurship, 6(1), p. 68.

Bigsten, A. and Tengstam, S., 2015. International coordination and the effectiveness of aid. *World Development*, 69, pp. 75–85.

Boons, F. and Lüdeke-Freund, F., 2013. Business models for sustainable innovation: State-of-the-art and steps towards a research agenda. *Journal of Cleaner Production*, 45, pp. 9–19.

Cali, M. and Te Velde, D.W., 2011. Does aid for trade really improve trade performance? *World Development*, 39(5), pp. 725–740.

Cook, P. and Uchida, Y., 2003. Privatisation and economic growth in developing countries. *The Journal of Development Studies*, 39(6), pp. 121–154.

Easterly, W., 2003. Can foreign aid buy growth? *Journal of Economic Perspectives*, 17(3), pp. 23–48.

Frankfurt School-UNEP Centre/BNEF, 2018. Global trends in renewable energy investment 2018. Frankfurt am Main. Retrieved from www.fs-unep-centre.org (accessed 07 September 2019).

Gabriel, C.A., 2016. What is challenging renewable energy entrepreneurs in developing countries? *Renewable and Sustainable Energy Reviews*, 64, pp. 362–371.

Gabriel, C.A. and Kirkwood, J., 2016. Business models for model businesses: Lessons from renewable energy entrepreneurs in developing countries. *Energy Policy*, 95, pp. 336–349.

Gabriel, C.A., Kirkwood, J., Walton, S. and Rose, E.L., 2016. How do developing country constraints affect renewable energy entrepreneurs? *Energy for Sustainable Development*, 35, pp. 52–66.

Jones, S., 2015. Aid supplies over time: Addressing heterogeneity, trends, and dynamics. World Development, 69, 31–43.

Kennard, M. and Provost, C., 2016. How aid became big business. *Los Angeles Review of Books*, 09 May. Pulitzer Center. Retrieved from https://pulit zercenter.org/reporting/how-aid-became-big-business (accessed 07 September 2019).

Kosack, S., 2003. Effective aid: How democracy allows development aid to improve the quality of life. *World Development*, 31(1), pp. 1–22.

Lighting Global, 2019. Lighting Africa. Retrieved from www.lightingglobal.org/ where-we-work/lighting-africa/ (accessed 08 September 2019).

Martinot, E., 2001. Renewable energy investment by the World Bank. *Energy Policy*, 29(9), pp. 689–699.

Martinot, E., Cabraal, A. and Mathur, S., 2001. World Bank/GEF solar home system projects: Experiences and lessons learned 1993–2000. *Renewable and Sustainable Energy Reviews*, 5(1), pp. 39–57.

McGillivray, M., 2005. Is aid effective? World Institute for Development Economics Research (draft), Helsinki, ca. February (mimeo).

Molina-Gallart, N., 2014. Strange bedfellows? NGO: Corporate relations in international development: An NGO perspective. *Development Studies Research: An Open Access Journal*, 1(1), pp. 42–53.

Monroy, C.R. and Hernández, A.S.S., 2008. Strengthening financial innovation in energy supply projects for rural exploitations in developing countries. *Renewable and Sustainable Energy Reviews*, 12(7), pp. 1928–1943.

Moyo, D., 2009. *Dead Aid: Why Aid Is Not Working and How There Is a Better Way for Africa*. New York, NY: Farrar, Straus and Giroux. ISBN: 0374532125.

OECD, 2014. OECD development co-operation peer reviews: United Kingdom 2014, OECD development co-operation peer reviews. OECD Publishing. Retrieved from http://dx.doi.org/10.1787/9789264226579-en (accessed 08 September 2019).

OECD/DAC, 2018. Aid at a glance. Retrieved from www.oecd.org/dac/financing-sustainable-development/development-finance-data/aid-at-a-glance.htm (accessed 07 September 2019).

OECD/DAC, 2019. Official development assistance: Definition and coverage. Retrieved from www.oecd.org/dac/stats/officialdevelopmentassistancedefinitionandcoverage. htm (accessed 07 September 2019).

Oxfam, 2016. *Accountability and Ownership: The Role of Aid in a Post-2015 World*. Oxfam Briefing Paper, September. Cowley, Oxford, UK.

Schaltegger, S., Hansen, E.G. and Lüdeke-Freund, F., 2016a. Business models for sustainability: Origins, present research, and future avenues. *Organization and Environment*, 29(1), pp. 3–10.

Schaltegger, S., Lüdeke-Freund, F. and Hansen, E., 2012. Business cases for sustainability: The role of business model innovation for corporate sustainability. *International Journal of Innovation and Sustainable Development*, 6(2), pp. 95–119.

Smith, N.C. and Crawford, R.J., 2008. Unilever and Oxfam: Understanding the impacts of business on poverty (A) and (B). *Journal of Business Ethics Education*, 5, pp. 63–112.

Stubbs, W. and Cocklin, C., 2008. Conceptualizing a "sustainability business model". *Organization & Environment*, 21(2), pp. 103–127.

UNEP (United Nations Environment Programme), 2013. Global trends in renewable energy investment 2013. Frankfurt School, UNEP Collaborating Centre for Climate & Sustainable Energy Finance, Bloomberg New Energy Finance, German Federal Ministry for the Environment, Nature Conservation and Nuclear Safety, United Nations Environment Programme, Germany.

World Bank, 2019. *Doing Business 2019: Training for Reform*. A World Bank Group Flagship Report, 16th edition. International Bank for Reconstruction and Development/The World Bank, Washington, DC, USA.

World Bank and IFC (International Finance Corporation), 2013. *Doing Business 2013: Smarter Regulations for Small and Medium-Size Enterprises*. Washington, DC, USA: Worldbank and International Finance Corporation.

6 Defining and measuring success

Defining success

Individual actors can bring about change. In fact, particularly in challenging environments such as emerging markets, we rely partially on these actors to defy the status quo and catalyse transitions to new social innovations. In the sustainable energy transition in emerging markets, renewable energy enterprises (REEs) face an enormous challenge, as they are often characterised as peripheral or non-dominant actors within the renewable energy industry (see Chapter 1). That is, while fossil energy incumbents, international aid and development organisations (IDOs), governments and non-government organisations (NGOs) might constitute and reinforce the status quo (i.e. they are the dominant actors), REEs aim to change the status quo (and are therefore conceptualised as peripheral actors). How, therefore, would such enterprises define success?

'Success' is a subjective and contested construct. Particularly in the current climate as societies and civil society place greater demands on enterprises to expand their definition of success beyond simply profits, contemporary enterprises must dedicate considerable resources to reimagining their own definition of success. In emerging markets, the inescapable socioeconomic and ecological challenges formulate an imperative for enterprises of all kinds to look beyond profit-seeing behaviours to their contributions to societal and environmental welfare. For REEs in particular, the sustainable energy transition is well underway. To ignore the implications of this transition for new approaches to enterprise and value creation could be to the detriment of these enterprises. Therefore, I observed that REEs define their success not only by conventional financial measures, but also by their contribution to realising the sustainable energy transition in emerging markets. Indeed, I found that even the most conventional, profit-seeking REEs measured their success by a combination of indicators of enhanced distribution and uptake of their renewable energy technology (RET) product and their ability to become and remain self-sustaining in the long-term. In fact, the more strongly the entrepreneurs held on to beliefs and values about the importance of achieving societal and ecological outcomes, the more adamant they were about the need for new definitions and indicators of success.[1]

Therefore, I define successful renewable energy enterprise as follows. It is *the creation and procurement of social, ecological and financial value by a self-sufficient renewable energy enterprise that enhances the distribution and uptake of RET products in emerging markets.*

Based on this definition, this final chapter serves two purposes. The first is to outline and describe the key alternative metrics used by REEs in emerging markets to measure their success on these parameters. In the section 'All about the Metrics' I refer to and build upon my previous work, which suggests that socially-motivated REEs in emerging markets are averse to financial growth in the traditional sense (Gabriel et al., 2019). For the benefit of nascent REEs and the researchers interested in studying them in emerging markets, in this section I provide descriptive detail on these alternative measures. The second purpose of this chapter is to characterise successful REEs in emerging markets. In the section 'The Successful Renewable Energy Enterprise in Emerging Markets', I present and discuss the findings of the analysis and comparison I undertook of the discursive strategies of successful versus unsuccessful REEs. Therefore, the resulting final characterisation includes business model features as well as specific discursive strategies for success in emerging markets.

All about the metrics

Conventional measures of enterprise success focus solely on the achievement of the enterprise's stated goals and objectives, inadvertently ignoring the *means*, processes or strategies used by the enterprise to achieve these goals. For enterprises that aim to achieve social and ecological goals in emerging markets, the means are just as or, arguably, more important than the ends. For example, REEs who embrace an aid-independent logic of value creation (see Chapter 5) must concern themselves with not only the goal to co-generate financial revenue, but also with the effective execution of processes of value co-creation and co-configuration with stakeholders in emerging markets. Yet, even the literature on socially-and ecologically-motivated enterprise focuses solely on alternative and inclusive measures of performance in terms of achieving their end goals (*cf.* Austin, Stevenson and Wei-Skillern, 2006 and Mair and Marti, 2006). However, performance measures that include consideration of the means used to achieve these goals better reflect the peculiar priorities of the enterprise.

Scholars who study socially-and ecologically-motivated enterprises acknowledge and appreciate the differences in their priorities (*cf.* Bacq and Janssen, 2011; Eckhardt and Shane, 2003 and Douglas, 2013). Indeed, in contrast to conventional profit-seeking enterprises, such enterprises prioritise opportunities to solve social and/or ecological challenges, such as the sustainable energy transition in emerging markets. Thus, socially-and ecologically-motivated entrepreneurs tend to have different priorities, motivations and resource mobilisation strategies than their commercially oriented counterparts (Austin, Stevenson and Wei-Skillern, 2006; Mair and Marti, 2006; Doherty, Haugh and Lyon, 2014). Moreover, as I demonstrated in preceding chapters, successful REEs who pursue an aid-independent business model may use different and idiosyncratic means to achieve their co-creation goals, depending on their own motivations and experiences (Lim, Oh and De Clercq, 2016; Mary George et al., 2016; De Carolis and Saparito, 2006). This means REEs may engage in value creation and configuration processes that are distinct from those of conventional profit-seeking enterprises. Therefore, these processes ought also to feature in the metrics used to gauge the success of these enterprises.

Another reason to consider alternative measures of performance for REEs in emerging markets is that they operate their enterprises within some of the world's most challenging and penurious contexts. Indeed, REEs address a myriad of challenges neglected by market economies, governments and other dysfunctional institutions in emerging markets (Santos, 2012; Pathak and Muralidharan, 2017; Estrin, Mickiewicz and Stephan, 2016). They aim to provide solutions to the socioeconomic and environmental challenges faced, often filling deep institutional voids in such markets. However, these enterprises remain challenged in such contexts by issues such as the absence of a specialised legal form for socially-and ecologically-motivated enterprises (Littlewood and Holt, 2015) and limited local financial resources (Ault and Spicer, 2014; Bruton, Ahlstrom and Obloj, 2008; Littlewood and Holt, 2015). Regions such as sub-Saharan Africa are complex social and cultural contexts that likely influence REEs' self-perceptions, venture organisation and activities on the ground (Rivera-Santos et al., 2015; Ault and Spicer, 2014; Bruton, Ahlstrom and Obloj, 2008). Therefore, one cannot assume that conventional measures of performance are important to all REEs in these contexts (Khoury and Prasad, 2016; Gabriel et al., 2019).

Finally, as I emphasised in Chapter 1 of this volume, it is important to highlight the perspectives and experiences of REEs operating in some of the world's least developed regions because the issue remains largely unaddressed in the least developed of the world's emerging markets to date (Khoury and Prasad, 2016; Kolk, Rivera-Santos and Rufín, 2014; Prahalad, 2005; Seelos and Mair, 2005). Indeed, it is important to draw upon a wider variety of economic and institutional contexts and take lessons from research in under-represented, least developed regions such as those I studied from 2012 to 2018.

To measure the success of REEs in emerging markets using both goals-and means-focused metrics, in addition to conventional measures of growth and profitability, I propose three indicators: *Uptake, Inclusiveness* and *Self-Sufficiency* (Table 6.1). I define each construct as follows. *Uptake* refers to the extent of distribution and widespread availability and use of the REE's products and/or services. *Inclusiveness* is the depth and breadth of the REE's co-creation activities with a variety of stakeholders including, most importantly, RET end-users in emerging markets. *Self-Sufficiency*

Table 6.1 Uptake, Inclusiveness and Self-Sufficiency: success measures for renewable energy enterprise in emerging markets

Success Measures	Suggested Indicators[2]	Implications for Means and Processes Used	Implications for Goals Achieved
Uptake	• Number of products sold • Electricity generated • Proportion of need met by enterprise's product(s) • Household volume and percent ownership of the enterprise's product(s) • Price of products offered • Affordability and appropriateness of products offered	• Selective market segmentation within niches • Embeddedness within end-user communities • Reverse Innovation • Solutions designed for remote communities	• RET products increasingly available and widely used by end-users • Rate of change in number of RET projects managed by the enterprise • Project success rate by percentage of outcomes achieved
Inclusiveness	• Rate of access to increasingly poorer end-users in the Base of the Pyramid (BOP) • Proportion of REE's employees and/or business partners that are members of BOP communities	• The enterprise offers tailored financing options to end-users, e.g. microcredit, micro-franchising, pay-as-you-go • The enterprise's business model integrated with livelihoods within end-user communities • The enterprise employs and partners with people from BOP communities • The enterprise promotes RETs with productive uses in communities (urban and rural)	• Lower rates of energy poverty among end-user communities • A higher percentage of end-users who can afford RET products offered • New jobs created by the enterprise, both directly and directly
Self-Sufficiency	• Number and success rate of active RET projects • Number, success rate and value of RET projects • Proportion of cost of RET products borne by the REE itself • Leverage, i.e. ratio of equity to grants • Ability to reinvest in social impact and value co-creation activities	• The enterprise consistently facilitates generation of social and financial value for end-users, to maintain reliable customer base • The enterprise consistently reinvests the generated profits in social impact and infrastructure, i.e. distributes, rather than accumulates value • Percentage of aid funds retained by the enterprise	• High proportion of costs borne by the REE itself • The enterprise consistently generates revenues • The enterprise consistently generates surplus • High ratio of equity to grants

measures the REE's ability to sustain its business model indefinitely by generating and sustaining revenues to be re-invested in Uptake and Inclusiveness activities.

Notably, these metrics roughly correspond to the three aspects of the aid-independent logic of value creation I proposed previously in Chapter 5 (see Figure 5.3). That is, while Uptake measures the effectiveness of co-creation of value between key business partners and end-users, Inclusiveness is an indicator of the extent and effectiveness of revenue co-generation with end-users-turned-business-partners. Finally, Self-Sufficiency relates to sustainability of the REE's model of revenue generation. These constructs are not necessarily alternative in the sense of having never been used by enterprises. Instead, my aim is to highlight those indicators I consider appropriate and already in use by successful REEs in emerging markets. In the article by Gabriel et al. (2019), I identify 14 additional performance measures for REEs in emerging markets. Each of these 14 indicators may be classified under one of the three indicators I discuss here. Specifically, as illustrated in Table 6.1, I outline implications for the enterprises' goals and value creation processes in emerging markets.

For instance, REEs measure their Uptake in emerging markets with indicators such as the number of products or systems sold and proportion of electricity demand met by those products. Within this indicator, to ensure their RET products are increasingly available and widely used in emerging markets, REEs focus on understanding their specific niche within the market and ensure the products offered are appropriate for end-user communities. In addition, to ensure their business models and activities are truly inclusive, some REEs challenge themselves to serve the poorest of the poor at the Base of the Pyramid (BOP) and/or ensure that the voice of the BOP is heard within the organisation itself. This can be achieved by REEs who hire members of communities at the BOP and offer RETs for productive uses that enhance livelihoods in such communities. Finally, REEs can measure their Self-sufficiency by understanding the extent of their dependence on aid and other grants as a source of income. For instance, they can consider their ratio of equity to grants, with the aim to enhance the proportion of equity, or leverage, the RET entrepreneurs contribute. When combined, higher rates of Uptake and Inclusiveness can potentially enhance Self-sufficiency, as both lead to more revenue for the REE and more secure and lasting partnerships (e.g. customer loyalty, legitimacy and social capital) in emerging markets.

In the next section, I discuss success from the perspective of REEs' ability to contribute to the sustainable energy transition in emerging markets. I recognised over the years that much of their success depends on REEs' relationships and partnerships within the industry, both locally and internationally. Indeed, REEs that contribute to co-development of new products and approaches and become involved in public discourse around energy access and poverty are not only visible publicly, but they also enhance their legitimacy. By engaging in these activities, REEs become attractive local business partners, further enhancing their relationships and chances of success. Therefore, I aimed to understand the potential connections between these relationships and the REEs' intention to contribute to sustainable energy transition in emerging markets.

The successful renewable energy enterprise in emerging markets

What strategies should REEs use to ensure they can successfully contribute to the sustainable energy transition in emerging markets? Is there a relationship between their intentions to realise change in emerging markets and the types of discourses in which they engage to encourage change? Over the years, the REEs I studied take action and use their voices, individually and collectively, to generate discussion around the cause of sustainable human thriving in emerging markets. They engaged in both verbal and written treatises, with the aim to generate support for their endeavours. These actions, treatises and behaviours are referred to as discursive strategies. Therefore, in this section, I present and discuss findings from a website analysis I conducted, which enabled a comparison of the publicised change intentions and discursive strategies of successful and unsuccessful REEs in emerging markets. To achieve this, I isolated the evident change intentions of the 30 REEs with websites available in English, and I then undertook a qualitative exploration of the specific discourses in which they engage via their websites. Finally, I compared these discourses between failed and surviving REEs. This means I used the REEs' websites as discursive objects in this case. Discursive objects are documents, monologues or technologies, for example, that comprise the means by which people communicate with target audiences. The REEs' websites were insightful discursive objects, as they are the platforms used by REEs in emerging markets to advance their cause and promote a transition to sustainable energy technologies in their respective locales.

Websites as discursive objects

The internet is the ideal discursive platform of our digital age and the ultimate level playing field. It provides enterprises in often-remote parts of emerging markets with a convenient and common place that is open all day long to interact with the world around them. In recent years, the role of internet in shaping enterprise strategy and operation has drawn increasing discussion (Higson and Briginshaw, 2000; Lipitakis and Phillips, 2016). Websites are useful objects to study an enterprise's discursive interactions (both direct and indirect) with its local and international stakeholders.

Website content and design has also emerged as an important issue (Rosen and Purinton, 2004). Recent studies on the topic of website design focus on the contributions that website design can make in several domains. First, it is an important tool to establish and maintain relations with stakeholders by acting as a detailed and comprehensive collection of information about the enterprise – its interests and strategic goals, for example (Eighmey and McCord, 1998; Blanco, Sarasa and Sanclemente, 2010). Second, if information transfer is efficient and the online experience is personalised, updated and well organised, there are customer satisfaction advantages to be gained (Cyr, Head, Larios and Pan, 2009; Zhou, Lu and Wang, 2009; McDowell, Wilson and Kile Jr, 2016). Finally, the increased use of websites by enterprises in emerging markets has created unparalleled opportunities for participation in global markets and, by extension, the ability to take one's message to wider and more diverse audiences than ever before (Ilieva, Baron and Healey, 2002; Rahimnia and Hassanzadeh, 2013).

In emerging markets, REEs rely on their websites to display the products, technologies and services they offer, highlight social and environmental impact, communicate the aims, objectives and scope of their enterprises, and highlight the technical and regional expertise and experiences of the enterprise. Crucially, websites are also an important platform to isolate and understand the REE's key stakeholders and the various ways it engages with these stakeholders. Indeed, one can learn a great deal about the desire and willingness of an REE to contribute to the sustainable energy transition from its website. Therefore, I surmised that the business website serves as an insightful discursive object through which I could investigate and compare REEs' discourses with their stakeholders in emerging markets.[3]

Website evaluation is an established research subject and method, and it is a useful tool to assess website quality and understand the strategies of businesses (Rocha, 2012; Hernández, Jiménez and Martín, 2009). However, researchers recognise that it is difficult to construct a standard technique or widely accepted framework for website evaluation, as different organizations have their own goals and objectives and these differences are reflected in their website content and design (Chiou, Lin and Perng, 2011). Therefore, to maintain the integrity of the research process, I adapted my evaluation of the 30 websites to the specific aims of the research. I used the coding frameworks and cues outlined in Appendix 2 as the basis of the analysis. I coded the content of each website based on each of the themes listed in the first column of Appendix 2. I read the entire contents of the REEs' websites and coded the content at one or more of these themes as appropriate. For example, each time a website mentioned an objective to improve social conditions, I coded the sentence into the 'social change' theme. Two researcher assistants coded all 30 websites independently, and then I reconciled the coding of both researchers.

Propositions

How REEs position themselves to influence change could directly influence their chances of success and survival. Therefore, I aimed to understand the relationship between their discursive strategies for social change and their survival. I explored four propositions, whose relationship I illustrate in Figure 6.1. My analysis confirmed all of my postulations, notably with the exception of Proposition 1 (P1).

Proposition 1: intent to influence change and website content and quality

Research suggests that website content and quality are intentionally constructed. The enterprise is a single level of organization in a broader constantly changing system (Lemke, 1999). In order to survive in dynamic environments REEs need to coordinate market information from different levels (e.g. individuals, government and the economy) to capitalize on the communication potential of their website and gain recognition or opportunity (Kim, 2014). On the macro-level, there is the argument that websites as part of discursive strategy are insightful reflections of an enterprise's potential to transform contexts (Stanfill, 2014). There is also qualitative research that demonstrates how firms use website design to influence change at the

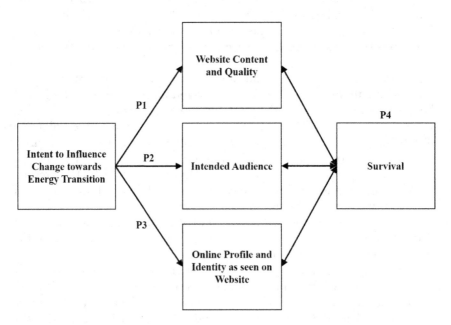

Figure 6.1 The propositions and discursive relationships explored

micro-level (Rosen and Purinton, 2004). In addition, from a practical perspective, changes in strategy must be matched by changes in website content and quality to effectively convey the intended message. Previous website evaluation studies suggest that informational fit-to-task, perceived usability and communication style and effectiveness of a business' website are aligned with the overall strategy of the business (Kim and Stoel, 2004; Flavian, Guinaliu and Gurrea, 2006; Sobo, Herlihy and Bicker, 2011). Ideally, REEs whose strategy includes an intent to catalyse the sustainable energy transition in emerging markets should have good quality websites with content that fits and conveys these intentions. Therefore, my first proposition examined *what* kind of change the REE envisages and the relationship with website content and quality (see Figure 6.1).

> *Proposition 1 (P1): REEs who intend to influence the sustainable energy transition in emerging markets will have better quality and condition of their websites and content than REEs who do not intend to influence the sustainable energy transition.*

To address this proposition, I first appraised the extent to which the websites provide an indication of the REEs' intent to influence change towards the sustainable energy transition (P1, 2 and 3). I considered word and phrase cues such as the ones shown in Appendix 2 an indication of the REEs' intention to influence economic, environmental, health-related or social change – that is, the REEs' intention to improve these conditions in the emerging markets in which they operated. I categorised websites that provided no clear indication of the REEs' intent to influence change under the theme 'Does not intend to change/Not obvious'. Second, to assess each website's content and quality (P1), I used Hasan (2009) and Hasan and Abuelrub (2011)'s framework. Based on this framework, each independent coder assessed four criteria: the Content, Design, Organisation and User-friendliness of each website, as shown in Appendix 2. I gave each of the 30 websites a score, between one and five, depending on the extent to which they fulfilled these criteria.[4] Websites with a score of '1' did not meet any of the content and quality criteria, and websites with a score of '5' indicated high quality content that met all the criteria.

Proposition 2: intent to influence change and intended audience

Successful discourse requires communicators to tailor their messages to their intended audiences. Indeed, REEs must adjust and tailor the information they share for different recipients to have the desired impact (Stank, Keller and Daugherty, 2001). As Shropshire and Hillman (2007: 63) noted, there is "evidence that firms vary widely in their stakeholder management strategies and that stakeholder management is related to shareholder value creation".

Thus, enterprises will adjust their discursive strategy to suit their intended audience. My second proposition explored *who* is the target of REEs' discursive strategies in emerging markets (see Figure 6.1).

> *Proposition 2 (P2): The kind of change envisaged by REEs will be consistent with the intended audience of the REEs' websites.*

To address this proposition, the next step of my analysis involved coding the websites according to the audience(s) they intended to target (P2). I explored each enterprise's target customer group (organisations or households), as well as geographical focus (national, regional or international) and technical level (targeted to the layperson or technical experts) of the content on each website. I used word and phrase cues (examples provided in Appendix 2) to indicate the intended audiences of the REEs and coded the website content accordingly. However, determining intended audience required an additional stage of analysis. I considered the specific audiences mentioned on each website (e.g. specific NGOs or IDOs) to determine whether they were economic, environmental, social or health-related stakeholders. This process revealed who the REEs perceive as key allies in their bid for change.

Proposition 3: intent to influence change and web profile and identity

Enterprises increasingly recognise the significance of the internet in promoting institutional change (Vallaster and von Wallpach, 2013). An enterprise's media profile and identity result from management's active engagement in simultaneous interactions between interdependent stakeholders. The enterprise's web profile and identity are likely to affect consumers' responses to, conceptions of and interest in new products and technologies. For instance, end-user ambivalence towards certain RET products might be relieved in the context of firms who use images in promotional reports, websites and the media (Buchanan-Oliver, Cruz and Schroeder, 2010). In particular, websites could provide opportunities for indirect engagement between the enterprise and its stakeholders and intended audiences in emerging markets. Indeed, Hernández, Jiménez and Martín (2009) emphasized that the website is an effective means of matching and influencing the perceptions and opinions of the enterprise's target audience. Therefore, my third proposition focuses on *how* REEs enter into discourse with their target audiences through their websites. Specifically, I examined the words and imagery used by the REEs to influence the sustainable energy transition in emerging markets (see Figure 6.1).

> *Proposition 3 (P3): The kind of change envisaged by REEs will be consistent with the online profile and identity of their enterprises as reflected on their business websites.*

To address this proposition, I assessed the web profiles and online identities of each REE (P3) through a content analysis of frequently used words and images on the websites, as well as the logos of each enterprise. I also investigated the most commonly used words in the names of the enterprises. For frequently used images, I noted if and how many times each of the 30 websites used a particular motif – once, twice, or thrice or more – and coded the websites accordingly. For frequently used words, I observed the popularity and frequency of specific words: 1–3 times, 4–6 times, or more than 6 times on a single website (refer to the Appendix 2). 'Other' words were also noted, which occurred in fewer than ten of the websites I studied. Finally, I appraised the names of the enterprises themselves, to determine popularity in the case of specific words such as 'eco', 'energy' or 'power'.

Proposition 4: discursive strategy and survival

There is no consensus about the degree to which firms who intend to compete should participate in discursive strategy. However, most scholars agree that enterprises dedicated to fulfilling their strategies in the environments in which they operate benefit from reconciling intended audience demands for a sense of individuality, freedom and self (Caruana, Crane and Fitchett, 2008). They also benefit from trying to influence and co-create the market by facilitating exchanges and interactions between various stakeholders (Hodgson, 2000; Holt, 2002). Enterprises that trivialise discursive strategies are confronted with lower chances of survival than their counterparts (Hendry, 2000). Rahimnia and Hassanzadeh (2013) found discursive strategies displayed on websites have an important effect on e-marketing and e-trust effectiveness, but the effect of the informational dimension is greater than that of design. Thus, with the near ubiquity of business websites, enterprises' online stakeholder relationships have dramatically increased in prevalence, complexity, and financial and strategic importance. Therefore, my final proposition, Proposition 4, assesses whether specific discourses enhance REEs' chances of survival in emerging markets (see Figure 6.1).

> *Proposition 4 (P4): The discursive strategies used by REEs relate to their survival in emerging markets.*

I monitored the survival of each of the REEs (P4). In the years between data collection and analysis and writing this book, I monitored the website activity of all 30 REEs and checked in on the enterprises periodically. I did this to determine the business survival rate of our REEs. Of the 30 REEs with websites in English, 23 were still operational after three years. I did not treat this observation as an indication of survival rates more broadly. Instead, I looked at the key differences in discursive strategy (as seen via the websites) between the seven that did not survive and the 23 that survived. Hence, I began to formulate implications for nascent REEs who might be considering their use of a website to promote and advance their enterprise and the sustainable energy transition in emerging markets.

Appendix 3 provides a summary of my conclusions on these propositions. The only proposition for which I could find no support was P1 – overall, there was no evidence to suggest that REEs who seemed more committed to influencing change had a better quality web presence than those without stated intentions to influence change. I noted, however, that REEs who expressed a strong desire to improve health conditions (such as the occurrence of respiratory diseases due to exposure to traditional cookstoves) in emerging markets specifically, did operate better quality websites than those with an expressed focus on economic, environmental or social change. I found some support for Propositions 2, 3 and 4. For P2, REEs that focused on enabling economic change focused on communicating and collaborating with stakeholders that influence economic conditions such as businesses, banks and local government. Likewise, for those focused on social and environmental change in their respective markets, I found support for my third proposition (P3) as well. For instance, REEs whose intentions suggest a strong focus on improving environmental (i.e. natural ecosystem) factors, used mainly environment-related words and imagery in their discourses and messages with stakeholders (compare Appendices 2 and 3). I found the same for those with economic, social and health-related change intentions. Finally, I found some support for P4 as there was strong evidence to suggest that the combined strength and effect of the REEs' discursive strategies influenced their chances of success in emerging markets.

The discursive strategies of successful renewable energy enterprises

In this section, I summarise and discuss the key discursive strategies used by successful REEs in emerging markets. I provide details of the specific factors evident from their web presence that contribute to overall success in Table 6.2. The discursive strategies outlined in Table 6.2 are those with the strongest results among the 30 REEs whose web presence I analysed.[5] That is, they are the factors reflected by the largest percentage of surviving REEs.

For instance, although they are motivated to provide solutions to social and environmental challenges in their respective markets, I found that REEs that seemed to downplay these motivations survived, while others with an almost exclusive focus on these aspects did not. Specifically, REEs whose discursive strategies emphasised the health and economic benefits of renewable energy and their intention to transform these aspects of the market for renewable energies accounted for 100 percent and 92.3 percent of surviving REEs, respectively. I argue this is consistent with the REEs' tendency to treat NGOs, IDOs, MNEs and other commissioning organisations as customers instead of the end-users themselves (refer to Chapter 5). Indeed, 100 percent of the REEs whose discursive strategies suggest a focus on technically proficient audiences, instead of the layperson audiences that normally characterise end-users in emerging markets, survived.

Table 6.2 Discursive strategies of successful renewable energy enterprises in emerging markets[1]

Discursive Strategies	Survival rate for REEs	Notes
Focus on changing economic and health conditions	Economic conditions (92.3%) Health conditions (100%)	83.3% of REEs with intention to change environmental conditions survived, while 88.2% of those with intention to change societal conditions survived.
Target technically proficient audiences	Technically proficient audiences ONLY (100%)	Only 71.4% of REEs that targeted layperson audiences and 70.6% of those that targeted both layperson and technically proficient audiences survived.
Target both households and businesses as customers	BOTH households and businesses as customers (83%)	In terms of targeted customer segments, 75% of REEs that focused only on households survived compared to 33% of REEs that focused only on businesses.
Target international audiences	International audiences (100%)	REEs that targeted audiences on a national or regional scale had 71% and 69% success rates, respectively. REEs whose websites did not communicate a clear geopolitical scale for the impact of their businesses had a 0% success rate.
Use popular words and imagery in web profile/ identity	Business name: Eco (100%), Global (100%), Light (100%), Renewable (100%), Resource (100%), Sun (100%), Sustainable (100%), Systems (100%), Uncommon name (100%) Frequently used words: Clean (100%), Climate change or Global Warming (100%), Electricity or Electric (100%), Hydro (100%), 'Wind' (100%) and Social (83%) Frequently used images/motifs: People (100%), The Sun (100%)	In addition, REEs who used nature and/or abstract nature and space motifs (33%), as well as technological motifs (27.3%), had lower survival rates than those who used mostly built environment motifs (42.8%).

1 Note that percentages total over 100% because categories were not mutually exclusive, e.g. REEs could demonstrate intentions to influence more than one type of change or serve more than one category of customer.

Moreover, it does not appear advantageous to select either households or businesses only as customers. Instead, REEs whose discursive strategies seemed to target a mix of household and commercial customers were more likely to survive the four years between 2013 and 2017 (83 percent). In general, success rates are high regardless of REEs' focus on promoting their enterprises and communicating their messages on national (71 percent), regional (69 percent) or international (100 percent) scales. Instead, what seems important is to portray a clear geopolitical target for one's discursive strategies; indeed, the REEs for which I could not discern a clear focus nationally or otherwise had not survived. It is perhaps not surprising, though, that those with a clear international focus were still in business when I started Study II in 2017. Indeed, they were larger more mature REEs, whose business models were already dependent upon their relationships with international actors such as IDOs and MNEs.

Finally, I also noted that REEs who discussed wind and hydropower frequently experienced a higher rate of success than those who discussed solar energy frequently. I inferred this might be because wind and hydropower providers are likely larger, well-established businesses with considerable infrastructural and network support. This means they are less likely to fail than the majority of solar providers who often provide smaller scale RET products to end-users. Small scale solar providers are also more likely to be solely dependent on aid funding – yet another factor that might affect their survival and success in emerging markets.

Key success factors for renewable energy enterprise in emerging markets

In summary, the insights revealed in Part II of this volume point to particular Key Success Factors (KSFs) that enable REEs who distribute RET products and systems to overcome the strategic and operational challenges they face in emerging markets. Specifically, successful distributors of RET products and systems:

- Leverage unique sociocultural knowledge and embeddedness in local communities as a core competency to compete and/or collaborate with international aid and multinational enterprises (MNEs) in emerging markets

(Chapter 4)

- Adopt specific market niches but may or may not collaborate intensely with other REEs in emerging markets

(Chapter 4)

- Develop aid-independent business models for long-term self-sufficiency

(Chapter 5)

- Target a combination of households and businesses as key customers

(Chapter 6)

- Measure success based on RET product uptake and the inclusiveness and self-sufficiency of their business models

(Chapter 6)

- Utilise discursive strategies that communicate their intention to contribute to the sustainable energy transition to international, technically proficient stakeholders

(Chapter 6)

In Part III of this book, I illustrate how these factors might be operationalised in the business models of real-life REEs, using the case studies of two successful enterprises operating in emerging markets in the Africa and Asia-Pacific regions.

Notes

1 I discuss the REEs' perceptions of indicators of their success in an article published in the journal, *Alternatives: Global, Local, Political*, titled "Performance beyond Economic Growth: Alternatives from Growth Averse Enterprises in the Global South" (Gabriel et al., 2019).
2 Based on Gabriel et al. (2019).
3 I acknowledge that websites are not the only means to understand the discursive strategies and success of REEs in emerging markets. However, when I first began Study II, I noted that all the still-surviving REEs still maintained active websites and a web presence overall, while those that were no longer operational no longer maintained websites. I inferred that whether they had operational websites could be a good way to gauge overall success of the enterprises. Furthermore, on the websites of the surviving REEs were blogs, news articles and other information through which the REEs themselves communicated not only their activities, but also their passion and intention in emerging markets. Thus, having collected copies of all website data in Study I, including for those REEs that did not survive until Study II, I was able to compare the websites and discourses of surviving and non-surviving REEs in emerging markets.
4 Hasan (2009) and Hasan and Abuelrub (2011) can be consulted for a comprehensive overview of the indicators and specific checklist used to assess the content and quality of the websites.
5 In my research, I used survival as an indicator of success. I inferred this was an acceptable and in many ways powerful conflation, because my appraisal of all four positions around discursive strategy suggests the REEs' intent to influence change (the definition of success I used in this study and presented at the start of this chapter) is indeed related to their survival.

References

Ault, J.K. and Spicer, A., 2013. The institutional context of poverty: State fragility as a predictor of cross-national variation in commercial microfinance lending. *Strategic Management Journal*, 35(12), pp. 1818–1838.

Austin, J., Stevenson, H. and Wei-Skillern, J., 2006. Social and commercial entrepreneurship: Same, different, or both? *Entrepreneurship: Theory and Practice*, 30(1), pp. 1–22.

Bacq, S. and Janssen, F., 2011. The multiple faces of social entrepreneurship: A review of definitional issues based on geographical and thematic criteria. *Entrepreneurship & Regional Development*, 23(5–6), pp. 373–403.

Blanco, C.F., Sarasa, R.G. and Sanclemente, C.O., 2010. Effects of visual and textual information in online product presentations: Looking for the best combination in website design. *European Journal of Information Systems*, 19(6), pp. 668–686.

Bruton, G.D., Ahlstrom, D. and Obloj, K., 2008. Entrepreneurship in emerging economies: Where are we today and where should the research go in the future. *Entrepreneurship: Theory and Practice*, 32(1).

Buchanan-Oliver, M., Cruz, A. and Schroeder, J., 2010. Shaping the body and technology. *European Journal of Marketing*, 44(5), pp. 635–652.

Caruana, R., Crane, A. and Fitchett, J., 2008. Paradoxes of consumer independence: A critical discourse analysis of the independent traveller. *Marketing Theory*, 8(3), pp. 253–272.

Chiou, W.C., Lin, C.C. and Perng, C., 2011. A strategic website evaluation of online travel agencies. *Tourism Management*, 32(6), pp. 1463–1473.

Cyr, D., Head, M., Larios, H. and Pan, B., 2009. Exploring human images in website design: a multi-method approach. *MIS Quarterly*, 33(3), pp. 539–566.

De Carolis, D.M. and Saparito, P., 2006. Social capital, cognition, and entrepreneurial opportunities: A theoretical framework. *Entrepreneurship: Theory and Practice*, 30(1), pp. 41–56.

Doherty, B., Haugh, H. and Lyon, F., 2014. Social enterprises as hybrid organizations: A review and research agenda. *International Journal of Management Reviews*, 16(4), pp. 417–436.

Douglas, E.J., 2013. Reconstructing entrepreneurial intentions to identify predisposition for growth. *Journal of Business Venturing*, 28(5), pp. 633–651.

Eckhardt, J.T. and Shane, S.A., 2003. Opportunities and entrepreneurship. *Journal of Management*, 29(3), pp. 333–349.

Eighmey, J. and McCord, L., 1998. Adding value in the information age: Uses and gratifications of sites on the World Wide Web. *Journal of Business Research*, 41(3), pp. 187–194.

Estrin, S., Mickiewicz, T. and Stephan, U., 2016. Human capital in social and commercial entrepreneurship. *Journal of Business Venturing*, 31(4), pp. 449–467.

Flavian, C., Guinaliu, M. and Gurrea, R., 2006. The role played by perceived usability, satisfaction and consumer trust on website loyalty. *Information and Management*, 43(1), pp. 1–14.

Gabriel, C.A., Nazar, S., Zhu, D. and Kirkwood, J., 2019. Performance beyond economic growth: Alternatives from growth-averse enterprises in the Global South. *Alternatives: Global, Local, Political*, pp. 1–9.

Hasan, L., 2009. Usability evaluation framework for e-commerce websites in developing countries. (Doctoral dissertation, © Layla Hasan). Loughborough University, Loughborough, UK.

Hasan, L. and Abuelrub, E., 2011. Assessing the quality of web sites. *Applied Computing and Informatics*, 9(1), pp. 11–29.

Hendry, J., 2000. Strategic decision-making, discourse, and strategy as social practice. *Journal of Management Studies*, 37(7), pp. 955–978.

Hernández, B., Jiménez, J. and Martín, M., 2009. Key website factors in e-business strategy. *International Journal of Information Management*, 29(5), pp. 362–371.

Higson, C. and Briginshaw, J., 2000. Valuing internet business. *Business Strategy Review*, 11(1), pp. 10–20.

Hodgson, D.M., 2000. *Discourse, Discipline and the Subject: A Foucauldian Analysis of the UK Financial Services Industry*. Hampshire: Ashgate.

Holt, D.B., 2002. Why do brands cause trouble? A dialectical theory of consumer culture and branding. *Journal of Consumer Research*, 29(1), pp. 70–90.

Ilieva, J., Baron, S. and Healey, N.M., 2002. Online surveys in marketing research: Pros and cons. *International Journal of Market Research*, 44(3), pp. 361–376.

Khoury, T.A. and Prasad, A., 2016. Entrepreneurship amid concurrent institutional constraints in less developed countries. *Business & Society*, 55(7), pp. 934–969.

Kim, J., 2014. Web accessibility-based website design and realization: With focus on T-Cast-integrated website. *Korea Science & Art Forum*, 15, p. 167.

Kim, S. and Stoel, L., 2004. Apparel retailers: Website quality dimensions and satisfaction. *Journal of Retailing and Consumer Services*, 11(2), pp. 109–117.

Kolk, A., Rivera-Santos, M. and Rufín, C., 2014. Reviewing a decade of research on the "base/bottom of the pyramid" (BOP) concept. *Business & Society*, 53(3), pp. 338–377.

Lemke, J., 1999. Discourse and organizational dynamics: Website communication and institutional change. *Discourse & Society*, 10(1), pp. 21–47.

Lim, D.S.K., Oh, C.H. and De Clercq, D., 2016. Engagement in entrepreneurship in emerging economies: Interactive effects of individual-level factors and institutional conditions. *International Business Review*, 25(4), pp. 933–945.

Lipitakis, A. and Phillips, P., 2016. On e-business strategy planning and performance: A comparative study of the UK and Greece. *Technology Analysis & Strategic Management*, 28(3), pp. 266–289.

Littlewood, D. and Holt, D., 2018. Social entrepreneurship in South Africa: Exploring the influence of environment. *Business & Society*, 57(3), pp. 525–561.

Mair, J. and Marti, I., 2006. Social entrepreneurship research: A source of explanation, prediction, and delight. *Journal of World Business*, 41, pp. 36–44.

Mary George, N., Parida, V., Lahti, T. and Wincent, J., 2016. A systematic literature review of entrepreneurial opportunity recognition: Insights on influencing factors. *International Entrepreneurship and Management Journal*, 12(2), pp. 309–350.

McDowell, W.C., Wilson, R.C. and Kile Jr, C.O., 2016. An examination of retail website design and conversion rate. *Journal of Business Research*, 69(11), pp. 4837–4842.

Pathak, S. and Muralidharan, E., 2017. Economic inequality and social entrepreneurship. *Business & Society*, 57(6), pp. 1150–1190.

Prahalad, C.K., 2005. *The Fortune at the Bottom of the Pyramid: Eradicating Poverty through Profits*. Philadelphia, PA: Wharton School Publishing.

Rahimnia, F. and Hassanzadeh, J.F., 2013. The impact of website content dimension and e-trust on e-marketing effectiveness: The case of Iranian commercial saffron corporations. *Information & Management*, 50(5), pp. 240–247.

Rivera-Santos, M., Holt, D., Littlewood, D. and Kolk, A., 2015. Social entrepreneurship in sub-Saharan Africa. *Academy of Management Perspectives*, 29(1), pp. 72–91.

Rocha, Á., 2012. Framework for a global quality evaluation of a website. *Online Information Review*, 36(3), pp. 374–382.

Rosen, D.E. and Purinton, E., 2004. Website design: Viewing the web as a cognitive landscape. *Journal of Business Research*, 57(7), pp. 787–794.

Santos, F.M., 2012. A positive theory of social entrepreneurship. *Journal of Business Ethics*, 111(3), pp. 335–351.

Seelos, C. and Mair, J., 2005. Social entrepreneurship: Creating new business models to serve the poor. *Business Horizons*, 48(3), pp. 241–246.

Shropshire, C. and Hillman, A.J., 2007. A longitudinal study of significant change in stakeholder management. *Business & Society*, 46(1), pp. 63–87.

Sobo, E.J., Herlihy, E. and Bicker, M., 2011. Selling medical travel to US patient-consumers: The cultural appeal of website marketing messages. *Anthropology and Medicine*, 18(1), pp. 119–136.

Stanfill, M., 2014. The interface as discourse: The production of norms through web design. *New Media & Society*, 17(7), pp. 1059–1074.

Stank, T., Keller, S. and Daugherty, P., 2001. Supply chain collaboration and logistical service performance. *Journal of Business Logistics*, 22(1), pp. 29–48.

Vallaster, C. and von Wallpach, S., 2013. An online discursive inquiry into the social dynamics of multi-stakeholder brand meaning co-creation. *Journal of Business Research*, 66(9), pp. 1505–1515.

Zhou, T., Lu, Y. and Wang, B., 2009. The relative importance of website design quality and service quality in determining consumers' online repurchase behavior. *Information Systems Management*, 26(4), pp. 327–337.

Part III

Case studies

In Part III of this book, I briefly tell the stories of two renewable energy enterprises (REEs) operating in emerging markets: Power Providers, operating in Tanzania, and A-Wing, operating in Indonesia. I have been fortunate in my research and interactions with renewable energy enterprises around the world that they all gave generously of their time and experience to help me understand their journeys in the renewable energy industry. I have not included them all in my research, as some agreed only to more informal conversations rather than to be the subject of my formalised research endeavour. Nevertheless, on aggregate, whether or not they are the subject of my research, all the REEs who shared their stories with me contributed to the writing of this book. In particular, three REEs agreed to be identified as illustrative case studies of renewable energy enterprise: Illumination Solar, Power Providers and A-Wing.

In 2018, I published the story and business strategies of Illumination Solar as a case study for use in higher education classrooms. I believed, as I do now, that these stories hold great value for students of sustainable business as well as for students interested in the sustainable energy transition in emerging markets. Hence, the case study is available via Ivey Publishing or Harvard Business School Publishing for educators interested in giving students a taste of the real-life challenges and dilemmas faced by these enterprises as they navigate the renewable energy industry in emerging markets. The case synopsis is as follows:

> In October 2017, Shane Thatcher, co-founder of Australian social enterprise Illumination Solar (Illumination), had mixed feelings. He was rethinking his company's Give Power campaign. After five marginally profitable years designing and supplying portable solar lights (solar lanterns) to some of the world's most energy impoverished communities, including refugee camps, Thatcher had decided to market his products to Australian customers for outdoor uses such as camping and hiking. Under the Give Power campaign, Illumination donated one solar lantern to a community in need, for every solar product purchased by Australian

customers. However, this strategy was not successful. Thatcher's main goal for his company was to sustainably provide good quality solar lights to impoverished people in developing countries. To reach that goal, he wondered which strategy to follow: return to the original business model, re-structure the Give Power campaign, or come up with something entirely new to generate higher profits?

Source: Gabriel, Stanley and Thatcher (2018), page 1.[1]

In this section, I tell the stories of the remaining two enterprises in brief (Power Providers and A-Wing) as a way of bringing to life some of the challenges I described previously. These include logistical and competitive challenges (as described in Chapters 3 and 4, respectively) as well as challenges associated with aid flows in emerging markets (as described in Chapter 5). My aim is also to demonstrate the real-life implications of the ideas I proposed in the previous chapters of this book, in particular, key features of an aid-independent logic of value creation (Chapter 5) and alternative measures of success for REEs in emerging markets (Chapter 6). I believe the insights from these case studies are most important and useful for nascent enterprises in the renewable energy industry in emerging markets. Importantly, they remind readers of the underlying social and environmental motivations that drive many renewable energy enterprises in emerging markets.

Case study 1: Power Providers, Tanzania

> *An axiom of business is that it should be economically viable, generating from its sales more than those sales cost, plus overheads. That is a necessary principle for starting a business but not a sufficient one: many entrepreneurs never look beyond that principle and indeed their measure of success is how big that surplus can be and how rich they can get. But it is surely better to judge an enterprise on its contribution to the wellbeing of society and not just on how big it is*
>
> (O'Hanlon and Abbott, 2012).

The preceding quote is an excerpt from John O'Hanlon and Jeff Abbott's 2012 feature article on Clive Jones and his renewable energy enterprise (REE), *Power Providers Company Limited*, which continues to operate in Tanzania. Like them, I too was struck by Jones' integrity, humility and commitment to a cause much bigger and more important than, simply, profits. Although institutionally de-incentivised, his resolute commitment to do the right thing and his relentless pursuit of a transition to more sustainable energy production were uplifting and inspiring. He was and remains to this day, in my opinion, the epitome of entrepreneurship-for-good. With his permission, his is the first of two case studies I will share. I have drawn from numerous sources to tell this story, including Power Providers' own website and web pages,[2] O'Hanlon and Abbott (2012)'s article, my own conversations with Jones and several other web articles and sources, all of which have been cited accordingly, with additional information provided in the list of references at the end of this chapter.

Mission

To provide our clients with affordable and reliable power by installing high quality renewable energy systems with great service.

Vision

Power Providers will continue to pioneer the mainstreaming of renewable energy in the Tanzanian power sector in order to contribute meaningfully to the strengthening of Tanzania's power security and a wider distribution of power nationally.

Enterprise history

In 2007, along with three Tanzanian partners, Clive Jones founded Power Providers Company Limited. All sources that describe Jones' motivation for starting Power Providers report the same underlying incentive: Jones believed strongly that fossil fuel alternatives, in particular renewable energies, were a necessary transition for sustainable human development and survival. In addition, when he started Power Providers, he was acutely aware of the growing need for quality solar energy, especially in the most remote areas in Tanzania. Power Providers serves a range of clients from individual households, hotels, schools and hospitals, to tour operators, farms and industrial organisations (O'Hanlon and Abbott, 2012).

Meet Clive Jones

Jones is a British national, who has been living in Tanzania for over 35 years. He has an academic background as an environmental biologist. Unable to find employment in his field, he travelled first to India, then to Africa. He says, "I mobilised my lifestyle to enable me to travel" (O'Hanlon and Abbott, 2012). In Tanzania, on a work trip for an expeditionary overlanding company he fell in love with the wildlife of East Africa. This was the beginning of his career in tourism. Jones explains he worked in the safari industry from 1981 for 10 years: "For four years I ran primate trips – Tanzania's tourist industry was in its infancy and I was in heaven, in the heart of the Serengeti plains with a truckful of clients and hardly another soul in sight!" (O'Hanlon and Abbott, 2012).

In my last conversation with him before writing this book, Jones explained the industry eventually became more established and crowded, and his interest waned as clients desired luxury instead of hands-on experiences in nature. So, he eventually returned to academia and worked in wildlife and natural resource management and conservation. He worked with NGOs like the Frankfurt Zoological Society and facilitated Tanzania's accession to the international Ramsar Convention, setting standards for wetlands management (O'Hanlon and Abbott, 2012). O'Hanlon and Abbott (2012: 4) summarised Jones' experiences in wildlife conservation as follows:

> *After a period working with the legendary wildlife film-maker Hugo van Lawick, Jones was engaged by the African Wildlife Foundation to manage the Manyara Ranch, a 45,000-acre asset sandwiched between Tarangiri National park and Lake Manyara National Park. The ranch is in a very important wildlife corridor, he explains, on land used by pastoralists, notably Maasai, and farmers: 'My mandate was to manage this ranch to find the balance point between the communities and the wildlife, while encouraging sustainable models of tourism.' One of the problems of running a remote station like the Manyara Ranch is providing energy to scattered facilities, with no chance to connect to the grid – and in any case Tanzania enjoys an erratic mains electrical supply to only 10 per cent of the population. The solution for the office, cattle sheds and accommodations at Manyara was found in solar power, charging an array of batteries to provide a continuous, reliable electricity supply.*

By that time, Jones had a family to raise and realised that although he could have positive impact on the natural environment, his conservation work did not cover his expenses. He craved the opportunity to do work with potential long-term positive impacts on the natural environment, and he eventually built on his technical skills to start a renewable energy business. Given his experience until then, solar power was the natural choice.

The Power Providers business model

Power Providers uses a renewable energy Distributor business model (i.e. Type III). Solar energy is its core business – it designs, supplies and installs high-quality solar power solutions. Indeed, Power Providers is a full service renewable energy enterprise, providing all varieties of renewable energy services and power systems, including solar power systems, backup/battery power systems, solar water heating, solar water pumping and renewable energy consultancy, among others. "We like to engage the client closely in the design process. A crucial part of the work", he says, "is education. Clients can't be expected to understand about renewable energy and its advantages" (O'Hanlon and Abbott, 2012: 5).

As good solar providers should, Power Providers supports its clients throughout the entire process, starting with detailed assessment of their power requirements for at least the next five years. "You need to have a system that will last for the duration of the battery bank," says Jones. According to O'Hanlon and Abbott (2012), Jones explained further, "You do not want to grow out of your battery bank – you want to grow into it. We nurture their engagement in renewable energy opportunities. We are one of the few companies in Tanzania that will do that, and I think that gives us an edge." Power Providers also considers each client's budget and operating costs.

When I asked why Power Providers has not diversified away from solar energy, Jones explained, "hydro is very specialised and not particularly local-ised around here. Wind – there is no data in Tanzania, and I refuse to supply wind turbines to clients unless I know it will work. Solar is much more reli-able, very mathematical, and it's a proven resource".

Power Providers employs about fourteen people, with a range of skills from LEED and installation technicians and engineers to managers, accoun-tants and storekeepers, all of whom were Tanzanian at the time. The valuable local knowledge possessed by Power Providers' staff means the company is well embedded locally and possesses an excellent understanding of local socioeconomic and sociocultural conditions in Tanzania. In fact, Jones explained, "Everyone I have on my staff has been trained by myself. The design engineer is a university graduate; I put him through a few courses, and I gave him access to some of the proprietary designs that I made, which he has improved immensely. So he's an in-house product". By training and employing Tanzanian staff, Power Providers is not only deeply embedded, but also inclusive in its approach.

When asked whether Power Providers has strong competition in the Tan-zanian renewable energy industry, Jones responded:

> No, but they're starting to come along. What gave us our edge why we have never advertised and why we are so busy is because we are pro-fessional. Finding a professional in any sector is a challenge. But now there are more professionals and there are one or two big companies coming in because East Africa is seen as a gold mine. But I do not think the competition is a problem because there is still a massive amount of demand out there, more than the existing business capacity. So there is a massive opportunity.

Indeed, Power Providers enjoys an excellent reputation for not only supply-ing quality systems, but also for its after-sales services and professionalism. With service, integrity and professionalism literally written into its core val-ues,[3] the company provides professional and reliable support for its clients. On its webpage, Power Providers relates an experience with one of its clients regarding maintenance of one its installed systems. The client echoes Jones' sentiment about professionalism:

> Power Providers installed a backup system in a private property in Aru-sha seven years ago where the system has worked flawlessly since that time. Recently we received a call from the client to investigate a system

failure. Our technicians discovered that the voltage stabilizer installed to provide TANESCO power conditioning on the backup system had failed. We removed the stabiliser, performed the repairs and re-installed. The client was delighted with the way we performed our role and said as much when completing our service feedback form. Kudos has to be extended to our technicians who embody the professionalism that we extol:

"Power Providers consistently shows professionalism in an area that historically doesn't get 'professionalism'. Hope this expands to other industries!"

About 30–50 percent of Power Providers' customers are commercial, of which a significant portion are in the hospitality industry. The rest of Power Providers' customers are from the agriculture, hotel, education and community services or domestic sectors. Jones explained the company has large demand for its domestic systems, but it tends to focus on installation of the larger solar power systems. I once asked Jones if he viewed marginalised communities at the Base of the Pyramid (BOP) as a viable customer segment. The response he provided echoes my own research findings from the last seven years. It also plainly reflects the many challenges caused by the influence of international aid and development organisations (IDOs) in emerging markets, which I discuss in previous chapters of this book (see Chapters Four and Five, for example, for further explanation of these challenges):

No, I actually deliberately steer clear of it. In order to approach marginalised communities with a business model, you need to be able to find a large number of whatever you're providing at a very low margin to a distributed environment. Not only that, you are providing them with stuff you're pioneering because you have no idea whether they want it or not. And my position is to build this company up to a point where it is more secure before looking at marginalised communities. And I'm still not convinced that providing one solar panel, or one light to these houses is the way forward. I think that a distributed micro-grid is more the way forward on a community level, which would then produce the power centrally and then distribute them to different outlets. I don't see the current model as a permanent business model. I mean what the money should be doing, instead of going to aid, it should be going into seed money and soft loans for companies in a difficult business environment – supportive accounting systems, administrative systems, compliance – instead of forcing a company to change its business plan in order to address rural communities. The whole objective should be to build sustainable business opportunities in the country.

Jones has started discussing micro-grid options with possible collaborators, as a distributed alternative to the centralised national grid, especially for end-users who need power but are unable to afford the associated upfront costs.

Key success factors for Power Providers

Similar to other enterprises involved in distributing renewable energy technology (RET) products, Jones and Power Providers now face the challenge of scaling up (see Chapter 3). Jones explained this is especially challenging in the region because "the prospect of finding new staff is very, very daunting". Indeed, Jones dedicates considerable resource to training his staff. His focus on explicitly hiring local staff, as well as his focus on service, professionalism and delivering high quality systems to clients, has won Jones and Power Providers the trust and support of local Tanzanians, which bodes well for its performance on my proposed 'Inclusiveness' measure of success for renewable energy enterprises in emerging markets (see Chapter 6).

In addition, Clive Jones' own explanation of the reasons Power Providers has grown so organically provides support for my proposed 'Self-Sufficiency' measure of success for renewable energy enterprises in emerging markets (see Chapter 6). From start-up to growth and now at the point of considering scaling-up further, Power Providers has been wholly self-funded. Jones re-invests the company's profits into its value creation processes and infrastructures. The credit offered by local finance institutions is unattractive to most businesses and can potentially hinder rather than enhance a company's ability to become self-sufficient.

Recently, in response to his persistent efforts, for three consecutive years the KPMG/Citizen Annual Awards recognised Power Providers as one of the Top 100 Midsized Companies in Tanzania (O'Hanlon and Abbott, 2012). At the time of writing, Power Providers had installed the largest solar water pumping system in Tanzania.[4] In addition, having built up from nothing to a million dollar turnover in its first five years, by any definition Power Providers has done well. Jones once remarked, "If you ask around, I think people will tell you they think we are a very big company, because we have a big presence and ten years of experience at our backs". Indeed, Power Providers' reputation and presence precedes it, even on the internet. Jones explained that his company has thrived on word of mouth referrals. Yet, it is not the company's commercial and economic success that Jones relishes most. Instead, Jones is most proud that he has and continues to contribute to the transition away from fossil fuels in Tanzania. Despite the significant political and commercial inertia Jones experiences, his strong conviction and dedication to environmental sustainability drives the enterprise and defines its goals and core values.

Case study 2: A-Wing International, Indonesia

The electrification rate in Indonesia was about 65 to 70 percent at the time of interview. This meant that approximately 60 to 80 million people did not have access to electricity in the country, and they were mostly located in the Eastern parts of Indonesia. In fact, for Eastern Indonesia alone, the electrification rate was less than 50 percent. In Indonesia, especially in regions without electricity access, the use and introduction of renewable energies is highly anticipated as a solution to energy access and energy poverty challenges in some of the country's most remote communities. Ironically, Eastern Indonesia is also known for its huge renewable power generating potential. However, given the remote locations of communities in Eastern Indonesia, and the geographical obstacles that hinder delivery of renewable energy technologies (RETs) to these communities, supply chain logistics and access have been identified as a major stumbling block. Yet, renewables continue to attract much attention in Indonesia for its potential to generate electric power on remote islands and in the suburbs of urban areas, especially in Papua. Indeed, it is seen as a solution to the range of energy challenges faced.

In response to these challenges, A-Wing International,[5] a manufacturer of wind power generators and desalination equipment, specialises in small wind power generators, seawater desalination equipment, and research and development on products that make effective use of renewable energy. A-Wing is driven by the ethos of "Electricity in places without electricity and water in places without water" and takes seriously its mission to deliver wind power to as many locations as possible. A-Wing conducts sales and construction both at home and abroad, and through its collaborations with local NGOs in Indonesia and Bangladesh, the enterprise delivers Japanese technology to villages and areas without electricity.

Mission

Micro wind turbines – Making energy a sustainable local source.

Vision

1   To provide total energy solutions based on our innovative micro-wind turbine technology.
2   To work towards a sustainable society, relying on natural renewable energy sources.
3   To improve quality of life through locally generated, clean energy.
4   To supply regions without access to electricity with energy and water through our technology.

Enterprise history

Ananda Setiyo Ivannanto co-founded A-Wing International in April 2010 after he graduated from university in Japan. A-Wing International is an Indonesian manufacturer and distributor of wind energy technologies. It was founded when Ivannanto received venture funding from a Japanese partner, Hirohide Nakamura, to work together to bring Japanese designed wind turbines to Indonesian communities.

Ananda Ivannanto has 10 years' experience and expertise in renewable energy, environment and business consultancy. He spent more than 15 years establishing strong relationships with Japan for education, business and social ventures. Although Ivannanto did not invent this particular model of wind turbine himself, the inventor of the technology (his Japanese partner) is heavily involved in A-Wing as an equity-contributing partner. Indeed, Ivannanto's Japanese partner provided financial support during the enterprise's start-up phase, as well as technical and logistical support for installation and maintenance. Ivannanto's business partner, Hirohide Nakamura, has been described as a serial entrepreneur with almost 50 years' experience in various Japanese companies, including ten years at Director level in a listed company and ten years investing in various businesses related to renewable energy and environment. Nakamura is passionate about dedicating the remainder of his life to impactful social enterprises that benefit those that need it most.

Meet Ananda Setiyo Ivannanto

An Indonesian native, in 2010 Ivannanto was keen to leverage the partnerships he had established with a Japanese wind turbine manufacturer to enhance the sustainable energy transition in his home country. When his Japanese partner corporation received 50 million yen of Official Development Assistance (ODA) funds (i.e. 'aid') for projects in Bangladesh, Ivannanto had the opportunity to sell the technology in Bangladesh and expand A-Wing's customer base. Some of the money received as aid was re-injected back into the enterprise to cover its operational activities. Another very small portion of it was allocated to activities in the countries outside of Japan that A-Wing targets as potential customers. Mainly, however, Ivannanto explained that the enterprise receives its funds from the sale of wind turbines and other equipment. As customers often experience difficulty accessing these turbines and other equipment, A-Wing takes its role as distributor seriously and maintains close connections with utilities and/or providers of other supporting products related to renewable energy.

In addition, Ivannanto spent the first three years after the enterprise was founded trying to build legitimacy and a professional network. As he explained, "it is quite difficult to start a business in Indonesia if you really don't know people around." Therefore, Ivannanto said that he spent three years largely building relationships with government officials, potential NGOs, funders and investors, universities and potential customers as well. Ivannanto divided his time between building these important relationships and developing his own business model. Particularly in the first three years after A-Wing was founded, Ivannanto persisted in his search for angel investors or other financial support for the enterprise.

A considerable proportion of the difficulty Ivannanto and his team face in the wind energy sector in Indonesia is because the vast majority of the country's wind resources are located along the Eastern side of Indonesia. With good wind speeds, it would be ideal to try to harvest some of this wind energy. However, A-Wing's lack of operational support and financial investment at start-up meant it could not venture too far afield to assess the actual needs of end-users in these communities. Therefore, A-Wing decided to work much harder to leverage the connections he established in Jakarta in those first three years after he founded the enterprise in 2010. However, this became an important turning point for the enterprise, as Ivannanto realised how difficult it was to be successful without depending on the input and artefacts of others. Instead, he decided to try to provide whole solutions for end-users. He explained, "what we were trying to do at first is we only sold the wind turbine, but this did not work." This experience taught Ivannanto that, in Indonesia, and perhaps in other countries, sometimes just providing a technology is not enough. REEs need to provide whole solutions and give beneficiary communities the chance to understand how the technology works. In essence, REEs must rely on their embeddedness within beneficiary communities and leverage their knowledge of the communities' needs, norms and habits to design and deliver whole solutions that work (Chapter 5).

The A-Wing business model

A-Wing operated under a largely Distributor business model in its early days (i.e. Type III), but later scaled-up to an Integrator model (i.e. Type IV), as it became involved in all aspects of the RET and renewable energy sources (RES) supply chains. A-Wing's products include a small wind power generator, desalination equipment and a battery system that makes full use of renewable energy. The company's new wind power generator was developed by A-Wing in collaboration with the Indonesian Academy of Sciences (LIPI). It was recognized as a recommended product for use in non-electrified areas such as those in Eastern Indonesia. In addition, the A-Wing windmill is made up of five parts that can be easily installed on site, and it has been recognised for its long product life. Finally, A-Wing aims to make its newly developed wind power generator a low-priced model that matches the local situation in some of Indonesia's most remote communities. For instance, having concluded that local production of the new generator is indeed possible, A-Wing's priorities now include redesigning the generator to suit the needs of local end-users. This will be an important factor to ensure that the company's products are appropriate to the local needs and sociocultural preferences of end-users in emerging markets. Indeed, A-Wing's localised production and product design processes (including consulting with local experts and communities) will ensure it continues to achieve Inclusiveness in its business model well into the future (see Chapter 6).

Thus, A-Wing's business model is a response to a specific, identified need and to renewable energy potential available to be exploited in certain regions. However, another challenge to be considered is after-sales service and support – that is, ensuring that end-users are able to manage and maintain the technologies installed. Ivannanto explained he believes the approach of the government of Indonesia could be problematic. Its approach is to encourage solar panel manufacturers or players to assist with the installation of solar energy projects in Tanzania, but the scope of the projects is usually only the first three months. This means that once the first three months have elapsed, the international solar manufacturers and installers leave and are no longer available to provide support or maintenance for end-users. "There's a lot of cases where the solar panel doesn't work anymore and nobody is there to repair or maintain it. Then, because the manufacturers give ownership of the solar panels to the government and the government gives ownership of the panel to the community, then no one with the skills to maintain these systems has access to them".

When asked who A-Wing's main customers were, Ivannanto explained, "The customers that we normally have at the moment mostly are universities or research institutes from many places in Indonesia. There's one from Borneo, one from Sumatra, several in Java Island". Universities across Indonesia were purchasing A-Wing's wind turbines for research purposes. Such partnerships were extremely important to A-Wing, as they provided an aid-independent source of income for the company (see Chapter Five). Ivannanto disclosed, "They have been really good partners with us because that's how we grow our business. Until we become fully commercial – when the financial and policy support catch-up – we rely very much on these kinds of customers".

Key success factors for A-Wing

A-Wing has had such considerable success that it has attracted the attention and support of other renewable energy enterprises in Indonesia. As a result, to date A-Wing has partnerships with several other renewable energy firms in Indonesia to form the A-Wing Group, where partners offer completely different, yet complementary, products and services. This approach helps A-Wing achieve some of the 'Uptake' and 'Inclusiveness' aims of the enterprise (see Chapter 6). One of the companies, Awina Sinergi[6] Indonesia, is known within the A-Wing Group for providing technology transfer and system development support to A-Wing for its wind turbine technology. Awina Sinergi was established in 2018 to provide environment related technology, renewable energy investment and business collaboration between Japan and Indonesia and all other countries. In addition, research and investment consulting company for Asian and African countries, AAI Co., Ltd. was established in 2012 in Kurume City, Fukuoka. AAI's focus is doing research, business consulting and investment for Asian and African countries and worldwide. In addition, biomass R&D company, GEC Bio Co. Ltd, joined A-Wing Group in 2017. Indeed, A-Wing's development into a group of companies highlighted how essential it is to collaborate with perceived rivals on the market.

Nevertheless, Ivannanto is not worried about losing his competitive edge or diluting the good reputation he has built in Jakarta. Instead, he highlighted the following six factors, which he believes demonstrate A-Wing Group's inimitable core competencies (A-Wing Group, 2019: 21):

1   Ten+ years' experience with building renewable energy business from the start. Ivanannto claims the majority of other REEs in the market have fewer than five years' experience.
2   Strong network with Japanese investors, technology owners and general trading companies, which cover all of the supply chain in renewable energy business.
3   Strong connection to strategic ministries such as Energy and Mineral Resources, State Own Enterprise, Agriculture, Environmental and Forestry, Ocean and Fisheries, Maritime Affairs and Economic Affairs in Indonesia.
4   Strong partnerships with local government such as North Sumatra, West Sumatra, DKI Jakarta, West Java, East Java, South Sulawesi, East Nusa Tenggara and also Regent Government Association.
5   Established presence and networks overseas in other Asian and African countries such as Bangladesh, Ethiopia, Philippines, Vietnam, Malaysia and Singapore.
6   Professional and lean management team to ensure fast movement to make strategic business decisions effectively.

Indeed, between 2010 and 2013, A-Wing Group established branches in other countries in Asia, including Japan, Bangladesh and Thailand, and at the time of writing had sold its products in numerous other countries and cultures as well. Ivannanto explained, "We have sold one in East Timor, Timor Leste and we sold also to Pakistan. If you see it from our partner's point of view, we have sold our wind turbine in 10 countries in total" (refer to 'Uptake' in Chapter 6). In addition, when asked how A-Wing measures its success, Ivannanto explained, "Well, we seek profit, but we seek more to create changes in people's lives. So actually, letting our technology change the lives of the people is actually our most top priority and after that of course to run the operation of the company. Our main core principle is to provide electricity to places where they don't have electricity, so that's how we run our operation" (refer to 'Uptake' and 'Inclusiveness' in Chapter 6). Indeed, A-Wing, too, gauges its performance and success in emerging markets by alternative standards – not only profits. Like many other REEs operating within these challenging environments, A-Wing's founders continue to do their share to contribute to the sustainable energy transition and enhancement of sustainable human thriving in emerging markets.

Notes

1   Case Study available from Ivey Publishing (Product Number: 9B18M152) and Harvard Business Publishing (Product Number: W18618-PDF-ENG).
2   Power Providers' website: https://powerproviders.co.tz/

3 Power Providers' Mission, Vision and Values available here: www.powerproviders-store.co.tz/about/
4 More information on this project available here: www.linkedin.com/posts/power-providers_largest-solar-water-pumping-system-in-tanzania-activity-6561532000 266670080-aFjG
5 A-Wing International's website: www.awing-i.com/english/index.html
6 Awina Sinergi's website: http://awina.co.id/our-group-2/

References

A-Wing Group, 2019. *A-Wing Group: Integrated Sustainable Solutions for a Better World*. Jakarta, Indonesia.

Gabriel, C., Stanley, M. and Thatcher, S., 2018. *Illumination Solar: Delivering Energy Poverty Solutions*. Case Study, Ivey Publishing.

O'Hanlon, J. and Abbott, J., 2012. Power providers company limited. *Business and Belief*. Retrieved from www.bus-ex.com/article/power-providers-company-limited (accessed 09 September 2019).

Appendices

Appendix 1

Indicators of human development and well-being, based on UNDP 2015 human development report[1]

Countries represented in the study	HDI Index	HDI Rank	Health (Life expectancy at birth)	Education (expected years of schooling)	Income/Composition of resources (GNI per capita (2011 PPP$))	Inequality (adjusted inequality (IHDI))	Gender (Gender development index GDI)	Poverty (Multi-dimensional poverty index, HDRO specifications)	Work, employment, vulnerability (employment to population ratio (% ages 15+))	Human Security (Homicide rate (per 100,000 people))	Trade & Financial Flows (exports & imports (% of GDP))	Mobility & Communication (mobile phone subscriptions per 100 people)
Barbados	0.785	57	75.6	15.4	12,487.60	-	1.018	0.004	62.5%	7.4	96.8%	106.8
Belize	0.715	101	70.0	13.6	7,614	0.553	0.958	0.030	56%	44.7	127.2%	50.7
Cambodia	0.555	143	68.4	10.9	2,948.90	0.418	0.89	0.211	82.3%	6.5	139.5%	155.1
Cameroon	0.512	153	55.5	10.4	2,803.40	0.344	0.879	0.26	67.4%	7.6	49.6%	75.7
Chile	0.832	42	81.7	15.2	21,290.20	0.672	0.967	-	58.1%	3.1	65.5%	133.3
Costa Rica	0.766	69	79.4	13.9	13,413.40	0.613	0.974		58.2%	8.5	73.9%	143.8
Ecuador	0.732	88	75.9	14.2	10,605	0.570	0.980	0.015	65.7%	12.4	60.8%	103.9
Ethiopia	0.442	174	64.1	8.5	1,427.70	0.312	0.84	0.537	79.0%	12	41.5%	31.6
Fiji	0.727	90	70	15.7	7,492.50	0.616	0.941	-	50.5%	4	136.4%	98.8
Ghana	0.579	140	61.4	11.5	3,852.00	0.387	0.885	0.144	66.2%	6.1	89.4%	114.8
Guatemala	0.627	128	71.8	10.7	6,929.20	0.443	0.949	-	65.8%	39.9	58.6%	106.6
India	0.609	130	68	11.7	5,497.50	0.435	0.795	0.282	52.2%	3.5	53.3%	74.5
Indonesia	0.684	110	68.9	13	9,788.40	0.559	0.927	0.024	63.5%	0.6	49.5%	126.2
Kenya	0.548	145	61.6	11	2,761.60	0.377	0.913	0.226	61.1%	6.4	50.9%	73.8
Lao PDR	0.575	141	66.2	10.6	4,680.10	0.428	0.896	0.186	76.6%	5.9	83.4%	67
Nigeria	0.514	152	52.8	9	5,341.10	0.32	0.841	0.279	51.8%	20	31.0%	77.8
Panama	0.780	60	77.6	13.3	18,192	0.604	0.996	-	62.8%	17.2	154.8%	158.1
Papua New Guinea	0.505	158	62.6	9.9	2,462.80	-	-	-	70.7%	10.4		44.9
Philippines	0.668	115	68.2	11.3	7,915.20	0.547	0.977	0.033	60.6%	8.8	59.9%	111.2

Senegal	0.466	170	66.5	7.9	2,188.10	0.305	0.883	0.278	68.7%	2.8	73.6%	98.8
Somalia	-	-	-	-	-	-	-	-	-	-	-	-
South Africa	0.666	116	57.4	13.6	12,122.30	0.428	0.948	0.041	39.2%	31	64.2%	149.7
Tanzania	0.521	151	65	9.2	2,411.50	0.379	0.938	0.335	86.0%	12.7	49.5%	62.8
Thailand	0.726	93	74.4	13.5	13,322.90	0.576	1	0.004	71.7%	5	143.8%	144.4
Tonga	0.717	100	72.8	14.7	5,069	-	0.967	-		1	80.5%	64.3
Trinidad and Tobago	0.772	64	70.4	12.3	26,090.00	0.654	0.985	0.007	60.4%	28.3	103.2%	147.3
Uganda	0.483	163	58.5	9.8	1,612.60	0.337	0.886	0.359	74.5%	10.7	50.7%	52.4
Zambia	0.586	139	60.1	13.5	3,734	0.384	0.917	0.264	68.8%	10.7	81.6%	67.3

Appendix 2

Coding framework used for website analysis

Theme	Examples of cues used (if applicable)	Illustrative excerpts from websites (if applicable)[2]
REEs' Intent to Influence Change towards Energy Transition (P1, P2, P3)		
REE Does not Intend to Influence Change/Not Obvious from Website	Not Applicable	We believe that energy efficiency in building is the cheapest way to reduce carbon emissions and also the quickest way to do so. Provide the best energy solutions for our clients at the lowest cost while reducing their carbon footprint
REE Intends to Influence Change		
Economic Change	productivity, income, socio-economic	Increase family income and contribute to economic growth Increase economic productivity We aim to reduce the burden of high electricity prices and thereby promote social and economic development.
Environmental Change	environmental issues, carbon dioxide	Supporting global environment conservation effort and climate change Our vision is to help protect the environment.
Health-related Change	health benefits, safe drinking water	Burning fossil fuels releases a wide range of pollutants, adversely affecting the health of individuals. Solar cooking does not burn these fuels. By switching to our light, customer households no longer inhale noxious fumes, minimizing their risk of cancer and other kerosene related illnesses.
Social Change	community self-reliance, local socio-economic improvement	We are about the provision of sustainable resources primary to human daily existence, namely energy and water Develop renewable energy projects with high return on investment and social impact
Website Content and Quality (P1)		
Content (Score 1–5)	timeliness, relevance, variety of presentation, accuracy, objectivity, authority	Not Applicable

Design (Score 1–5)	attractiveness, appropriateness, colour, image/sound/video, text	Not Applicable
Organisation (Score 1–5)	indexing, mapping, consistency, linking, logo, domain	Not Applicable
User-Friendliness (Score 1–5)	usability, reliability, interactive features, security/privacy, customisation	Not Applicable
Intended Audience (P2)		
Customers		
Organisations	solutions for your organization, project for business	We are geared towards business-to-business, business–to-government transactions and sustainable energy projects. Power tariff rate that best fits your energy usage pattern, operational needs and business objectives
Households	rural households, village, families	. . . to empower the local villagers and the marginal groups in urban area Our product is now being used by more and more families.
Both	As above	We are a social enterprise working toward to energy/electricity solutions for people and communities Whether your requirement is large or small, we can provide you with the solution.
Geographical Level		
National	nation, domestic market	Various community development projects and energy in Indonesia We are an engineering firm that undertakes the design, supply and installation of renewable energy system packages for the various industrial sectors of our Nation's economy.
Regional	region, local rural areas	We are centrally located in the South Pacific and offer products and services tailored to the region.
International	global level, overseas market	Our mission is to reduce poverty in emerging markets. Our products have provided light to 2 million people in 22 countries.
Technical Level		

(Continued)

(Continued)

Theme	Examples of cues used (if applicable)	Illustrative excerpts from websites (if applicable)[2]
Layperson	installation, consulting, audit	We will be on hand to help you throughout the entire project, from the energy audit and assessment of your location to suggesting the size and type of system as well as the final installation. Our expert knowledge and experience ensure that we have the right skills and tools to configure a working solution for you and that it will provide the expected results based on your energy requirements.
Technically Proficient	optimum production performance, link up various energy sources, creation and innovation	Treat the sediment in anaerobic reactors, transforms this effluent into more worms and humus to fertilize soil Combined with our matching Wind + PV hybrid controller, our small wind turbines are the ideal solution for remote homes, independent parking lot and sign lighting and back-up power systems.
Both	As above	. . . transforming the way Africa generate its power, fuels its vehicles, designs and constructs its buildings, manufacture its products, delivers and fitters its water We specialize in the consulting, design and implementation of renewable energy systems, back up power systems, micro grids, water supply and sustainable solutions for green building.
Web Profile and Identity (P3)		
Business Name	Not Applicable	e.g. 'Energy', 'Eco', 'Electric', 'Global', 'Sun', 'Power'
Frequently Used Words	Words appear 1–3 times, 4–6 times, or more than 6 times on a single website	e.g. 'Energy', 'Renewable', 'Electricity'/'Electric', 'Solar', 'System', 'Wind'
Frequently Used Images	Specific motifs appear once, twice, or thrice or more on a single website	i.e. Nature (e.g. landscapes, farms, trees, plants), People (children, women, families, technicians), Built Environment (e.g. buildings, huts, construction sites), Technology (e.g. photovoltaic (PV) modules, wind turbines, batteries, solar lamps), Abstract Nature and Space (e.g. sunlight, solar flares, planetary views) or Stock Images (i.e. images clearly (from the researchers' perspective) procured from stock image sources).

Appendix 3
Summary of conclusions on propositions

Propositions	Finding
Proposition 1 (P1): REEs who intend to influence the sustainable energy transition in emerging markets will have better quality and condition of their websites and content than REEs who do not intend to influence the sustainable energy transition.	Could not be supported
Proposition 2 (P2): The kind of change envisaged by REEs will be consistent with the intended audience of the REEs' websites.	
Specifically: *REEs who envisage economic change targeted mainly economic stakeholders, REEs who envisage social change targeted mainly societal stakeholders, REEs who envisage environmental change targeted mainly environmental stakeholders, and REEs who envisage health-related change targeted mainly health-related stakeholders.*	Supported
Proposition 3 (P3): The kind of change envisaged by REEs will be consistent with the online profile and identity of their enterprises as reflected on their business websites.	
Specifically: *REEs who envisage economic change used mainly economy-related words and imagery, REEs who envisage social change used mainly society-related words and imagery, REEs who envisage environmental change used mainly environment-related words and imagery, and REEs who envisage health-related change used mainly health-related words and imagery.*	Supported
Proposition 4 (P4): The discursive strategies used by REEs relate to their survival in emerging markets.	Supported

Notes

1 All data shown were sourced from the UNDP's 2015 Human Development Report (UNDP, 2015). 'HDI' stands for 'Human Development Index', and items in bold font are the lowest scores in the particular human development category.
2 Quotes have been de-identified to preserve the entrepreneurs' anonymity.

Index

Figures are in italic; tables are in bold.

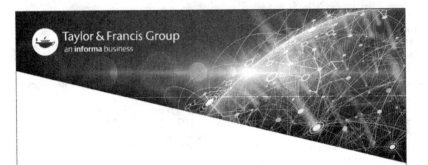

Printed in the United States
by Baker & Taylor Publisher Services